Materializing Memory

Archaeological material culture and the semantics of the past

Edited by

Irene Barbiera
Alice M. Choyke
Judith A. Rasson

CEU

nka
Nemzeti Kulturális Alap

BAR International Series 1977
2009

Published in 2016 by
BAR Publishing, Oxford

BAR International Series 1977

Materializing Memory

ISBN 978 1 4073 0509 7

© The editors and contributors severally and the Publisher 2009

Design by Krisztián Kolozsvári

The preparation of this book has been co-funded by the National Cultural Fund of Hungary.

C E U   **nka**
Nemzeti Kulturális Alap

BAR Publishing is the trading name of British Archaeological Reports (Oxford) Ltd.
British Archaeological Reports was first incorporated in 1974 to publish the BAR
Series, International and British. In 1992 Hadrian Books Ltd became part of the BAR
group. This volume was originally published by Archaeopress in conjunction with
British Archaeological Reports (Oxford) Ltd / Hadrian Books Ltd, the Series principal
publisher, in 2009. This present volume is published by BAR Publishing, 2016.

Printed in England

BAR
PUBLISHING

BAR titles are available from:

BAR Publishing
122 Banbury Rd, Oxford, OX2 7BP, UK
EMAIL   info@barpublishing.com
PHONE   +44 (0)1865 310431
FAX   +44 (0)1865 316916
www.barpublishing.com

MATERIALIZING MEMORY

ARCHAEOLOGICAL MATERIAL CULTURE
AND THE SEMANTICS OF THE PAST

TABLE OF CONTENTS

NOTES ON MEMORY-WORK AND MATERIALITY

John Chapman

Abstract

In seeking to draw together some common threads on the work of remembering and forgetting from the chapters of this volume, I use these thoughts to focus on three aspects of recent research on memory, which are grounded in archaeology but which have wider applicability to the historical and anthropological chapters in this collection. These three aspects are a brief history of the study of memory (see the quote by Nietzsche); the notion that memory – whether commemoration, remembrance or forgetting – involves cultural work on the part of individuals or groups; and the plurality of memories and who is best served by remembering or forgetting (see the quote by Camus).

> *"... the past has to be forgotten if it is not to become the gravedigger of the present" (Nietzsche 1983)*

> *"Remembrance of things past is just for the rich. For the poor it only marks the faint traces on the path to death (Camus 1994: 62)*

Introduction

Climo and Cattell (2002: 1) assert that "without memory, the world would cease to exist in any meaningful way." How can this assertion be squared with Nietzsche's opposite view, expressed in the quotation above? While Climo and Cattell emphasise the scaffolding which memory creates for the social world to hang its past upon, Nietzsche is fearful that the world's failure to obliterate the terrible deeds of the recent past will prevent future reconciliation, if not the basis for moral behaviour. One way of resolving this gap in perception is to consider that forgetting is just as much part of the process of memory building as is remembering. Every space that has been cleared of memory opens up a potential area for new or revived memories. This is part of the long-term, dynamic dialectic that connects past to present – a dialectic in which Nietzsche and Climo and Cattell find themselves on opposite sides. As we shall see, it is almost impossible to discuss remembering without addressing the complementary aspect of forgetting. Both terms also conjure up a significant relationship not only with material culture but also with people, places and things – the identity triad for studies of the past and the present. In this foreword, I hope to be able to offer some insights into these relationships. It is my hope that the discussion, which is focussed primarily on archaeological materials from prehistory and early history, will have wider relevance to the anthropological and historical approaches to memory that are well represented in this collection.

I start with some observations on the way in which memory has been studied in recent archaeology. The present volume was conceived at a session in the European Association of Archaeologists' Annual Meeting in September 2004, in Lyon, France (for details, see the "Introduction," this volume). The time since that session has been a busy time for memory studies and it may be helpful if these very recent years were put in a longer-term context of how memory has been studied in archaeology since the 1980s.

The history of memory studies in archaeology

Zoe Devlin (2007: 1) has noted that there has been a boom in memory studies over the last 25 years. While the pioneering works of Sigmund Freud (1900) and Maurice Halbwachs (1925) on memory made a major impact on the human sciences at the time of their publication, there was a lack of focus in memory studies into the late 1970s. Paul Connerton (2006: 315) observes that earlier studies of "memory" fell under different terms, such as the history of *mentalités*, myth, or oral history, popular culture, commemorative rituals or autobiography – without anyone seeking to link these under general rubric of "memory". This was indeed Connerton's (1989) achievement, in writing *How Societies Remember*. For Connerton (1989: 104), the social body was constituted in a double sense: constructed as an object of knowledge or discourse AND culturally shaped by its actual practices and behaviour, especially in habitual performances. This insight, coupled with Connerton's distinction between commemorative ceremonies and the two forms of bodily social memories – inscription and incorporation – has formed the foundations for the studies of memory ever since (for early elaborations on inscription and incorporation, see Battaglia [1992] and Rowlands [1993]). A useful elaboration of the forms of memory was advanced by Assmann (1992), who differentiated four kinds of memory: mimetic memory, the transmission of practical knowledge from past to the present; material memory, the history contained in objects; communicative memory, the traces of the past in language and communication; and cultural memory, the transmission of meanings from the past as explicit historical reference and consciousness.

The role played by archaeology in this memory boom was remarkably muted, considering that the backward-looking nature of archaeology meant that a focus on memory was supposedly "inevitable" (van Dyke and Alcock 2003: 3). Apart from the Mike Rowlands' article, published in *World Archaeology* in 1993, little explicit theorising on either individual or social memory appeared in the archaeological research of the 1990s. In Olick and Robbins' (1998) review article on memory, a lengthy list of disciplines contributing to studies of social memory includes anthropology but excludes archaeology. Several reviews of memory in archaeological research cite the 1998 *World Archaeology* volume No. 30, No. 1, on the "Past in the past," as the beginnings of a new trend in studying memory. However, while all of the 11 papers make implicit reference to the importance of memory, only one author (Michael Dietler) nominates "memory" as one of his keywords, while only three authors – Dietler (1998), Manning (1998) and Holtorf (1998) – explicitly discuss the role of memory in their case studies. The same is true of articles/book chapters which even refer to "memory" in their titles (e.g., Cummins 2000), while in two of Richard Bradley's books, discussion of memory is limited to brief recapitulation of Connerton's distinction between insciption and incorporation, together with Rowlands' comments (Bradley 1998: 2000). An exception to this research is Jonathan Last's (1998) discussion of Bronze Age barrow burials, in which the role of memory is vital in stressing the use of the memory of embodied differences by elites to maintain their position.

The development of memory studies in archaeology can be readily identified by comparing two pairs of writings. In each pair, we can contrast the implicit and relatively underdeveloped role of memory in the argument of the earlier piece – a role that increases in importance in the second work to a pivotal position. In the first pair, written by Richard Bradley, his *World Archaeology* article (1998a) makes brief mention of Connerton's arguments, while, in his book on *The Past in Prehistoric Societies* (Bradley 2000a: 12-14, 109-111), there is an interesting elaboration on Connerton's ideas, as well as the idea that monuments were intended as memorials – an attempt to formulate the memories of the future. The second pair was written by Howard Williams. We can contrast the implict use of memory theory in his *World Archaeology* 1998 article and his introductory chapter in an important contribution to mortuary studies entitled *Archaeologies of Remembrance: Death and Memory in Past Societies* (Williams, H. 2001). Williams is correct to note that ancient graves were **not** discussed as a way of communities remembering their own societies until very recently (2001a: 4-6). In the same way, two years later, Susan Alcock (2002: 19) could state that "specifically *archaeological* research into the dynamics of social memory remains by and large at a relatively early stage." It is thus the turn of the millennium that marks the emergence of a body of research incorporating explicit archaeological analyses of social memory, with H. Williams' (2001) edited volume supplemented by monographs by Susan Alcock (2002) on the importance of memory in the Greek past and an influential collection edited by Van Dyck and Alcock (2003a). A generally supported conclusion was H. Williams' (2001a: 9) recognition of the importance of the combination of literacy, orality, and materiality in the production of social memory. An important correction to typologically-oriented studies of memory was made by Alasdair Whittle (2003, esp. Chapter 5), through his notion of memory as fluid, dynamic, and creative and his avoidance of definitions of forms of memory in favour of diverse rememberings and uses of the past.

Nevertheless, memory studies could hardly be said to have gained a foothold in the upper échelons of post-processual theory as long as several influential approaches continued to neglect social memory (e.g., Chris Tilley's [2004] phenomenological approach to the materiality of stone; Boivin and Owoc's [2004] collection on the cultural perception of the mineral world; Fowler's study of personhood in archaeology and anthropology (Fowler 2004); and Cummings and Pannett's (2005) collection on the materiality of stone – with the welcome exception of the chapter by Andy Jones [2005]). It was in this context of a still-hesitant appreciation of the role of social memory that the "Memory" session of the Lyon EAA Annual Meeting of 2004 emerged as a new point of departure.

It was indeed left to Andy Jones to inscribe social memory irreversibly onto the archaeological *tabula* with his all-encompassing volume on *Memory and Material Culture* (Jones, A. 2007). In this volume, Jones succeeds in integrating social memory studies with Peircean semiotics and an active theory of material culture, in which "**both** objects **and** people are engaged in the process of remembering, in that objects provide humans with the ground to experience memory" (ibid., 22). Jones covers an extensive terrain, tackling the memories inscribed in LBK long-houses, as well as the monumentalising Scottish Neolithic, with its houses, megalithic tombs, rock art and sacred landscapes. The result is a carefully-constructed theory of how memory works, not only in the human mind but also beyond it, not in the Merlin Donald (1991) sense of extended symbolic storage but as a way of experiencing and interpreting the world rather than merely reproducing it.

A sure sign of the emergence of a research theme with wide resonance is the publication by BAR of a clutch of recent doctorates. Thus, in 2007 and 2008, three such volumes appeared – indicating start-dates around 2004/5: Clack's discussion of the environmental relations of the Wachagga of Kilimanjaro and their implications for landscape archaeology (Clack 2007); Dev-lin's dissection of archaeology and history in respect of remembering the dead in Anglo-Saxon England (Dev-lin 2007); and Jones' eff orts to move heaven and earth to understand landscape, death and memory in the Ace-ramic Neolithic of Cyprus (P. Jones 2008).

Th e sophistication of Devlin's approach far surpasses that of the other doctorants, with her wide-ranging treat-ment of persons, objects, and places. She identifi es the deceased's body as the most important Early Medieval mnemonic object, as the framework for adding memories through material culture (2007: 34). Following Geary's (1994: 20) re-working of the old Lévi-Strauss tag that objects are "good to remember with," Devlin maintains that it is not just any old object that can trigger memo-ries for anyone – but that the actor needs to engage with the past events represented by the object (2007: 22-25). Anglo-Saxon cemeteries are categorised as technologies of memory, with their organisation and layout produc-tive of processes of remembering and forgetting. It is the landscape of the cemetery itself – not the graveside scene – that projects memory forwards and this is what later people engage with (2007: 49-58).

It is Clack (2007), however, who carries off the (consolation) prize of coining the term "memoryscape", after Ingold's (1993) pioneering term "taskscape", Morley's (2006) "soundscape", and Finlay's "lithicscape". Clack describes a variety of outworkings of "memoryscape" with two principal senses (2007: 5-6): a cognitive sense, as an expression of the convergence zone between culture, emotion, and memory; and a phenomenological sense, as a refi nement of mental maps (cf. maps of meaning: Küchler 1993). Clack uses this term as a scaff olding for his entire study but the problem is that the term is over-determined by its indexing to the views of scholars who each hold a markedly diff erent set of theoretical precon-ceptions: to Schama's (1996) "landscape memory", to Donald's (1991) external symbolic storage, as well as be-ing inherent in the dwelling process (Th omas, J. 2001). Th e conclusion of Clack's ethno-archaeological study is also rather disappointing for telling us what we already suspected: "the sacred landscapes of the Wachagga in-form and choreograph their being-in-the-world" (2007: 78-79).

P. Jones (2008: 134) claims that memory is central to her monograph on the Aceramic Neolithic of Cyprus, but this is not the overall impression that one is given. Her attempted distinction (2008: 140) between figurines and skulls as deliberate mnemonics, while other mundane objects may not have been intentionally used for memory-work, is unconvincing. More useful, however, is the dialectic she establishes between remembering and forgetting as shown in respect of objects: their creation led to mnemonics for the dead, while their destruction, disposal or deposition led to forgetting (2008: 146).

This series of observations should not be treated as a comprehensive review of memory studies in archaeology but it does convey a sense of the direction of research since social memory made a theoretical impact on the discipline since 2000. We now turn to a different question, concerning the progress that archaeologists may have made in the ways in which they conceptualise the work necessary to produce social memory.

Memory-work as cultural work

It is to the credit of Mike Rowlands (1993) that he emphasised that remembering is a form of work, as with building monuments and memorials, while drying, chopping, cutting, and burning were all forms of the work of forgetting, often important in the mortuary domain. I should like to maintain that Connerton's (1989) two forms of bodily memory practice – incorporation and inscription – are in fact present in all acts of material-based memory-work. Memory-work involved both the human body or bodies, as well as extensions of the human body (tools, facilities, resources, etc.), in two ways: there was an incorporated memory of accomplishing the work itself, as well as an inscription of the memory by that body into the object of work. This approach is directly relevant to two of Assmann's (1992) kinds of memory: mimetic memory and material memory. The use of written documents for Assmann's other forms of memory – communicative memory and cultural memory – also implicates embodied skills, viz. the memory-work involved in inscribing memory-trace onto various media. To the extent that cultural reliance on oral history was mediated by material objects in performances, this principle of the linkage between incorporation and inscription is also valid for oral history as well.

The specificity of memory-work is important in providing a basis for remembering. In this connection, it is worth recalling Halbwachs' comment: "But if a truth is to be settled in the memory of a group, it needs to be presented in the concrete form of an event, a personality or a locality," (1941: 159; cited in Alcock 2002: 25) to which we might add "objects" and "processes" for the sake of completeness. Let us consider in turn one example of each from the general literature on memory, as well as examples of these forms as presented in this volume.

9

Events

Events, or commemorative ceremonies, link past to present through invariant form and continuity of prescribed bodily practice (Connerton 1989). An excellent example for the European Iron Age is the series of ceremonial executions that led to the burial of "bog bodies" in North West Europe (Williams, M. 2001). The combination of often seemingly bizarre rites and often multiple means of "killing" the victim led M. Williams to the explanation that these highly theatrical practices were deliberately staged so as to fix the event in the memories of the audience. These events are reminiscent of Whitehouse's (1995) *imagistic* mode of religiosity, based as it is upon non-verbal iconic imagery, episodic or autobiographical memory, when unique schemata are produced from sensual arousal and cognitive shocks. Such traumatic events do indeed evoke affective episodic memories, leading to the formation of localised solidary communities (Whitehouse 1995). The variability of the bog executions can be accounted for by the incorporation of gradual change in this mode of religiosity, because new images do not require changes in other parts of religion. Such events would also come under the rubric of "timemarks" (Chapman 1997) – the temporal equivalent of "landmarks", which serve to highlight an event of particular significance to the community in the social memory and from which time could be "plotted" in a necessarily non-linear way. The medieval equivalent of timemarks are discussed in the chapters by Fiano and Hornickova in the context of the funerals, processions, and ceremonies which the royal elites utilised as rituals of remembrance.

Persons

One particular type of person is the "dividual" – a person whose formation depends not upon a unified, fixed bodily shell but on the relationships which s/he has with other people and objects (Strathern 1988; Fowler 2004). Defined in contradistinction to an individual, the dividual has classically been recognised as typical of Melanesian society but recent research in Balkan prehistory and other times/places has led to the identification of a form of personhood in which dividuality is at least as significant as individuality (Chapman 1997; Chapman and Gaydarska 2006). It was Deborah Battaglia (1992) who put the question, in the context of Sabarl mortuary exchange: "How to maintain Connerton's dichotomy between inscription and incorporation for dividuals?" when their memory – the memory of their relationships – is embodied in the objects carrying their personhood. The problem that Battaglia enunciated was that, as long as "their" objects circulate, the body of the newly-dead dividual is only apparently dead (cf. Rowlands 1993). In the Sabarl case, there is a gendered system of gifts proper to mortuary exchange: men exchange pigs, valuables, money and other durables, while women exchange ephemeral things produced by women. The difference is that male durable objects continue as mnemonics, unlike the female ephemera, which are not associated with memory outside the exchanges. To resolve this cultural issue, the Sabarl have created a memory screen to block memories of the newly-dead. Food and things gathered in memory of the newly-dead dividual must be dispersed and given away, as part of the work of forgetting. The final forgetting of the deceased is achieved only after the final mortuary feast, perhaps years after the death). Thus, the Sabarl constitute the body as the site of both remembering, through inscription in funeral feasts, and forgetting, through what Battaglia (1992: 13) calls counter-inscription, through the dispersal and burial of goods and food (cf. Devlin 2007 for the Anglo-Saxon body).

Persons who were as much dividual as individual pose questions in the understanding of prehistoric societies, not only in the ways that such personhood was formed through the life-course but also in the ways that their deaths could be finally forgotten. To the extent that inalienable objects – *Spondylus* shell rings, polished stone ceremonial axes, highly decorated pottery, royal or Church emblems – which incorporated long-term personal or social memories remained in circulation, the work of forgetting became much more difficult, with the possibility that closure would never be achieved. However, burial or destruction would help to erase the memories of the person, if that was what was required for the community.

Places

The significance of a place has recently been strongly linked to its associated memory traces (Bradley 2000a; Jones, A. 2007; Devlin 2007). A good example of the way that past dwelling places were incorporated into the present comes from the island of Crete, where the standing ruins of Mycenean palaces or towns, such as Knossos, Phaistos, Ayia Triadha, Palaikastro, Amnisos, Tylisos, and Komnos, became the focus for Early Iron Age deposition some 500 or 600 years after the fall of the palaces (Prent 2003). The selection of the specific place within the abandoned Mycenean site was important; deposition occurred near to, or on, the finest ashlar masonry walls – the pinnacle of Mycenean architecture splendour. The focus of deposition concerned elite practices, such as sacrifical dining and the associated aristocratic tripod-cauldrons, as well as objects linked to male warriors, such as weaponry and shields. However, other uses were made of the Mycenean ruins, such as stone quarrying and occasionally re-settlement. The Iron Age groups used these Mycenean sites in claims over territory or trading harbours. It is interesting that intensive re-use of past sites took place at the time when the reading of Homer was popular. Here, memory-work was dedicated to the linking of physically specific places of evident, but unclear, antiquity to Homeric epic writing about a glorious Mycenean (? Greek) past redolent with palace life, feasting, sacrificial offerings, and warfare. Such practices, so magnificently described in Homer, were indexed by the deposition of related objects in places where it was assumed that such practices took place.

Several chapters in this volume present interesting linkages between memory-work and places. Both Fiano and Hornickova discuss the self-referential way in which the foundation of medieval churches, monasteries and royal palaces were used in memory-work celebrating the nature of the places and, in particular, their founders and the fame of the holy relics stored there. In Majocchi's chapter, the ruling classes of Milan and Pavia used the memories incorporated in the royal palaces to wage propaganda wars for territorial control. Closer to some of the prehistoric studies of place referred to above, Kilmurray makes a strong case for the uses of megalithic monuments as places of active memorialisation, at least in part for the reason that the Neolithic generation is far shorter than the 25 years usually quoted and was most often, on average, a 15-year generation. This has important implications for Neolithic demographics as a whole, such as the notion that most monuments were probably built by teenagers, and also for memory transmission, which , for Kilmurray, was the prime function of monuments. Lastly, Rasson takes a single street in Los Angeles – Olvera Street – as an example of the Mexican and Franciscan contributions to the long-term development of California, its changing functions and its ultimate consumption by the Los Angeles heritage industry.

Objects

Since objects are at the centre of this collection of essays, one can readily find illustrations of the significance of each class of thing for memory-work. Thus, while Spat discusses the metal peacock standard which symbolises the Peacock Angel of the Yezidi people, Hornickova underlines the role of holy relics in the attempted conversion of Protestant Prague to its former Catholic faith, Barbiera explains the significance of weapons and jewellery in the Early Medieval Lombard graves which replaced the overtly inscribing Roman tradition of memorialisation, and Choyke extracts a wealth of social information from mundane bone tools, for which intergenerational curation is the key to memorialisation.

I wish to supplement these examples by turning to the work of Katerina Lillios (2003), whose study of engraved slate plaques in the Iberian Copper Age posits some remarkable conclusions about these usually highly decorated, brilliant and colourful objects. The plaques are normally buried in collective tombs, in numbers sometimes exceeding 100 examples in a single tomb. Of the one to two thousand plaques known, no two plaques are identical, a sound enough reason to identify the aspect of individuality and personal association for an artifact

class. The core of Lillios' research is an exploration of Lisboa's (1985) idea of a heraldic function for plaques. Lillios' working hypothesis is in two parts: the design motifs on the base are emblematic of lineage affiliation, while the number of horizontal registers shows the generational distance between the deceased and an important ancestor. Five data sets are explored in relation to this interpretation, all of which fail to falsify the idea. Thus, Lillios concludes that the burial of the plaques identified particular individuals at death, recording their lineage history and memorialising their being (ibid., p. 146). If Lillios is correct, this study pushes back the use of heraldic devices into deep prehistory and provokes comparisons with medieval uses of such devices. Provided that such objects were not created especially for the mortuary domain, there was great potential for the display and mobility of a plaque during an individual's lifetime, with memory-work involving both commemorative display and the inscription of memory onto the finely-made plaques.

Processes

Processes of dwelling have become central to the notion of inhabitation of a landscape (Johnston 1998; Ashmore and Knapp 1999). However, it was Kovacik (1999) who identified memory as the key aspect of the dwelling process through his definition of a settlement as "a dynamic construction of space and time that preserves, or perhaps encapsulates, the collective memory of a group" (ibid., 1999, 160). Kovacik goes on to observe that structured deposition can have an important role in processes of memory, as illustrated by the procurement and deposition of carnivores and birds of prey in the changing built environment of Pueblo settlements. For Kovacik, Pueblo house foundation deposits linked the house into the community, with deposition as an act of remembrance, even when done in a mundane manner (see also Hendon 2000 on storage, caches and burials). The interpretation that acts of deposition index previous acts and objects is important in the creation of place-value in a settlement and enhances much recent work on dwelling.

Another point that Kovacik makes (ibid., 1999, 162) is that, after a place is settled, memory acts as an "agent" to maintain the location's importance. But in what sense can "memory" act as an "agent"? This notion tends to the reification of a portmanteau term concealing a diversity of practices and processes. Perhaps this is one form of memory-work that does not work! A more interesting alternative is the work of Andy Jones (2007) on the agency of things in memory-work. Jones (2007: 77) seeks to shift our focus from artifacts as the embodiment of culture to the use of things in cultural practices. For Jones, objects are the traces of past actions; their history can be read in its wear (similarly for cycles of architectural alteration and repair in monuments: 2007,

21-22). Thus, material culture is enrolled in the performance of remembrance, which must be practised if it is to work (2007: 49-50). Human emotions are introduced into this account through the notion that objects reference the past because of their sensual qualities, as well as directing attention to future experience also (2007: 62). Thus, the capacity for an object to produce an emotive reaction will depend on its sensual qualities (2007: 66). This is a challenging approach that grounds memory in memory-work – the everyday practices that index and cross-reference our quotidian things to the past and presence other people, places, and things.

Common to all of these concrete examples of memory-work is the importance of the work of interpretation (Bradley 2003: 224). Thus, "the re-making of the past in the past was both a creative act and an interpretation" (2003: 226). The ongoing tension between remembering and forgetting meant that the passage of time brought new combinations of "souvenirs" with which to demonstrate (or deny) an affiliation (e.g., the introduction of new human remains into megaliths, see Cummings [2001: 26]). This multiplicity of interpretational possibilities leads us to our third theme – the plurality of memories.

The plurality of memories

We return to my second quotation, to Camus' sardonic, class-oriented joke against Proust in foregrounding the survival of the memories of the elites rather than those of the poor (let them eat *madeleines*!). Just as the dominant history is the history of the victors rather than that of the vanquished, the upper classes rather than the workers, we may be certain that the differential capacity to mobilise and complete memory-work will have discriminated against the unnamed masses in prehistory and history. To the extent that post-modernist history, as much as the human sciences in general, has sought to uncover the pasts of the invisible Other by whatever means, a multiplicity of histories has been written to redress the biases and the class-based filters. In memory studies, we are still far from identifying the filters that affect different forms of memory-work, even if Alcock (2002: 23) has recognised that male, elite, and urban perspectives, almost inevitably, pronounced upon what was "worthy of memory" from the Classical past to produce a historical filter. If, to quote Alcock (2002: 16) again: "a plurality of concurrent, possibly conflicting and potentially competing memories is available to peoples at any given time," the question is to what extent have all of these competing memories survived? These will include the dominant memories of the dominant groups, as well as what Foucault (1977) has termed "counter-memories" – memories which challenge the dominant discourse (non-elites, women, etc., quoted in Olick and Robbins [1998: 126]).

In this volume, the dice are loaded in favour of elites, with royal or ecclesiastical leaders highlighted in the chapters by Barbiera, Fiano, Majocchi, and Hornickova. Even here, however, Fiano orchestrates a debate about the category of person responsible for the memory-work in aristocratic Pavia – whether it was the monks or the widows. Nonetheless, it is the artisans, the housewives, and the elderly who do much of the memory-work to reproduce the meanings of bone tools in Choyke's chapter, while it is the local ethnic Hispanic community who stand at the heart of Rasson's Olvera Street project. Indeed, it is precisely Olvera Street which is the best example in this volume of the outworkings of multiple memories and competing affiliations. Rasson identifies six different groups all of whom are "stake-holders" in the project: the local stall-holders, local amateur historians, local genealogical societies, the official links to the city of Los Angeles (who displaced the state of California as owning the project), the tourists who visit the Street in their hundreds and thousands, and part of the local Hispanic community, who now include a variety of Mexican public festivals in the street's calendar. But Rasson quotes a thoughtful visitor whose various family members all react to Olvera Street in different ways and whose memories of the place and its urban context are quite at odds with each other.

One useful analogy that may help with finding structure in such a plurality of memories concerns the views of the geographer Rob Shields on place-identity (Shields [1991]; for an archaeological inflection, see Chapman [1998]). Shields argues that people use particular discourses about places as a mark of their own "insider" status in the relevant communities, meaning that group affiliation is created through knowledge of discourses that locate places as particular kinds of places. The notion that cultural knowledge is central to group affiliation is reinforced by the idea that the essential marker of a cultural activity is the process of place-identification. The naming of a place marks an insertion into a symbolic realm of a material space whose meaning can be discussed only in the context of that symbolic realm of discourse.

Shields (1991) proceeds to develop a nested hierarchical scheme for spatial identities, identifying mythology, place-myth, and place-image. At the highest level, a mythology of place identities is a form of cosmology, comprising the overall system of similarities and differences among all known places. The communal mythology is formed by a set of place-myths. Place-myths represent the conflicting but often internally coherent versions of the identity of a particular place. It is often the case that different groups negotiate their own versions of a place-myth with other groups. It is also common for place-myths to change over time. Such place-myths consist of a collective set of place-images.

Place-images derive from face-to-face encounters with particular places and consist of discrete messages associated with real places regardless of their character in reality. People who visit places commonly construct their images through one or more processes: over-simplification, stereotyping and labelling. In this way, place-identities begin to be formed at the lowest level; they tend to be dominated by core images, often in the form of mental maps, which tend to remain embedded despite other changes.

These three levels of mythology, myth, and image operate as "insider stories" – as part of the symbolic construction of communal identities despite the polyvocality of images (Shields 1991: 262). Rather than denying collective image-formation or collective consciousness, Shields opposes group myths and private behaviour, claiming that the tension between group myth and personal experience forms the basis for social action. How do these ideas relate to the plurality of memory?

A hierachical suite of aspects of memory can be mapped onto the tripartite Shields' scheme with relative success. At the lowest level are the memories that each person may hold about self, other persons, places, things, events, and processes. Because these individual memories were personally experienced, often in an emotional context, they remain as core images for the persons concerned. At the next level up, consonant with place-myths, there is social (or collective) memory, which solidifies around both quotidian memory-effects and more permanent effects. There may well have been different groups with markedly diverging views about the importance of *their* memories relating to a specific monument (e.g., Stonehenge), person or object. Social memory crystallises out of a multitude of personal memories, some of which are shared more widely than others. The counterpart in memory-work of the highest level – place mythology – is the creation of a memory-based moral order created out of a negotiation over the needs, desires, and principles of the entire community. Julia Hendon (2000) has shown how issues such as storage can influence the location of individuals within a moral order, which in turn creates the conditions for future social practices. Hendon (2000: 50) asserts that: "Storage, whether 'utilitarian' or ritual, raises issues of secrecy, memory, prestige and knowledge that help construct the moral system within which people live." In a parallel approach, Robinson (1989) has emphasised the importance of a person's relationship to a known and identifiable place of settlement, which confers on that person moral and juridical rights. The relational field of people and their settlements is clearly underpinned by a chain of social memories that link proper conduct with a given settlement. The opposite – a person whose home settlement is not known – becomes not merely an "outsider" but an "outcast", a non-person with no legal basis for relating to another community.

The proposal for a nested hierarchy of memory that runs in parallel with Shields' (1991) hierarchy of place-identity shares with Shields' account the key role of "insiders" and "outsiders". Insiders – those who experienced the same, or a similar range of, memories as other people in the group – will have the common bonds of the past to create a shared identity. Those who have no such shared memories – the "outsiders" to your "insiders" – can only ever negotiate the meanings of people, places and things to which there is common access with the "insider" group. It is the individuals who share some memories as a result of a shared past but whose collective memory has foregrounded different facets of the past who are socially most problematic, because they challenge at a very basic level the "insiders" beliefs in their own remembered pasts. In complex societies, where there is no place to hide from the memory-based moral order of the dominant elites, counter-memories can still be created to act as a form of resistance to elite power.

Conclusions

Let me summarise my forethoughts to this volume by making four general observations. I started with a quotation from Climo and Cattell (2002: 1), who asserted that "without memory, the world would cease to exist in any meaningful way." There are signs that this truth has been taken on board more seriously by archaeologists and historians in the last decade than previously. In their enthusiastic yet uncritical acceptance of the memory research agenda, some colleagues have expanded the brief of memory to include, as with some short histories of the world, almost everything. A concern about this recent research trend has been raised by Devlin (2007) that the concept of social memory may become so diffuse and wide-ranging as to become meaningless. While Devlin's solution to restrict the notion of memory-work to the time of personal experience is surely too narrow, another approach is to make sufficiently strong linkages between the multiplicity of forms of memory and the use of things in Bourdieu-type cultural practices so that memory is always securely anchored to the material world (cf. Jones, A. 2007). This would summarise the materialist paradigm for the study of memory-work that is recommended here.

A second point concerns the dangers of assuming that memory-work will encapsulate the same range of practices whatever the form and aetiology of personhood in the relevant cultural context. Not surprisingly, the default position has been the Western individual. This chapter has made a start in discussing the very different practices necessary to bring the forgetting of that particular form of dispersed person – the Melanesian dividual – to a successful long-term conclusion. However, there are many different forms of dividual person known in anthropology, such as the South Indian dividual (Busby 1997), while the Polynesian concept of expanded personhood (Sahlins 1985) and the Jivaro notion of Amazonian personhood (Whittle 2003) introduce yet more differences in the ways of being human. It would be important for future studies of memory to achieve a better integration between contrasting forms of personhood and the appropriate forms of memory-work.

Turning to the contents of this volume, I see the main strength of the collection in the diversity of approach, time/place context of studies and the wide range of memory-work under discussion. It is rare to find an in-depth study of a Los Angeles street rubbing shoulders with chapters on the memory-uses of the royal palace of medieval Pavia, the impact of Neolithic demographics on the construction of megalithic monuments and the mundane but eloquent testimony of bone tools in the materialisation of inter-generational family commemoration. The Department of Medieval Studies at the Central European University of Budapest should be congratulated on the range of research – not only historical but also archaeological and ethnographic.

Finally, a comment on two theoretical aspects of memory studies where this collection could have recalled the previous research literature on memory rather better. Memory research since Connerton (1989), Battaglia (1992) and Rowlands (1993) has identified a key area of memory studies as the dialectic between remembering and forgetting. This dialectic is implicitly present in this collection (e.g., the way, in Fiano's chapter, in which the inhabitants burnt down the Lombard royal palace of Pavia in 1024 without stopping its use as a mnemonic support for further generations of royal elites) but the studies would all have been strengthened by close attention to this dialectic. Secondly, recent studies of material memories have focused closely on the reasons for the selection of certain classes of artifacts for mnemonics rather than the overlooking of other classes (e.g., Devlin's (2007) criticism of H. Williams' (2003) analysis of early medieval bone combs as mnemonic devices). This point can be broadened to refer to all cases of persons and all forms of places, as well as all categories of object, that have been selected to bring particular embodied characteristics to the task of memory-work. A clear, explicit statment of the rationale behind the selection of specific people, places, and things would have lent even more weight to the often sophisticated arguments in this collection.

Acknowledgements

I am grateful to Alice Choyke for inviting me to set down some thoughts on her volume. I trust that the result will be to her taste and that she does not regret her invitation. I am also naturally grateful to the contributors of all the chapters for making my reading into social memory much more stimulating and diverse. Thanks are due, as always, to Bisserka for her comments on earlier, less comprehensible drafts.

Bibliography

Alcock, S. E. 2002. *Archaeologies of the Greek Past. Landscape, Monuments and Memories*. Cambridge: Cambridge University Press.

Ashmore, W. and Knapp, A. B. (eds.). 1999. *Archaeologies of Landscape. Contemporary Perspectives*. Oxford: Blackwell.

Assmann, J. 1992. *Das kulturelle Gedächtnis: Schrift, Erinnerung und politische Identität in frühen Hochkulturen*. Munich: C. H. Beck.

Battaglia, D. 1992. The Body in the Gift: memory and Forgetting in Sabarl Mortuary Exchanges. *American Ethnologist* 19, No. 1, pp. 3-18.

Boivin, N. and Owoc, M. A. (eds.). 2004. *Soils, Stones and Symbols. Cultural Perceptions of the Mineral World*. London: UCL Press.

Bradley, R. 1998. Ruined Buildings, Ruined Stones: Enclosures, Tombs and Natural Places in the Neolithic of South-West England. *World Archaeology* 30, No.1, pp. 13-22.

Bradley, R. 1998. *The Significance of Monuments*. London: Routledge.

Bradley, R. 2000. *The Archaeology of Natural Places*. London: Routledge.

Bradley, R. 2000a. *The Past in Prehistoric Societies*. London: Routledge.

Bradley, R. 2003. The Translation of Time. In *Archaeologies of Memory*. R. Van Dyke and S. E. Alcock (eds.). Oxford: Blackwell, pp. 221-227.

Busby, C. 1997. Permeable and Partible Persons: A Comparative Analysis of Gender and Body in South India and Melanesia. *Journal of the Royal Anthropological Institute* 3, No. 2, pp. 261-278.

Camus, A. 1994. *The First Man* (translated by D. Hapgood). London: Penguin.

Chapman, J. 1997. Places as Timemarks – The Social Construction of Landscapes in Eastern Hungary. In *Landscapes in Flux*. J. Chapman and P. Dolukhanov (eds.). Oxford: Oxbow Books, pp. 137-162.

Chapman, J. 1998. Objects and Places: Their Value in the Past. In *The Archaeology of Prestige and Wealth*. D. W. Bailey (ed.). BAR International Series 730. Oxford: BAR Publishing, pp. 106-130.

Chapman, J. and Gaydarska, B. 2006. *Parts and Wholes. Fragmentation in Prehistoric Context*. Oxford: Oxbow Books.

Clack, T. A. R. 2007. *Memory and the Mountain. Environmental Relations of the Wachagga of Kilimanjaro and Implications for Landscape Archaeology*. BAR I-1679. Oxford: BAR Publishing.

Climo, J. J. and Cattell, M. G. 2002. Introduction: Meaning in Social Memory and History: Anthropological

Perspectives. In *Social Memory and History: Anthropological Perspectives*. J. J. Climo and M. G. Cattell (eds.). Walnut Creek, CA: Altamira Press, pp. 1-36.

Connerton, P. 1989. *How Societies Remember*. Cambridge: Cambridge University Press.

Connerton, P. 2006. Cultural Memory. In *Handbook of Material Culture*. C. Tilley, W. Keane, S. Küchler, M. Rowlands, and P. Spyer (eds.). London: Sage, pp. 315-324.

Cummings V. 2000. Myth, Memory and Metaphor: The Significance of Place, Space and Landscape in Mesolithic Pembrokeshire. In *Mesolithic lifeways. Current Research from Britain and Ireland*. R. Young (ed.). Leicester Archaeology Monographs No. 7. Leicester: University of Leicester, pp. 87-95.

Cummings, V. 2001. Building from Memory. Remembering the Past at Neolithic Monuments in Western Britain. In *Archaeologies of Remembrance. Death and Memory in Past Societies*. H. Williams (ed.). London: Kluwer, pp. 25-43.

Cummings, V. and Pannett, A. (eds.). 2005. *Set in Stone. New Approaches to Neolithic Monuments in Scotland*. Oxford: Oxbow Books.

Devlin, Z. 2007. *Remembering the Dead in Anglo-Saxon England. Memory Theory in Archaeology and History*. BAR British Series B446. Oxford: BAR Publishing.

Dietler, M. 1998. A Tale of Three Sites: The Monumentalization of Celtic Oppida and the Politics of Collective Memory and Identity. *World Archaeology* 30, No. 1, pp. 72-89.

Donald, M. 1991. *Origins of the Modern Mind: Three Stages in the Evolution of Culture and Cognition*. Cambridge, MA: Harvard University Press.

Foucault, M. 1977. *Language, Counter-memory, Practice: Selected Essays and Interviews*. (translated by J. F. Bouchard and S. Simon). Ithaca, NY: Cornell University Press.

Fowler, C. 2004. *The Archaeology of Personhood. An Anthropological Approach*. London: Routledge.

Freud, S. 1900 (1997). *The Interpretation of Dreams* (translated by A. A. Brill). London: Wordsworth Editions.

Geary, P. J. 1994. *Phantoms of Remembrance: Memory and Oblivion at the End of the First Millennium*. Princeton, NJ: Princeton University Press.

Halbwachs, M. 1925 (1992). *On Collective Memory* (translated/edited by L. A. Coser). Chicago: University of Chicago Press.

Halbwachs, M. 1941. *La topographie légendaire des évangiles en terre sainte: étude de mémoire collective*. Paris: Alcan.

Hendon, J. 2000. Storage, Memory, Knowledge and Social Relations. *American Anthropologist* 102, No. 1, pp. 42-53.

Holtorf, C. 1998. The Life-histories of Megaliths in Vorpommern-Mecklenburg (Germany). *World Archaeology* 30, No.1, pp. 23-38.

Ingold, T. 1993. The Temporality of the Landscape. *World Archaeology* 25, No. 2, pp. 152-174.

Johnston, R. 1998. The Paradox of Landscape. *European Journal of Archaeology* 1, No. 3, pp. 313- 325.

Jones, A. 2005. Between a Rock and a Hard Place: Rock art and Mimesis in Neolithic and Bronze Age Scotland. In *Set in stone. New approaches to Neolithic monuments in Scotland*. V. Cummings and A. Pannett (eds.). Oxford: Oxbow Books, pp. 107-117.

Jones, A. 2007. *Memory and Material Culture*. Cambridge: Cambridge University Press.

Jones, P. L. 2008. *Moving Heaven and Earth: Landscape, Death and Memory in the Aceramic Neolithic of Cyprus*. BAR I-1795. Oxford: BAR Publishing.

Kovacik, J. J. 1999. Memory and Pueblo Space. In *Making Places in the Prehistoric World. Themes in Settlement Archaeology*. J. Brück and M. Goodman (eds.). London: UCL Press, pp. 160-177.

Küchler, S. 1993. Landscape as Memory: The Mapping of Process and its Representation in a Melanesian Society. In *Landscape, politics and perspectives*. B. Bender (ed.). Oxford: Berg, 85-106.

Last, J. 1998. Books of Life: Biography and Memory in a Bronze Age Barrow. *Oxford Journal of Archaeology* 17, No.1: 43-53.

Lillios, K. T. 2003. Creating Memory in Prehistory: The Engraved Slate Plaques of SW Iberia. In *Archaeologies of Memory*. R. Van Dyke and S. E. Alcock (eds.). Oxford: Blackwell, pp. 129-150.

Lisboa, I. M. G. 1985. Meaning and Messages: Mapping Style in the Iberian Chalcolithic. *Archaeological Review from Cambridge* 4, No. 3. pp. 181-196.

Manning, S. 1998. Changing Pasts and Political Cognition in LBA Cyprus. *World Archaeology* 30, No.1, pp. 39-58.

Morley, I. 2006. Hunter-gatherer Music and its Implications for Identifying Intentionality in the Use of Acoustic Space. In *Archaeoacoustics*. C. Scarre and G. Lawson (eds.). Cambridge: McDonald Institute for Archaeological Research, pp. 95-105.

Nietzsche, F. 1983. *Untimely Meditations* (translated by R. J. Hollingdale). Cambridge: Cambridge University Press.

Olick, J. K. and Robbins, J. 1998. Social Memory Studies: From "Collective Memory" to the Historical Sociology of Mnemonic Practices. *Annual Review of Sociology* 24, pp. 105-140.

Prent, M. 2003. Glories of the Past in the Past: Ritual Activities at Palatial Ruins in EIA Crete. In *Archaeologies of Memory*. R. Van Dyke and S. E. Alcock (eds.). Oxford: Blackwell, pp. 81-103.

Robinson, D. 1989. The Language and Significance of Place in Latin America. In *The Power of Place. Bringing Together Geographical and Social Imaginations*. J. A. Agnew and J. S. Duncan (eds.). Boston: Unwin Hyman, pp. 157-184.

Rowlands, M. 1993. The Role of Memory in the Transmission of Culture. *World Archaeology* 25, pp. 141-151.

Sahlins, M. 1985. *Islands of of History*. Chicago: University of Chicago Press.

Schama, S. 1996. *Landscape and Memory*. London: Fontana.

Shields, R. 1991. *Places on the Margin. Alternative Geographies of Modernity*. London: Routledge.

Strathern, M. 1988. *The Gender of the Gift*. Berkeley: University of California Press.

Thomas, J. 2001. Archaeologies of Place and Landscape. In *Archaeological Theory Today*. I. Hodder (ed.). Oxford: Polity, pp. 165-186.

Tilley, C. 2004. *The Materiality of Stone. Explorations in Landscape Phenomenology 1*. Oxford: Berg.

Van Dyke, R. and Alcock, S. E. 2003. Archaeologies of Memory: An Introduction. In *Archaeologies of Memory*. R. Van Dyke and S. E. Alcock (eds.). Oxford: Blackwell, pp. 1-13.

Van Dyke, R. and Alcock, S.E. (eds.). 2003a. *Archaeologies of Memory*. Oxford: Blackwell.

Whitehouse, H. 1995. *Inside the Cult. Religious Innovation and Transmission in Papua New Guinea*. Oxford: Clarendon.

Whittle, A. 2003. *The Archaeology of People. Dimensions of Neolithic life*. London: Routledge.

Williams, H., 1998. Monuments and the Past in in Early Anglo-Saxon England. *World Archaeology* 30, No. 1, pp. 90-108.

Williams, H. (ed.). 2001. *Archaeologies of Remembrance. Death and Memory in Past Societies*. London: Kluwer.

Williams, H., 2001a. Introduction. In H. Williams (ed.) *Archaeologies of Remembrance. Death and Memory in Past Societies*. London: Kluwer, pp. 1-24.

Williams, H. 2003. Material Culture as Memory: Combs and Cremation in Early Medieval Britain. *Early Medieval Europe 2003* 12, No. 2, pp. 89-128.

Williams, M. 2001. Tales from the Dead. Remembering the Bog Bodies in the Iron Age of North-Western Europe. In H. Williams (ed.) *Archaeologies of Remembrance. Death and Memory in Past Societies*. London: Kluwer, pp. 89-112.

World Archaeology 1998. Vol. 30. No. 1, "The Past in the Past."

INTRODUCTION

Irene Barbiera

Some of the papers collected in this volume were originally presented at the Xth annual meeting of the European Society of Archaeologists, held in Lyon in 2004, in a section entitled: *Social Change, Stability and the Use of Memory in Past Societies*. Since that time, many things have changed and the structure of the volume no longer properly represents the session as it was comprised then. New contributions were added and some other papers presented at the conference were not included in the volume. The present group of papers relate to a broad range of chronological periods, from prehistory until contemporary times since humans have always manipulated the physical world they find around them and still do today. The many ways different aspects of material culture can be used to construct and support social memory are considered in detail in the papers in this volume. The original core of the discourse from the conference, however, has still been preserved. The original idea was to consider how material culture was employed in different societies and in different cultural contexts in the past to transmit, preserve and invent memory in juxtaposition with social stability, change and transformations. Memory and forgetting have many faces and so does the way material culture is used as their physical manifestation. Each paper considers one or more aspects of material culture employed to create memory in both preserving and transforming social contexts.

One important aspect addressed in various papers is the way material culture was employed to reinforce power positions, social cohesion and stratification through the creation of collective memory materialized in special objects. This was particularly significant in phases of social transformations, when the elites needed to reinforce or establish their positions and therefore had to invest more energy in creating their public image. Particularly important in this regard were town monuments or significant places as well as special objects promoted exclusively by elites groups as a means of propaganda.

As Zsidi points out, public monuments particularly flourished in Aquincum towards the end of the AD 1st century, after the town become the capital of the province of Pannonia Inferior. In the context of this new role played by Aquincum, monuments were employed to perpetuate three levels of memory within the local population. The first level was aimed at emphasizing the importance of the local elites on an international level, by stressing their connections with Imperial authority, the second level aimed at advertising their public activities concerned with development of public space in the town. The third level was related to the creation of genealogies of eminent families through funerary monuments located on the main roads coming into the town. Stone was the material of social memory *par excellence* in Roman times, displaying long-lasting collective and private spheres of memory in public spaces. As family fortunes waned however, re-use of these monuments also shows that there was much on-going active forgetting.

This attitude of creating "*ville vetrines*" (Cracco Ruggini, 1989), towns where monuments spoke to the efforts which elites dedicated to their citizens continued during the Early Middle Ages although the types of monuments and buildings may have changed together with their functions. Majocchi shows in his paper how the Lombard kings made Pavia into their capital by promoting public constructions and creating instant memories in stone. The new kings made great efforts to create a worthy capital to reside in, the symbol of which was the new royal palace. In addition, churches, monasteries and the tombs connected to them also flourished in Pavia. These buildings spread after Christianization and were promoted by aristocratic groups to display their connection with the Church by offering citizens new buildings to pray in. Thus, in Pavia, the Lomabards created an image and memories of themselves as good Christian rulers through the media of material culture. The public space they created and the memory of themselves they left behind were later re-emphasised during the 12th-14th centuries when the commune of Pavia was in competition with Milan and later the emerging ruling family of the Visconti for control of the region. The role of Pavia as capital of the Lombard kingdom became a significant, valuable piece of history to be remembered. The surviving monuments were the tangible face of this particular past.

Places of memory did not always result from conscious political plans. This is the case of Olivera Street in 20ᵗʰ century Los Angeles as described by Rasson. The main square became a place of memory for Mexican folklore thanks to the initiative of an ordinary lady, from a non prominent family. Her idea was inspired by a romantic, nostalgic and paternalistic interest in indigenous culture which was widespread at the time among non-indigenous groups living in California. Later on, the place assumed a multi-layered meaning for various social groups. It was important for the self-identity of the Mexican indigenous minority but, at the same time, it become a place where the elites promoted public events through the use of particular physical 'props' recognized by a wide range of people including any citizen or tourists wanting to experience the flavor of this particular culture.

The flourishing of burial monuments in Neolithic Europe is also interpreted as a sign of significant social change. Construction of these large burial monuments became common, especially in the British Isles. The construction of these monuments must have been the result of better organized communities related to the presence of permanent settlements as Kilmurray has pointed out. Moreover, given that many people in the Neolithic may have had relatively short lives, several more generations than has been previously thought may necessarily have been involved in building and maintaining such monuments. As a consequence, the past they were meant to symbolize was multiple: they were built to represent the memory of historical events passed down though orality and they become the past itself, involving many distant generations. Also, from a social point of view, the fact that numerous generations were involved in such projects, suggests that some sort of grandiose plan, coordinated by stable chieftain kin groups and keyed to deliberately produce memory, seems to lie behind these constructions.

Besides monuments, special objects such as grave goods, or other symbols displayed during public rituals, ceremonies or visibly in every day social interactions were actively employed to both legitimate power positions and create an idea of continuity at a time when significant social changes were underway. Another group of papers in this volume are devoted to this aspect of material culture and memory.

Bone tools, from Neolithic and Bronze Age contexts in Hungary, discussed by Choyke, were often produced using identical technical styles and often following very similar formal models over hundreds of years. The use of and wearing of individual objects could also be transgenerational, connecting the past with the present and future on a number of different emotional levels for small, household level social groups and even individuals. The ultimate of abandonment of such long-lived styles also signaled the disappearance of the social constructs which supported their existence over such long time periods. Among more mobile groups, inhabiting settlements for only a few years, such special bone objects may have acted as a medium for cohesion within the community and kin groups. Produced and used for many hundreds of years, they incorporated a sense of belonging and past traditions. Reflecting a similar, parallel attitude, traditional ladies from Transylvania may be attached to certain, special traditional like combs as one more means to anchor themselves to family history and tradition as a reaction to the forces of modernization.

Majocchi shows that although the attitudes of the elites toward towns did not substantially change after the end of the Roman Empire, a time of great social transformation, other spheres of memory were transformed as a response to instability. For instance, some significant changes occurred in the way the dead were remembered in the context of cemeteries, as shown by Barbiera. Funerary inscriptions were only rarely employed in this period, and more lavish grave goods started to be deposited in graves. The ritual of the funeral and the symbolic deposition of grave goods had an important meaning for the creation, display and maintenance of the chosen identity of the deceased and their families. Possibly at a time when inscriptions and written words were not employed, more emphasis was given to symbolic rituals, perhaps to fire the communal imagination, an important repository for the memory of the deceased, which was otherwise only transmitted orally. It seems that in this period, when power positions between elites were less clear, rituals, with their recognized and appropriate objects, played an important role in the establishment of the new, emerging social order. Kin groups created an image of themselves for the future, by burying their ancestors in a magnificent and memorable manner. With greater social complexity, when the dynastic succession was unstable, as explained by Fiano, the display of the physical throne promoted funerals and commemorative rituals for the deceased kings. These rituals and the objects used in them, were meant to stress the strong connections with the new king and legitimize the succession as well as the new ruler's own power. In later centuries the church controlled more and more of these rituals of memory, performed to commemorate the anniversary of a particular death and meant to save the soul of the dead person. Ruling dynasties and aristocratic families gave donations to monasteries in exchange for prayers to save the soul of their ancestors. Material donations were recorded and their memory preserved. In this way, the putative position acquired by these aristocrats' souls in the otherworld became a reflection of the power and prosperity these individuals had achieved in this world. The prayers that they paid for were intended to memorialize these achievements.

Another example of the way material culture can be employed as significant symbol of memory at a time of social change is the peacock standard in Yezidi religion, investigated by Spät. The peacock god was the venerated symbol of this small religion whose practitioners are spread through parts of Iraq, Syria, Turkey, Iran, and the Caucasian states since the Middle Ages. The small bronze statuette is still displayed in processions during special religious events. These processions and rituals represent important moments for this religion since, until recently, it was transmitted orally. A special group of men, the so-called *qewwal*s, were in charge of keeping the memory of Yezidi religion and transmitting it from father to son. These individuals celebrated ceremonies and had special powers within the religious communities. These religious elites also had the right to employ small metal objects of supposed great antiquity sewn on bags which marked them as being different from other practitioners of this religion. The memory of the generations who used these objects as well as the connection of these individually old peacock standards with a constructed divine past serve to support and preserve religious beliefs within these far-flung, sometimes quite isolated communities. From the 1970s however, with the spread of literacy especially among wealthiest groups and Yezidis living in the European dispora, intellectuals started writing down their sacred texts. This fact has brought significant changes: the *qewwal*s have begun to lose their importance as the guardians of Yezidi religious belief. The way the religion was performed and transmitted changed, while rituals and processions with their special props lost their importance. In this context of transformation, the image of the peacock standard remained an important symbol of Yezidi religious identity, though in a different, standardized printed form. It is now found on books and written contexts and in this form is no longer such a valuable object in religious events. In this guise, the peacock standard has become an important vehicle for preserving communal memory. Thus, the peacock itself kept its function as a symbol of memory, even if the social order of the Yezidis, it is connected to in the traditional religion, has changed significantly.

Besides the efforts involved in creating credible memory, different kinds of identities may be expressed through the medium of material culture. The acts of remembering and forgetting as well as the selection of particular memories made visible (or invisible) some aspects of social identity. This is another important point addressed across the board in the papers collected in this volume. Gender and the role of men and women in the perpetuation of pubic and private memory is an important result emerging from various papers. Whilst in twentieth century Los Angeles, a women was actively involved in the creation of a public space (see Rasson in this volume), in previous societies, from prehistory to the Middle Ages, women seem to have been more invisible in the public sphere, with a few exceptions. Women, on the other hand, may have been more active in the preservation of private, kin-based group memories, for instance as mourners (Zsidi, Barbiera and Fiano) or as keepers of family, household traditions (Choyke). Their acts of remembering had clear social consequences when the kin groups these women belonged to were powerful (see Fiano).

In addition to gender, age was also an important category which impacted on the way material culture were utilized in remembering. As Kilmurray stressed in his paper, a significant aspect of the way group-built monuments and their memory operate on society is linked to demography and in particular individual life spans. Shorter life spans meant that there was less overlap between generations which in turn had important consequences for maintaining, reactivation, and transmission of social memory. At the same time, funerals played an important role in group memory of the life cycle and the social role of individuals at different stages in their lives (Barbiera and Choyke).

Memory also plays an important role in relation to other aspects of identity, remembered or forgotten in different contexts, in the maintenance of socially recognized ethnic boundaries (Rasson), kin group membership (Choyke, Barbiera, Zsidi), social rank (Zsidi, Majocchi, and Barbiera) and religious affiliation (Majocchi, Fiano, and Spat). Such identities are malleable and can be actively employed by different societies or particular social groups through deposition or use of special objects or monuments to select or invent a special past and by doing so enhance a particular identity for themselves. Even though many different strategies were developed by different societies in different periods, material culture seems always to have been particularly powerful as a tool of remembering in times of change and social stress to give a sense of authenticity and continuity to legitimate new situations or new power positions (Howsbow, 1972). Newly emerging artifacts or monuments or objects made more valuable by their association with an ancient constructed past were meant to create a direct link between the past, present and the imagined future.

GRANDMOTHER'S AWL: INDIVIDUAL AND COLLECTIVE MEMORY THROUGH MATERIAL CULTURE

Alice M. Choyke

Abstract

Particular types of prehistoric bone tools could be used over the lifetimes of individuals. Such objects would have embodied the memory of both their recent and far-distant constructed past for the groups who traditionally used them. Intensively used tools and ornaments made of osseous materials would have represented the experience and *savoir faire* of practitioners closely associated with them and their individual lifetime of memories. Some tools and ornaments may even have been exploited across generations, linking the more immediate past and present with the expected future. Examples of the various ways the long-term use of traditional bone objects worked to sustain social memory are presented here with descriptions of two types of recent traditional bone objects where the individual biographies are available. The first objects are bone combs owned and used by a middle-aged woman from a traditional Hungarian village in Romania. The second object is a bevel-ended tool used for burnishing and creasing leather in shoe-making. This tool type comes from a workshop in Sofia, Bulgaria, and is part of the tool kit used by these traditional artisans. Examples of carefully manufactured and well-worn bone tools and ornaments from Neolithic and Bronze Age contexts in Hungary will then be presented in light of the way ethnographically attested bone objects have been shown to represent both individual and group memories for their users.

Keywords: Central Europe, individual and group memory, *chaîne d'opération*, long-term use, bone tools and ornaments

***

Introduction

Individual and collective memory expressed by and through the traditional material culture surrounding and exploited by people is one way both individuals and social groups maintain continuity and cohesion. Traditional objects made and used by people in their everyday lives were surely used by people as references to the past in order to validate the present. Rejection of artifact manufacturing traditions (when an object ceases to be used for a particular task) can also be seen as a kind of forgetting, a reaction to inevitable changes in social structures through time. As Malinowski (1939) has pointed out, objects have social lives. These "material" lives were set in motion, circumscribed, animated, and integrated into the society that surrounded them and the cultural traditions they were a part of. Thus, worked osseous objects and ornaments have always been made and used according to such regular, accepted rules, accompanied by the "proper" gestures of practice. Some of these objects were utilized by individuals for many years, perhaps throughout their lives and even passed down to subsequent generations. At the same time, these tool and ornament types could be produced and used in more-or-less similar ways over the centuries and across generations. Now and in the past, the constant interplay between daily repetitive, expected experience contrasted with unique or unusual events as experienced by individuals that had the potential to disrupt custom and, potentially, over the long run, social cohesion. Thus, remembering by individuals and groups took place in a world of familiar objects ordered through social practice in such a way as both to provide a sense of continuity and to mark particular events. Social practices, encoded in the way tools were customarily made and exploited, represent one of the major ways, apart from speech, in which people have always engaged with the material world. The ordered gestures, almost ritualized, involved in tool and ornament production and function were first described in French literature on lithic production as *the chaîne d'opération* or *chaîne operatoire* but has since moved into the French bone tool literature and on into general archaeological usage.

Raday (1990:49) has pointed out that since mundane objects are inextricably tied to memory, people inevitably used them to establish links with both the personal and constructed group past. This kind of remembering helps sustain both personal and group identity. As people age, individual artifacts become increasingly associated with their personal memories. At the same time, the objects themselves become associated with the people who used them, at least by others in their immediate social circle. Thus, changes in the order of the way things are supposed to be done, in the way objects are made and the way they are used, can represent another kind of statement about various perceived or desired changes in an individual's life or the social order followed by a particular group of people. The word group is used in this paper to refer to any association of people within society based on a range of common recognized factors from profession, family ties, gender, age cohort, ethnicity, religion to even simple location.

The nature of worked osseous materials

Tools and ornaments made from osseous materials have a surprisingly enduring character. Thus, such objects may follow a person through various life stages in their existence, evoking over and over again the life situations of which they were once a part. The material world, particularly objects made from relatively tough, durable materials, often outlives its original context and even its original owners, becoming trans-generational. Even humble objects used in everyday activities can serve as monuments to individual efforts or social ideals of production and use, which, in turn, extend into a long ago, revered mythological past. In parallel, as societies underwent change connected both to outside influences and the natural tendency of humans to tinker with their lives, certain traditional objects naturally lost their signature value. Their production ceased or underwent important changes in technical and formal style, in a sense, they and the constructed memories behind them were forgotten.

At the same time, individual bone objects, together with the memory of ancient manufacturing and use traditions embedded within them, underwent continuous re-modeling throughout their use-lives. Patterns of breakage, renewal, and even re-use and discard were predictable and culturally established. These individual worked bone objects frequently display use, handling wear, and repeated repair that would have taken many years to produce. Such objects themselves might have formed part of individual memories, especially as an individual aged along with his or her tools. Such well-worn objects could become expressions of the personal experience(s) and *savoir faire* of the people who exploited them in the close knit household and village setting of the prehistoric milieu they came from.

Worked bone objects used in the small farming hamlets of the Early Neolithic Körös culture in Hungary may, in some cases, have been transported to each new settlement, actually lasting longer than settlements themselves, helping to create a sense of continuity for individuals through the memory of their previous manufacture and use contexts. These might be described as mobile memories woven around the customary, familiar activities of individuals past and present (Choyke

2007). Conversely, these well-used objects were sometimes thrown away before the end of their use life in acts of forgetting, perhaps coinciding with some dramatic event in the life of the individuals closely associated with them. Of course, many objects were simply broken and discarded or even lost and abandoned. The question of how to distinguish between the deliberate disposal and normal turnover of tools must be connected to patterns of discard displayed by particular kinds of artifacts as well as patterning in the kinds of places particular tool or ornament types were disposed of within ancient settlements. There is no such thing as a universal pattern in the way bone tools and ornaments were conserved or disposed of in the past. Each recognized social environment would have had its own rules and these rules may well have changed over centuries.

Sedentary, complex societies, apparently inhabiting politically defined territories and settlements which may have existed continuously for several hundred years, also adopted places of memory more intensely as part of the way they constructed ideas about the past, present, and future of their group. Traditional objects, however, including those made from bone, antler and tooth, would still have possessed the power to evoke both collective and individual memories through the traditional ways they were made and the length of time they were used.

Pinpointing memory maintenance associated with object types is a difficult business, especially in prehistoric periods where precise social contexts have been lost. It is proposed here, however, that worked osseous tools and ornaments meant to be used in a group setting or for display which are persistent in their style over long periods of time probably do represent varieties of memory related to preserving age, sex, and group identities. These may be associated with a particular community, all reinforced by their links to the past. It is exactly these very characteristic, planned tools and ornaments which often display the most intense wear and most often show signs of continuous repair in prehistoric settings, wear of a sort that most likely could only be produced over years of use.

Thus, objects, whether mundane, ornamental or unique, embody both cultural mores and become part of the human drama of existence. Even in the modern world, the presence of material things made and used by people in the present are interwoven into the fabric of people's memories of their individual life histories, the way the world was thought to have been experienced in the past and, finally, the way other people in the world are seen to experience life through the way they make and exploit these objects (Taylor and Cohen-Kiel 2003, http://www.cs.cornell.edu/ People/ Sengers/DomesticTech03/Taylor, last opened April 2009). In other words, material objects have often been used by people both in the past and the present as a means to formulate and represent coherent pictures of constructed individual and group history.

Long-term use of tools and ornaments and individual experience

The duration of the use-life of individual objects made from osseous materials has not been particularly researched; bone as a raw material is often seen as the plastic of prehistory. This relative indifference to this class of artifact is related to two factors. First, animal bone is readily available, devaluing its worth in the eyes of modern archaeologists who, generally speaking, have been brought up to believe that rarity is one essential factor of value. In fact, many other things may determine worth, including the appropriateness of a raw material for a particular kind of tool, long-term tradition, and the special anthropomorphizing characters associated with a particular species or skeletal element through myth or story (for a good example of such ascribed characters associated with particular animals and skeletal elements see Birtalan 2003). Secondly, there are also methodological problems associated with differentiating between tools exhibiting heavy handling wear from intensive use, especially on materials that promote polish such as leather or bark, and tools displaying heavy handling wear because they have been in use for many years. Nevertheless, researchers frequently encounter such polished, well worn objects on sites from all periods that have in all likelihood been exploited over long periods of time as well.

My personal realization that bone tools and ornaments may represent long-term experience on the part of their users and play their part in the construction of social memory, however, came from almost random encounters with the middle-aged and elderly owners (and users) of two modern objects previously used in traditional contexts in Eastern Europe. The advantage in these cases was that the individual tool biographies were available since the owners were still alive to be interviewed (Choyke 2006).

One aspect of tool-using behavior reflecting the cultural context for utilitarian, mundane objects is the length of time individual tools were intentionally kept and preserved by individuals or within particular social groupings. Looking at the proportions of ad hoc, barely used objects compared to heavily worn and curated ones on prehistoric sites in Hungary it is clear that, at different times and in different places, the attitude toward such objects could vary widely (Choyke 1997, 2001, 2005). Sometimes objects made from bone, antler, and tooth were cared for and continuously repaired for many years. At other times, the choice was made to throw them away well before the end of their potential use-lives.

One source of difficulty in comparing the length of time functionally similar bone tools were actually used is the striking variability in the quality of manufacture and intensity of use often recognizable within a single assemblage. Some ad hoc – expedient – objects display only minimal manufacture wear and appear to have been used only a few times before being thrown away (Choyke 1997, 2001). Other tools, some barely manufactured, are intensively used, apparently having become an individual's "favorite" tool. These objects are encountered in archaeological assemblages in varying frequencies depending on the particular site and local traditions of tool use. Some sites contain a high proportion of tools displaying signs of having been repeatedly curated and remodeled. Ultimately, some of these objects may actually have undergone such extreme remodeling that they were transformed into tools exploited for totally different purposes. As will be shown later, in extreme cases, worked bone objects may actually have been broken up and divided among select groups as talisman-like objects. When preservation of bone is good, such objects may display heavy handling polish, although otherwise they may or may not be carefully worked.

From time to time, but less often than might be supposed, bone tools occur that are carefully manufactured according to the precise technological rules of the given society. These tools and ornaments naturally broke as they were being used in various daily activities. At that point, the decision had to be made whether to repair them, by re-sharpening edges and points or re-drilling holes in pendants and beads. Again, depending on the cultural context and type of settlement, certain tools and ornaments traditionally appear to have been repaired and others thrown away with little or no attempt to conserve them. Equally, some kinds of tools and ornaments tend to display intensive use and handling wear. These repaired and intensively used objects give the strong impression, albeit a somewhat subjective one, of having been used for years. Thus, tools in a given assemblage were not only made following long-lived rules of manufacturing traditions but also represent a manufacturing continuum of quality and intensity of use (Choyke 1997, 2001). Given that traditional use of bone objects is rapidly disappearing around the world, probably experimentation will be the best way of distinguishing between archaeological bone tools used over short periods of time but very intensively and those used consistently over decades.

The purpose of this paper is NOT to suggest a methodology for identifying which tools are used intensively or over the very long term. That would require much additional thought and experimental work. Nor will I attempt to define tool use in terms of exact numbers of years. Rather, I will try to identify the phenomenon of well-made prehistoric objects produced according to precise rules over centuries, but also used over a lifetime or even lifetimes, by analogy with modern examples of bone tool production and use. The relative length of time such prehistoric objects remained in the possession of individuals or in circulation within a group has the potential to shed light on both individual and cultural memory.

First, two bone tools from known traditional contexts will be described along with their individual life trajectories.[1] The first are bone combs traditionally made by Roma artisans in Transylvania, in modern day Romania. The other is a bevel-ended burnishing tool made from a cattle metatarsal diaphysis that is still used by members of a group of elderly traditional shoe-makers in Sofia, Bulgaria (Choyke 2006, Fig. 1). An attempt will be made to draw parallels with Early Neolithic and Bronze Age implements and tooth ornaments from Hungary. Ornaments, in particular drilled teeth and tusks, are objects closely associated with both the mythical associations of the animal and certain protective qualities (Pétrequin and Pétrequin 2006: 110). They might also be associated with an individual who wore them for years. The length of time they may have been in use and possible strong associations with individuals or groups of individuals, however, may often have resulted in such objects developing a meaning within broader social collectives or groups beyond the village setting.

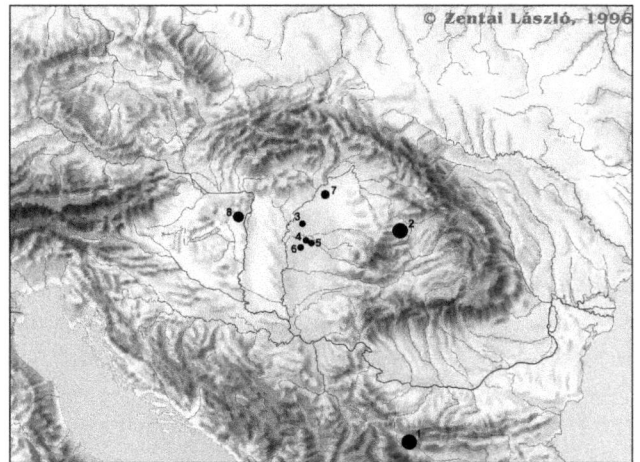

Fig. 1. Map showing all locations mentioned in the text: 1. Sofia, 2. Szék, 3. Ecsegfalva 23 (Early Neolithic), 4. Endrőd 39 (Early Neolithic), 5. Endrőd 119 (Early Neolithic), 6. Szarvas 23 (Early Neolithic), 7. Polgár-Csőszhalom-Dűlő 6 (Final Neolithic), 8. Százhalombatta-Földvár (Middle Bronze Age)

Tools as markers of time and memory

Although there has been much discussion in the literature of the social implications embedded in the serial motions and activities involved in technological production schemes (the *chaîne operatoire* construct), neither techniques of manufacture nor function will be considered here, but rather the after-life of objects. Tools and ornaments which continued in use in a community for long periods of people's lives played tacit roles in the continuous formation of personal and social memory by marking the passage of time and through their association with individuals or kinds of experience. This strengthening of memory was achieved through habituation and familiarity with individual objects and the way they were repeatedly and predictably used, repaired, broken, and discarded during daily life at settlements. In this context, objects in use for years are treated here as material reflections of life experience.

In contrast, the presence of barely used, ad hoc tools as well as better made objects, thrown away when they could still be repaired, testifies to acts of forgetting or diminishing the socially ascribed importance of certain tasks. This may become the case over time even within the same social setting so that objects associated with these tasks may be seen to have lost much of their importance as markers of time and experience.

Long personal use, however, may actually have added value to objects through association with a respected adult or elder. This would have reinforced tradition through reference to a remembered past possibly involving several generations (thus, an object could embody both custom and all previous users of a particular object). At the same time, a tendency to conserve objects as opposed to throwing them away when they break may also have been one way individuals conveyed tacit messages to other less apt or younger members of the group about their personal know-how, conservatism, and attitude to the work they were doing. This has been described as a kind of self-aggrandizing behavior in the literature (Dobres 2000).

In previous studies, I have discussed this manufacturing and use continuum (Choyke 1997) and have suggested that better quality, intensively made tools reflect the economic importance of the task they were used in. Conversely, I have suggested that more crudely made tools may reflect immediate tasks and the momentary needs of individuals. The relatively brief life-span of such tools means they are less able to make an impression on others (audience) except perhaps in the moment when they are discarded. Where these ad hoc tools are typical of an assemblage this suggests that the industries they were used in had lost, or in fact never had, core importance in people's lives.

Taking these arguments one step further, tools that are kept and curated over many years obviously link individuals through reinforced memory of the way a tool should be cared for and used in routine practices. Well-used tools, incorporated into sequential socially embedded routine practices (Pfaffenberger 1988: 148) become part of the continual reinterpretation and renegotiation that goes on within even the most conservative of social collectivities. Pfaffenberger (1992: 505) has called this a

---

1. I would like to gratefully thank Petar Zidarov for his generous agreement to share his data related to the traditional shoemakers' workshop in Sofia. I would also like to thank my good friend Zsuzsa Daniel from the Transylvanian village of Szék who has answered my infinite questions about a traditional way of life now rapidly dying out.

technological drama, although this implies a degree of conscious action among people using tools where the way tools are used and conserved over time is intended as a kind of explicit social discourse vis à vis a particular audience. Special prehistoric objects to be discussed later, such as Early Neolithic spoons with V-shaped bowls, ornamented antler axes, some animal-tooth ornaments or even odd fragments of heavily handled bone found at the Middle Bronze Age site of Százhalombatta-Földvár may well have been objects deeply embedded in their own particular ritual and mythic narrative, a dramatic narrative that was amplified by time, length of use, and continuous remodeling of the objects as they were used, broken, and repaired.

Tools and ornaments as markers of time and tradition

Bradley has said that time cannot be separated from social life. Our own time is dominated by linear clock time, but in the ancient past time must have been measured and understood in multiple and overlapping ways or even in a cyclical manner with "no single strand to be followed from the past to the future" (Bradley 2002: 5). The way particular tools and ornaments were used and conserved or discarded before the end of their working life was predictable and also served to mark the experience of the passage of time. In the case of tools and ornaments used over a lifetime or even on a trans-generational scale, the passage of time imbued them with special meaning with regard to reconfirmation of tradition.

Bone is brittle but tough. Tools and ornaments made from bone, antler or animal teeth can be used for years, decades even, given the proper conditions and cultural context. The span of a tool's life seems to have depended on four factors: 1. which skeletal elements were selected for manufacture; 2. the robustness of the tool or ornament; 3. the intensity of the work and the degree of impact stress inflicted on the working ends, and; 4. decisions by the users to repair and curate the tool or discard it before it had come to the true end of its working life.

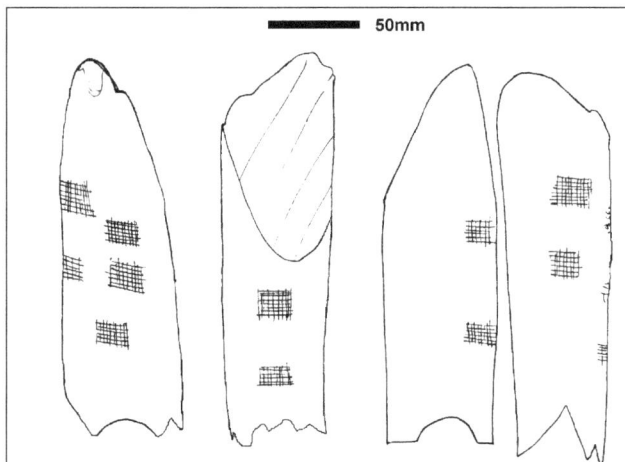

Fig. 2. Antler hammer/adze with worn incised design

Of course, some tools were simply lost or broken and discarded irrespective of general practice.

In general, long bones and teeth are very strong and resistant to damage. Tools made from ribs, however, have been found to wear at a much slower rate than those made from long bones (Christidou and Legrand 2005:389). Antler is less hard but more resistant to shock (Curry 1979; MacGregor 1985:25-29). Toughest of all are short bones such as astragali or phalanges. Worked astragali or phalanges, usually drilled and/or faceted, are very often found unbroken. Curiously enough, in the Carpathian Basin, worked astragali or phalanges became increasingly common as burnishers by the Middle Bronze Age, but rarely exhibit very intense use or handling wear.

Practitioners would have expected to repair tools made on more vulnerable bones more often and not expected to use these tools over many years without replacing them. Expectations about long-term durability must have later affected how quickly people decided to repair a broken object or make a new one instead. Clearly, a bevel-ended tool made on a cattle rib or long bone would be more durable then a small double point made on a split caprine rib, even if it was never used as more than some kind of toggle for clothing attachment.

Cristidou and Legrand (2005: 386-388) have pointed out that some awls are used with a twisting movement or with indirect percussion. Some scrapers may have been used with a scraping movement while others may have been used with a percussive gouging movement. Understandably, those tools used without percussion would incur less damage and last longer. Finally, tools and ornaments may have been chosen as "favorites" of an individual and therefore carefully taken care of. Such care may also have been a statement of conserving traditions – a tacit discourse about conservatism and thrift – in the face of different behaviors by other tool users in the group. Some tools and ornaments, of course, have explicit culturally received meanings and may also be inherently special because of who is allowed to use them. Such objects are more likely to receive special long-term attention as well. A case in point would be hammer/adzes made from the dense rose and beam segment of red deer (*Cervus elaphus*) antler. Dating to the early Middle Bronze Age and often found on sites of the so-called Hatvan Culture in Hungary. Some rare examples are distinguished by decorative designs on their surfaces. They are all found in relatively complete condition, displaying high handling polish compared to the analogous heavy-duty hammer-adze objects used in daily mundane activities (Fig. 2). The incised designs are always partially worn through handling (Choyke 1983: 183).

Long-term use: ethnographic analogies

The ethnographically attested objects that inspired this article comprise modern bone and horn combs from

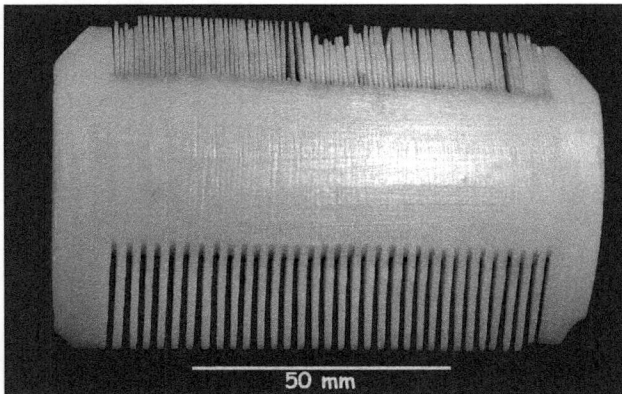

Fig. 3. Double-sided 15-year-old bone comb from Szék, Transylvania, in Romania

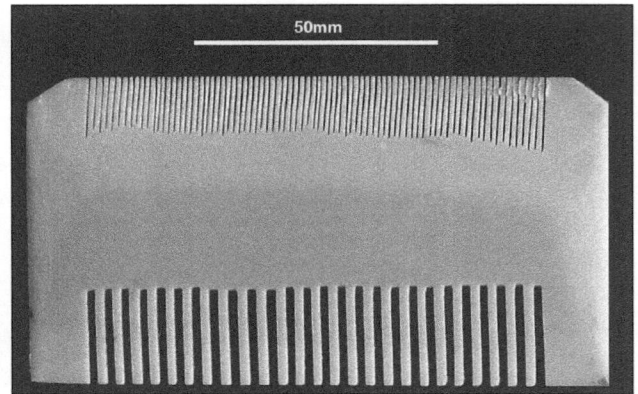

Fig. 4. New double-sided bone comb made by Roma craftsmen in Romania

Fig. 5. Close-up of wear on a 15-year-old comb

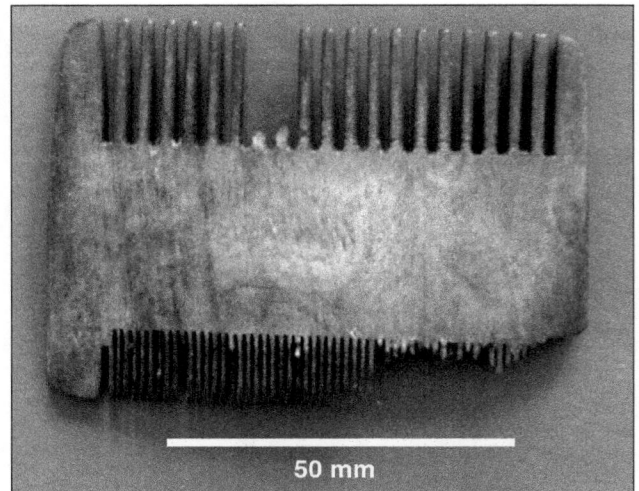

Fig. 6. Wear on family comb used on a daily basis by a four-member nuclear family over 40 years

a rural village setting and a shoe-maker's tool from an urban workshop setting. These objects have been described in detail elsewhere (Choyke 2006) but a brief review will be useful here.

The comb

This double-sided bone comb (Fig. 3) was used for at least 15 years by a 55-year-old Hungarian woman from the village of Szék in north-central Transylvania in Romania. The village is famous for its traditional music and folk crafts. Although for Budapest intellectuals it represents a mythical place of pure Hungarian tradition, nowadays, the village is pulling apart along age fault lines, with middle-aged and elderly people clinging to traditional ways of dress and deportment. The younger generation, influenced by television and continuous out-migration, actively shuns the "old ways". This rejection of tradition results in continual acts of cultural forgetting, often expressed as a rejection of dress customs. Many

different kinds of tools and ornaments have thus fallen out of fashion fairly rapidly over the last ten years. The bone combs, however, are particularly interesting because of their surprising durability and persistence.

Double-sided combs made of bone as well as cattle or water buffalo horn have been traditionally produced by Roma craftsmen in the surrounding area and are sold from time to time on market days in regional towns. The exact technique and sequence of their production, including flattening and cutting the bone or horn, remains elusive as these Roma craftsmen have repeatedly declined to be interviewed or photographed while they work. Clearly, these traditional craftspeople are losing some of their technological know-how because the newer, flatter bone combs (Fig. 4) are much less durable than older combs.

Seen within this changing cultural context, the long-term use of this comb (Fig. 3) has significance on different levels: Individual combs of my informant's generation, barring accident, were traditionally used and thriftily conserved over a lifetime, by women in particular. My informant's continued use of the comb represented a personal reaffirmation of a dying life-style. Her use of the comb within her family circle or among the group of women from Szék working as domestics in Budapest with whom she shared a room was a gesture of conservative reaffirmation with regard to other family members and her age cohort in the village. Many of these women still wear largely traditional dress although bits and pieces of this costume have undergone alterations over time and through exposure to outside influences. Thus, the whole process reflects the interplay and tension between the *habitus* discussed by Bourdieu (1977), "habituation, familiarity and repetition", and the inevitable contention and negotiation (Stark 1999, 28) that is taking place between members of what, to all intents and purposes, amounts to an age-cohort of women within the village. This natural social contention is exacerbated by the winds of change blowing through this rural community. Today, only five years after I began to be interested in these combs, very few of the village women continue to use them – including my own informant. Social cohesion within the village has less and less meaning for these women as children continue to leave the village.

Thus, when I asked my informant to take the life-histories of other comb-users, mostly elderly women still living in the village, we discovered that many of the older traditional women had recently thrown out still usable bone combs and purchased plastic ones, functionally neither better or worse than the old-fashioned bone or horn ones. It seems that even the older generation remaining behind in the village is beginning to reject the old ways, as embodied in such gestures of forgetting.

Nevertheless, it is clear that in the recent past these combs were used throughout the adult lifetimes of women. By using them even when the teeth were slightly damaged, women could display the virtues of cleanliness, thriftiness, and adherence to tradition. These combs were traditionally used in lieu of washing the long hair of women and children, to remove dirt (or sometimes even lice eggs) on a daily basis. My informant also used her comb twice daily even after the teeth began to break (see Fig. 3). Under magnification the marks of knife scraping and cutting during manufacture were almost totally obscured and there is some handling polish, but not as much as might be expected considering that hair has natural grease and graininess from dirt (Fig. 5).

In my informant's childhood, before modern ideas of hygiene inserted themselves into village thinking, it appears that comb use was not restricted to single individuals. The entire family used a single comb. Recently, I came into the possession of one of these old family combs that, not surprisingly, were considerably more worn but still usable after 40 years of intensive daily use (Fig. 6). After the combs ceased to be used (some time

Fig. 7. Shoemaker using tool

after the children left home to marry and the husband died) my informant's elderly mother stored them in the attic as personal mementos of the family's past. Archaeologically, they might well appear in the upper layers of a house feature as damaged but still usable objects. The fact of their preservation is related both to the intimate, long-term connection between the use of this comb and the family as well as to the fact that these combs still retained an emblematic significance in the mind of this older woman.

The shoemaker's tool

The second tool, a shoemaker's tool, represents one part of a complex tool kit belonging to three elderly master shoemakers who still carry out their trade in a small workshop in Sofia, the Bulgarian capital. All three shoemakers in this workshop use identical tool kits which they inherited from the masters who taught them their craft. The bone tools in question are used to smooth the leather of the shoe uppers into the space between the uppers and the sole prior to sewing or gluing on the sole (Fig. 7). They are also used to burnish the uppers, creating leather that is denser and more supple.

Their style of making shoes is traditional although the shoes they produce are now modern in style. Today, fewer people want to buy the inexpensive and beautifully made shoes they manufacture, preferring commercial shoes, and so their way of making a living is under increasing pressure. Most of their income comes from repairing poorly made but fashionable shoes purchased in commercial chain stores. These stores project an image of modernity which is apparently more important than durability to the modern population. Practicality and efficiency have little to do with these essentially culturally determined choices.

Each of the three shoemakers possessed a virtually identical version of this bone tool, made from a sturdy bone, probably a cattle radius diaphysis (Fig. 8). The shoemakers reported that these objects were at least 60 years old, having been customarily passed down from master to apprentice when the master retired from active work. The leather burnishers were thus used five days a week for periods of one half to one hour each day. The work does not require much strength or downward pressure, the leather is smooth and the tool itself is quite sturdy. The current shoemakers are the third set of people to have exploited these tools. Now, with no apprentices working for them and at the end of their professional lives, the shoemakers continue to employ these tools, much as the comb was used, to reaffirm their commitment to professional traditions and the dying art of shoe-making with which they totally identify themselves.

These bone burnishers, as well as all the other "old-fashioned" metal tools that the shoemakers use in the *chaîne operatoire* of their craft (Fig. 9, shown in order of their use) certainly could be described as transgenerational objects. Each of these men has worked in the shoe-making trade for 35 to 40 years, although formerly they were workers together in a small shoe-making factory elsewhere in Sofia. When the factory closed to make way for a facility with modern machines they moved to rooms on the ground floor of a "modern" apartment building in a working class suburb of Sofia. Their customers do not represent an old clientele but a cross-section of the people in the surrounding apartment blocks. As the shoemakers use these tools they also see each other using these tools together with the proper gestures each tool requires. Memories of a long past, including now-dead master shoemakers, are evoked within the framework of their present working practices. This manner of operating in the world of the past also sends a message to the outside, modern world in terms of the way the shoemakers see themselves. Memories are constantly produced and reproduced through long-term action and experience; created and recreated by the active technological production of many years. It is a process of creation and transmission, with the tools they use helping to materialize remembrance (Kwint 1999). The shoe-making tools, and among them the bone tool, do not represent crystallized memory but rather the organization and structure of their profession.

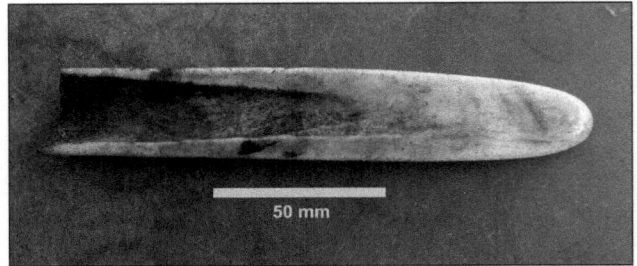

Fig. 8. Shoemaker's 60+ year-old burnisher

Fig. 9. Traditional shoe-making tools in order of use

The bone burnishing tools are well worn and stained although somewhat surprisingly lacking a high overall handling or use polish. After this length of time all marks of manufacture have long since been worn away and since the tools are said by the shoemakers to be virtually indestructible and are not used in high-stress activities the working end never needs to be repaired. The working end displays polish together with scattered striations (easily visible under 10× magnification) across the rounded working end. These striations run both parallel and vertically to the length of the tool (Fig. 10). Overall, there is less handling polish then might be expected, however, perhaps because the leather being worked comes to the workshop already in a highly processed, non-greasy state.

Perhaps it is not an accident that both the bone combs and burnishers, well worn and used over many years, are today in the possession of older people who cling to older traditions. Time and concepts of the past are critical elements in the way both the village women and the elderly shoemakers negotiate their places in the world with regard to the younger generation and provide a phenomenological backdrop for the construction of their identities.

The combs and the shoemaker's burnisher were used for many years. At a time when there are extreme shifts in local social organization both in Romania and Bulgaria, however, most of these objects are being discarded, some

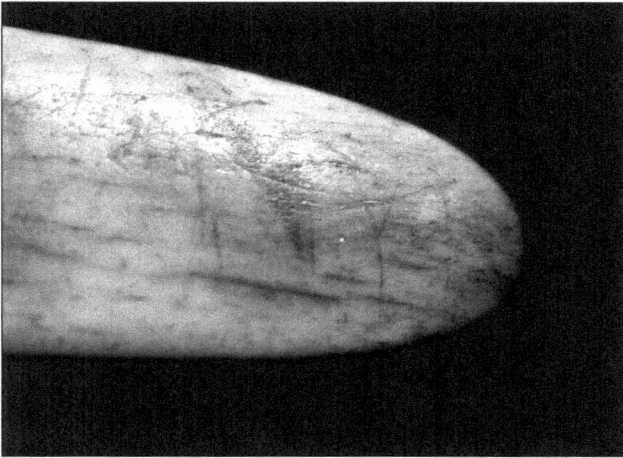

Fig. 10. Close-up of wear on working end of a 60+ year-old burnisher

well before they are completely worn out. This marks a change from previous periods, when both of these kinds of objects were carefully husbanded by the individuals using them. On a personal level, continued use of both the comb and the shoemaker's tools brings a personally reassuring sense of belonging somewhere in the world.

As the modern world encroaches on the lives of all the people using these objects, and the activities associated with them begin to lose value, the tendency seems to be to discard them. There will always be a few people who cling on and use their tools even more intensively because the tool use itself takes on a political expression of resisting change. In its extreme form, there are small groups of craftspeople in Hungary dedicated to re-vitalizing "old-fashioned" techniques and tools. Amongst these people there seems to be a tacit understanding that using archaic techniques and tools also means the practitioners support "good old-fashioned" social values.

Seen another way, within the small social groups where these objects from the imagined past are still being used, reputations are maintained though a fragile web of pre-scribed gestures and deliberate acts woven into the fabric of technological strategies and subsequent tool use (Sillar 1996:121). Learning the right way to make and use objects and displaying this know-how with confidence, skill, and flair, people created reputations among their peers. Tacit display to a target group using the "proper" comb to comb your hair or "proper" traditional tools of your trade, reinforced with the length of time an object has been used, represents one small way these people establish and maintain legitimacy within their target constituencies.

Parallels with these two long-used ethnographic examples can be drawn with prehistoric bone tools and ornaments (and, of course, tools and ornaments made of other raw materials as well). The set of objects to be considered here all seem to have had precise functions

within a production system. They can be found in all stages of use and dis-use from newly made to briefly used, moderately used, and used over the long term. If they were discarded before the end of their working lives, it was usually because they had been seriously damaged, irretrievably lost, and perhaps discarded following some event in the lives of their user(s). Of course, it is not possible to state precisely how many years these utilitarian and ornamental objects were in active use. Nor can anything be said now about the exact nature of their cultural context beyond their location at the village or household level. However, the fact that certain types of prehistoric bone objects seem to have been used only over the short term, what I have elsewhere termed Class II tools (Choyke 1997), while other objects have the potential to be cared for and preserved over many years is a signal that these objects are at least tacitly "agents" (Dobres 2000) in some kind of social discourse. Simply recognizing that duration of use could also have been another element in the overlapping networks of social negotiations within small-scale prehistoric societies represents a positive research step in enlivening our understanding of these ancient people.

Prehistoric tools and ornaments[2]

Conservatism in the use of certain tool and ornament types compared to a more profligate treatment of others may, thus, be a mechanism for the maintenance of social solidarity at the local community level, a way of signaling commitment to and competence in a piece of work. People may hang onto objects, repairing them and remodeling them in spite of the fact that the tools and ornaments are made from easily acquired raw materials and the manufacturing process involved in their production was neither difficult nor complicated. Clearly, there are some societies or segments of society where taking care of and preserving objects is considered to be an important, positive trait. The Wola people living in the highlands of New Guinea, for example, are reported as holding on carefully to potentially useful but perhaps never-to-be-used objects (Hardy and Sillitoe 2003).

Bone manufacturing of everyday objects in prehistoric Hungary would have largely been learned within the household. Thus, whether living in the small hamlets of the Early Neolithic or the larger villages at the end of the Neolithic or Middle Bronze Age, people would have relied especially on "habituation, familiarity, and repetition" in their daily round of activities to continuously reaffirm membership in particular social groups. Some heavily used, stereotypically manufactured house-

2. Here I would like to acknowledge Dr. Alasdair Whittle of Cardiff University who carried out the excavations at the Early Neolithic site of Ecsegfalva 23. The Bronze Age examples come from Százhalombatta-Földvár in Hungary. I would like to thank Dr. Magdolna Vicze, director of the Matrica Museum, Százhalombatta, for the opportunity to work on the bone tool assemblage from this site.

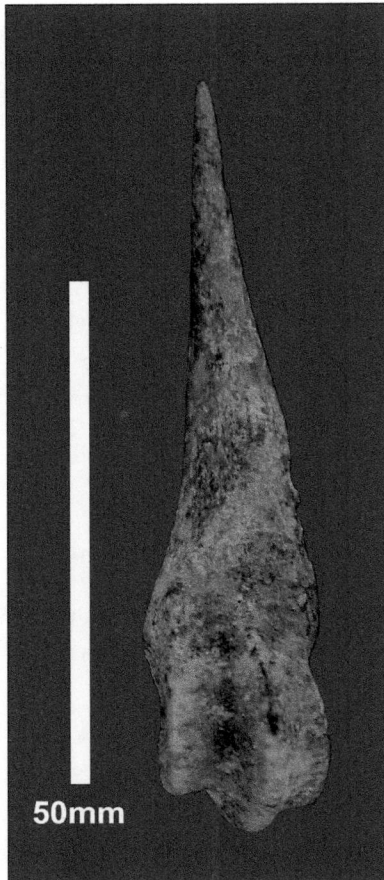

Fig. 11. Early Neolithic 'pencil-stub' caprine metapodial awl from Ecsegfalva 23 (after Choyke, 2007)

50mm

ruminant metapodium perforators (Class I; Schibler types 1/1 and 1/2, Makkay types XIII-XIV, Beldiman type DVM 4) retaining their epiphyseal ends represent a "classic" type since they are found on virtually all prehistoric sites from all periods where small ruminant bone was worked into tools. Metapodial bones are straight and naturally divided along the fusion line between the 3rd and 4th metapodia; skillful workers could potentially break them into four usable pieces to work into perforators, taking advantage of their natural fracturing qualities (Murray 1979: 28). Most typically, the articular condyle of the distal epiphysis was retained as a handle. During manufacturing, the bones were first grooved completely through the cortical bone of the diaphysis and in this case through the distal epiphysis as well (Clark and Thompson 1953). This style of manufacture is characteristic for awls on prehistoric sites in the Carpathian Basin and elsewhere, although the use of this style of bone tool manufacture tailed off in later prehistoric periods.

The metapodium perforators from the Early Neolithic Körös site of Ecsegfalva 23 in particular are heavily curated down to "pencil stubs" (Choyke 2006). Where the surface is intact, that is, not eroded from lying on the ground surface exposed to the elements, these objects can also display intensive handling polish (Fig. 11). This situation stands in contrast to observations made for the end of the Neolithic in the same region. Such awls occur in a great variety of sizes ranging from long new ones down to the pencil-stub size (e.g., Choyke 1997). The use life of such tools in basketry or sewing activities must have encompassed a number of years, certainly outliving the duration of individual settlements in the Early Neolithic period in this region if the assumption is correct that these small hamlets were not occupied continuously but that the inhabitants moved on after only a few years, returning only later to occupy more or less the same area. Several of the pencil-stub awls with intact tips, still in a usable condition, were discarded, abandoned or lost at this small site, as at other Körös and Criş sites (Makkay 1990, figure 10:7; Beldiman 1999-2000, fig. 2). Perhaps such tools, requiring planning, multi-stage manufacture, and amenable to continuous re-working, were closely associated with the individuals who used them and were discarded on the death of their owner or perhaps they were simply not considered worth carrying to the next settlement.

The spoons of the Starčevo-Körös-Criş cultural sphere are perhaps among the best known bone artifacts found at sites of this period. They are found consistently on almost all sites of these cultures over a broad region and are also the bone tools most likely to be reported in archaeological site reports for this period (Bačkalov 1979, plates XXIV9/13, XXV/8-10, Beldiman 1999-2000, figs. 6-8; Beldiman and Popuşoi 1993-1998; Kisléghi Nagy 1911, 148; Makkay 1990, 24-28, Nan-

hold tools and ornaments seem to have been particularly emblematic of the social self-identity of individuals, affecting not only consistency in technological style but also the intensity and length of their use. In this study, an object was considered intensively used over a long period if it had clearly been curated many times and displayed intensive handling polish on protuberant and concave surfaces alike. Sometimes the osseous materials these objects were manufactured from have an almost a melted appearance. Such objects are not common but nevertheless occur regularly on many of these sites. It must be admitted, however, that recognition of the degree and length of use for individual tools is still based on intuitively interpreted macro-features and a large amount of subjectivity. In the following pages, a few outstanding examples of intensively used objects made from osseous materials from prehistoric sites in Hungary are described. The list by no means covers the entire inventory or range of such "well-used" objects but is meant to convey a sense of what kinds of objects are available for study.

Early Neolithic examples from Ecsegfalva 23

Ecsegfalva 23 is a small Early Neolithic site of the Körös culture located east of the Danube near the center of the Great Hungarian Plain (see Fig. 1) Small

Fig. 12. Early Neolithic spoon with curated V-shaped bowl base from Ecsegfalva 23 (after Choyke, 2007)

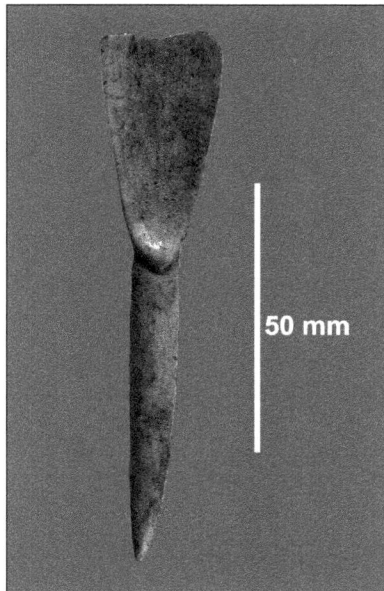

50 mm

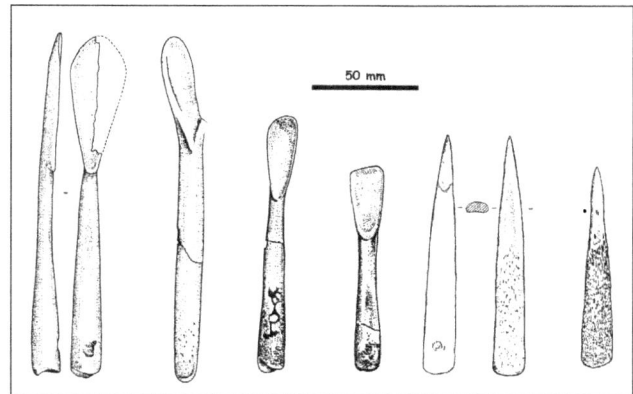

Fig. 13. Remodeling curation sequence in Early Neolithic spoon with V-shaped bowl base (after Makkay 1990)

dris 1972). In contrast to earlier ideas (Nandris 1972), these spoons can be made from the metatarsal bones of both wild and domestic cattle. The complete spoon from Ecsegfalva 23 was made from a domestic cattle or small aurochs metatarsal (Fig. 12). Such spoons were always curated and as a result they come in many different shapes (see Makkay 1990) although the V-shape of the spoon bowl always seems to have been preserved, probably deliberately; sometimes the bowls of the spoons were curated down to small points. The distal epiphysis, which was often retained in a heavily modified, pointed, form, marked a weak point on the handle part between the distal epiphysis and the diaphysis of the metatarsal. The final form of the spoons and all the re-working on the edge of the bowl and end of the handle part was carried out using abrasion over many years of use and reuse. Barring accidents, these objects must have lasted for the lifetimes of the people in the household where they were used. Furthermore, it may be important that in addition to their special shape, almost like a small abstract human head with a chin, they were made only from wild or domestic cattle bone. It is also curious that these beautiful, intensively used and curated objects, like the metapodial perforators, were often abandoned while still useful. Spoons also stand out particularly because they are often found with very glossy surfaces from both handling polish and the polish that comes from reworking with chipped stone tools. This shows that they were not simply tossed out on the ground but buried quickly. The spoons were continuously re-modeled and re-used and may have been used throughout an individual's lifetime, evolving into various forms but retaining the V-shaped base of the bowl part (Fig. 13). Again, if it is assumed that the small hamlets were only occupied for a few years, these represent objects that were carried from settlement to settlement.

Another special object with a wide distribution in the Early Neolithic of Hungary and points east are massive "hooks," usually made from long bone diaphyses of large cattle or aurochs (Makkay type XXIII). Massive "hooks" are also consistently represented in the archaeological literature on sites of the Starčevo-Körös-Criş cultural sphere (Kisléghi Nagy 1911; Bačkalov 1979, plates XVII/8-11, Makkay 1990, 40-41, 45; Beldiman 2000, figs. 5-7). Like the spoons, these objects are always glossy from intense handling polish, but unlike spoons they were not reworked when they broke. Their surfaces can be incredibly shiny and worn, with an almost melted appearance. The Ecsegfalva 23 specimen is so worn that marks from manufacture are obscured. The general appearance of this object, however, suggests that the final stage of manufacture must have included deliberate, intensive polishing of the cortical and medullary surfaces.

Such a degree of wear could only have occurred after many years. On sites, these massive hooks are always found broken, in particular by the area behind the rounded tip with the indentation next to it, as on this specimen from Ecsegfalva 23 (Fig. 14). These objects must have been part of individual adornment, discarded either when they broke or, possibly, they were broken deliberately (Chapman 2000). In the Körös region these hooks appear to have been locally manufactured exclusively from the long-bone diaphyses of wild cattle, particularly the humerus (see the sites of Endrőd 39 and 119 and Szarvas 23 in Makkay 1990, figures 13/13-18, 14/10).

Here again, this is a special object made exclusively from cattle bone. If it is true that cattle, and particularly wild cattle, were animals of major cultural significance and social value beyond simple economic use (Russell 1998:44), then the raw material might have enhanced the special symbolic meanings behind these hooks and, perhaps even

31

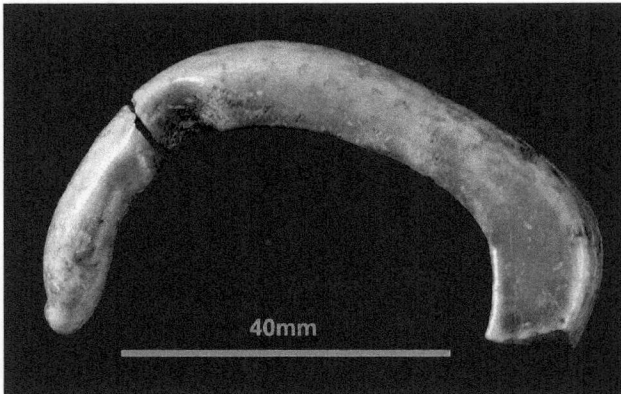

Fig. 14. Massive worn bone hook from cattle humerus from Ecsegfalva 23 (after Choyke, 2007)

Fig. 15. Cattle rib scrapers from Százhallombatta-Földvár (photo by author)

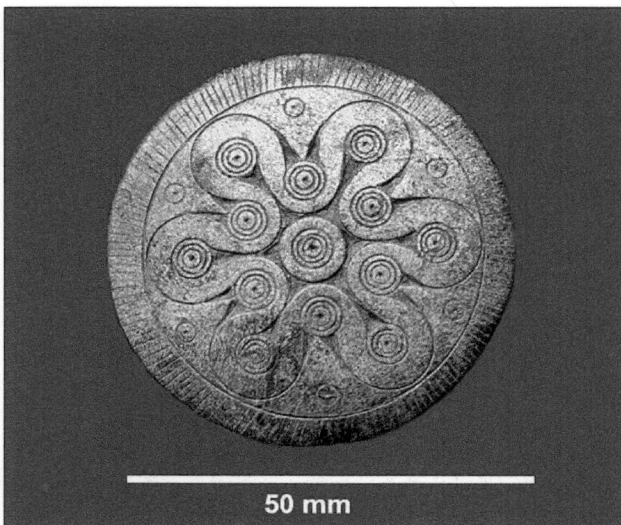

Fig. 16. Horse harness fitting from Százhallombatta-Földvár with worn incised design (after Choyke et al 2003)

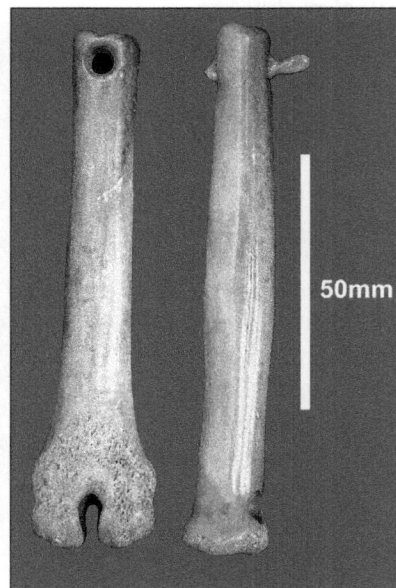

Fig. 17. A pair of heavily worn handle/grips from Százhallombatta-Földvár

who had the right to use them. These long-lived objects had intrinsic value derived from their form, their raw material, and long association with the individuals who wore or used them over many years of their lives.

Bronze Age objects from Százhalombatta-Földvár

By the Middle Bronze Age in Hungary, bone, although widely used, was more likely to be used to produce tools with shorter, less intense working lives tending toward the more ad hoc, Class II end of the manufacturing continuum (Choyke 1997, 2005). Nevertheless, even in this cultural context tools sometimes stand out in terms of the intensity of their use. Two examples of tools out of the many available have been chosen from the worked osseous assemblage of the Vatya culture tell site of Száz-halombatta-Földvár in western Hungary, lying on the banks of the Danube some 30 km south of Budapest (Poroszlai 2000).

The first type of object, characteristic of sites assigned to the Vatya culture, is made from cattle rib, not split except at the ends, which are beveled towards their distal ends (Fig. 15). The proximal ends are unfinished. Based on the high polish and parallel striations which often extend over the active end of such tools it seems likely that these rather crude but consistently produced objects were used to deflesh and scrape the inside of raw hides (Lemoine 1997; Cristidou and Legrand 2005:392). Christidou and Legrand have also pointed out that ribs used in burnishing and defleshing require substantially less repair than defleshers and burnishers made from mammalian long bones. Although these ribs mostly display moderate handing polish it is not surprising that from time to time some of these rib scrapers are found with a high handling and use polish covering all surfaces, protuberant and concave alike. It seems such tools may have been employed intensively and over relatively long periods of time. More attention paid to context

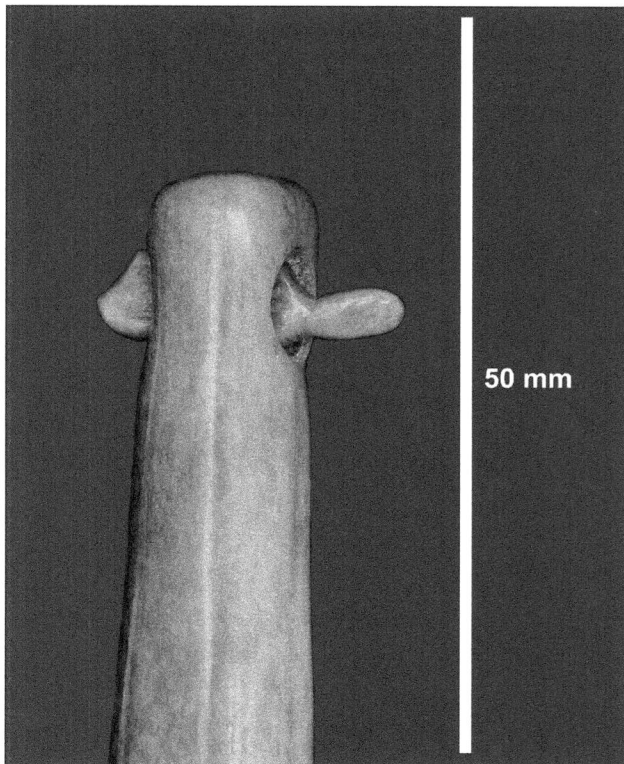

Fig. 18. Close-up of bone pin (used to hold leather strap in handle) from Százhallombatta-Földvár (photo by author)

might reveal that such well-worn although not elaborate tools tend to cluster in limited areas, the work area of a particular household. It might be inferred that the people using such tools would have been the elders of the society, repositories of experience and tradition in such small-scale societies.

Scrapers are generalized tools one that anyone living in this large and important Middle Bronze Age village-town might have used. People living at this settlement, however, would have been players in a strongly hierarchical society and it is likely that not everyone would have had the equal access or rights to certain sorts of resources. Conventionally, the most discussed artifact of this kind, usually made from antler, are horse harness fittings (for example Bökönyi 1960; Choyke 1979; Foltiny 1965; Hüttel 1981; Mozsolics 1962). These objects are made of antler and the incised designs are often worn in places (Fig. 16).

By the Middle Bronze Age, horse was much less common in the refuse bone remains than earlier, although there is evidence it was still eaten from time to time (Choyke et al. 2003). Clearly not everyone at the site of Százhallombatta-Földvár would have had their own horses or, perhaps, even the right to own them. In this context of restricted access to horses, a pair of highly worn handles or grips discovered during early excavations at the site (Kovács 1969) takes on new significance

(Fig. 17). The grips are made from complete sheep metatarsals. A leather strap of some sort seems to have been passed through the proximal end and fixed with a bone pin through a medio-laterally drilled hole just below the proximal epiphysis (Fig. 18). It is not unreasonable to suggest that these handles held the reins or whips for harnessed horses. These grips are beautiful objects, with the bone surfaces and edges having an almost melted appearance related to the intensity of their use and the length of time they were probably in active use, seemingly decades. Indeed, the level of wear is so extreme that it is not hard to imagine that these objects may have been passed down over several generations. Use of the same objects with a remarkably glossy and ancient appearance by members of the same social unit (family? clan?) would have given added emphasis to the rights and privileges they held with respect to whatever they used these handles for. Indeed, perhaps these grips were connected to horse handling. The grips were certainly still usable when they were abandoned and rapidly buried. This begs the question of why they stopped being used and why they were found as a pair so close to one another within the strata outside of any closed feature like a pit or a house.

Finally, another unique object from the Koszider-Vatya settlement levels at Százhalombatta displays signs of long-term use. The surface of this small piece of bone shows signs of manufacturing as well as a high degree of handling polish. This amorphous object looks like a fragment of some kind of tool or ornament that was exploited over many years, rounding all the worked surfaces and obscuring the manufacturing striations. In this case, this odd object must have come from a tool or ornament that was deliberately broken. Perhaps bits of it were then distributed among the appropriate people. It has a deep honey-brown color and is very glossy, as if it had been intensively handled or kept in a leather pouch. The wear on this piece of bone would have taken decades to develop (Fig. 19)

Prehistoric perforated teeth in Hungary

Another group of objects used both in personal adornment and as symbols is worth mentioning here briefly. Drilled teeth, used in necklaces with other decorative elements, sewn on clothing or woven into the hair are common enough finds on archaeological sites. Drilled incisors, canines or molar teeth came from dog, pig (wild and domestic), wolf, and bear; the latter two wild species often considered totem animals in various later folk mythologies in Eastern Europe. Even without considering the way these objects are worn, their very presence probably makes reference to an ancestral past and the roles the various animal species were said to play in that mythological past. Such drilled teeth probably had protective aspects related to that mythology. Their use

*Fig. 19.
Amorphous piece of
bone from a former
tool/ornament from
Százhallombatta-
Földvár (photo by
author)*

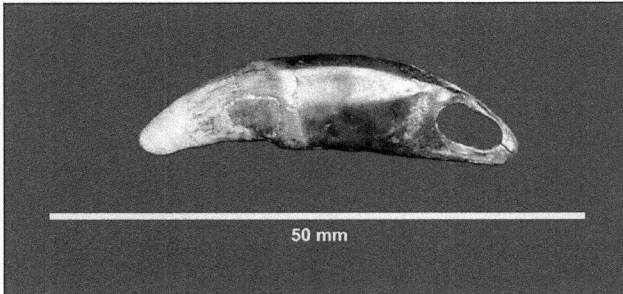

*Fig. 20. Drilled dog canine from Százhallombatta-
Földvár (after Choyke et al. 2003)*

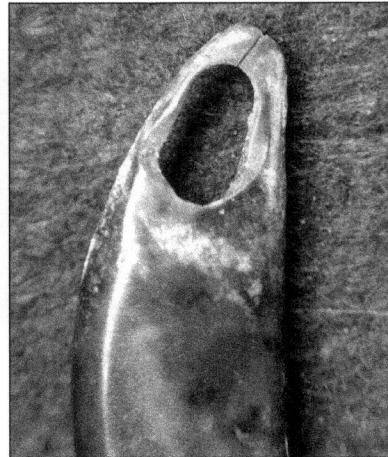

*Fig. 21. Close-up of
the worn hole in the
dog canine pendant
in Fig. 20, possibly
re-drilled from
Százhallombatta-
Földvár (photo by
author)*

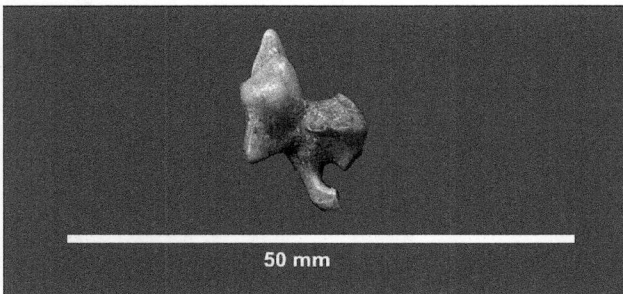

*Fig. 22. Drilled dog molar from Százhallombatta-Földvár
(after Choyke et al. 2003)*

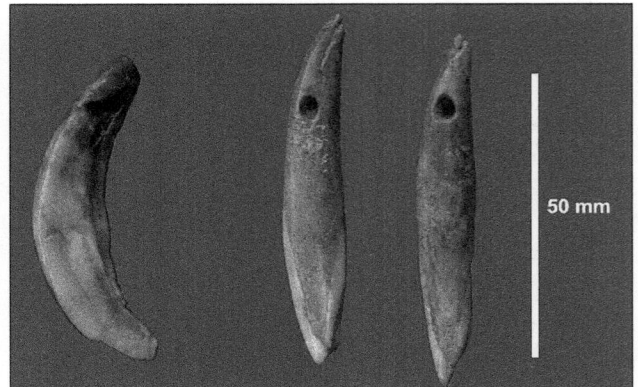

*Fig. 23. Three domestic pig incisor pendants with only
slightly worn holes Százhallombatta-Földvár (photo by
author)*

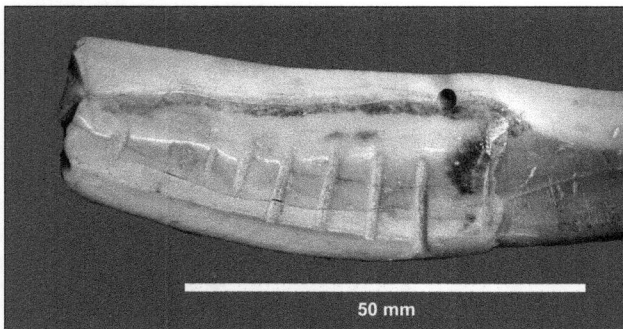

*Fig. 24. Close-up of wild boar tusk ornament with worn
incised lines from Százhallombatta-Földvár (photo by
author)*

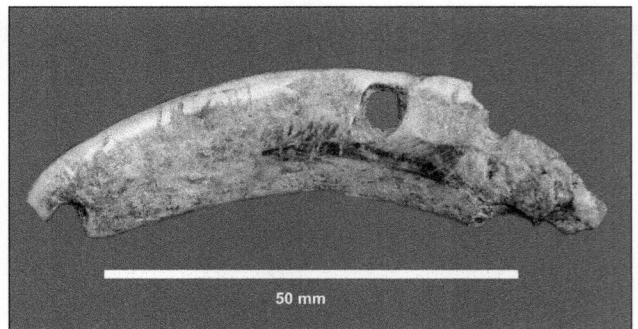

*Fig. 25. Drilled and re-drilled wild boar tusk from
Százhallombatta-Földvár (photo by author)*

may also have signaled hunting prowess. Wearing boar tusk and bear teeth may well have been gender and age-restricted. The long-term use of red deer canines, both real and copies, will also be discussed within a special Late Neolithic burial context.

All these tooth ornaments were personal goods. They will not be discussed here as decorations or carriers of symbolic meanings, however, but rather in terms of what seem to be signs of their long term-use. These signs include intensive wear around the suspension or attachment holes and even re-drilling as well as obscuring of manufacturing striations and polish. These kinds of wear suggest that these pendants/amulets were used for a relatively long time and perhaps even passed on to other people as a materialization of the relationships between generations.

Among the most common teeth found on prehistoric sites in the Carpathian Basin are drilled dog and wolf canines (or even molars, Figs. 20-22). In the Middle Bronze Age, intensively worn canines of brown bear occur regularly on sites although never in large numbers. Dogs and bear were apparently not eaten since they are hardly ever represented in the food refuse bones. Dog skulls are often found as so-called foundation sacrifices, however, so perhaps the teeth came from known animals and were meant to have a protective value. In any case, the perforations through the roots of the teeth are often highly worn around the holes, which sometimes needed to be re-drilled when the tooth broke across the original perforation (Fig. 21). These secondary suspension holes also wore thin in their turn. Given how hard tooth enamel is, this high degree of wear must certainly reflect long-term use. Drilled bear canines, found in the Carpathian Basin first and foremost on Middle Bronze Age sites, are also almost always highly polished and broken at the original holes, often with worn re-drilled suspension holes. One can imagine that the bear canine represented a hunting trophy of a species that in the past and today in Northern and Eastern Europe was regarded as an animal with special qualities as well as a formidable hunting quarry. The very degree of wear on such objects must have added to their value as old venerable objects worn by mature men with many years of hunting experience behind them.

Pig teeth, especially incisors or lower canines, are also often found on Middle Bronze Age sites in Hungary. Curiously, the suspension holes on the pig incisors are usually not heavily worn (Fig. 23) – at least compared to dog, wolf and bear canines. Boar tusk ornaments, drilled for suspension or attachment, on the other hand, almost always display heavy wear. Such lower tusks are always split, heavily worked and perforated, presumably to attach to clothing or to each other as some kind of a body ornament. One example from Száhalombatta-Földvár also has deeply incised lines on its inner surface. What is most relevant here is that some of the lines are almost

completely worn away, something which must have taken years to develop. All the edges of this particular object are rounded from years of rubbing against the soft material it was probably sewn to (Figs. 24). Another split boar tusk from the same site was re-drilled when it broke and the edges are also rounded from being worn over many years (Fig. 25). Perhaps the lines on the first tusk ornament represented some kind of particular accomplishment, the age and wear on the object reinforcing the depth of the wearer's experience (Spector 1991). Of course, there could be other explanations for the incised lines on the tusk. The parallel presented here is simply meant to show that decoration can also be used to refer to concrete events in an individual's life. Boar is also a dangerous game animal and one can imagine that wearing such objects was limited to the actual hunters as marks of their skill.

Deer canine teeth – a special case

One fascinating aspect of historic ethnographic attitudes toward wapiti upper canines, reported by McCabe (1982), is the way they were ascribed value in some Native American societies. Sewn onto clothing or strung on necklaces, such canines have been found archaeologically from North American sites dating back to 3000-5000 B.P. Prior to AD 1800 the use of wapiti teeth was restricted to women's dresses and was culture- and region-specific. Since each elk has only two canines and not all of them were suitable, it took time to gather significant numbers either through hunting or trading. Among the Arapaho, wapiti teeth were considered prestige items and could be inherited (and accumulated), representing family wealth and rank.

In prehistoric Europe, red deer canines have an even older history, stretching back to Paleolithic times. Even today, red deer canines are traditionally used in Central Europe in jewelry associated with hunting. Propeller-shaped beads meant to be strung in necklaces and most likely intended as copies of red deer canines were also widespread objects even in this early period (Taborin 2004: 27-29, 51,60, plate 31). Copies of drilled red deer canine also occur made in a variety of other raw materials. An interesting example of the use of real and, especially, copies of red deer upper canine teeth comes from the Late Neolithic of Hungary from the Polgár-Csőszhalom-Dűlő 6 horizontal site. Altogether, 11 graves, male and female, juvenile and adult, were found containing red deer canines and/or their blunt propeller-shaped imitation beads (Anders personal communication). The real stag canines at Polgár can be heavily used, sometimes displaying well worn suspension holes. The propeller-like beads may be so worn that they broke across the central hole and each end was re-drilled to form new beads. These new beads appear almost identical to real stag canines. The holes in turn undergo the

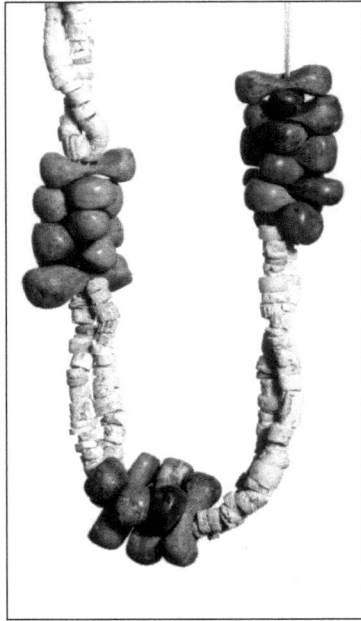

Fig. 26. Two necklaces of red deer copy beads clustered between rows of spondylus beads from Polgár-Csőszhalom-Dűlő 6 (photo Karoly Kozma)

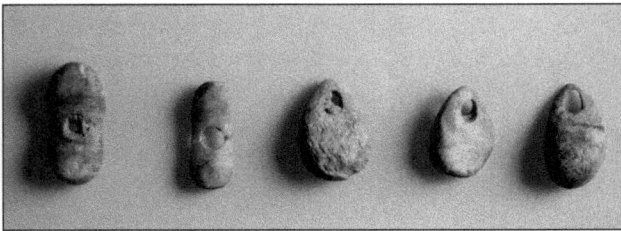

Fig. 27. Different degrees of wear on "figure-eight-shaped" beads from Polgár-Csőszhalom-Dűlő 6 (photo Karoly Kozma

same processes of wear and eventual breakage. With the exception of a necklace given to a woman well beyond her child-bearing years, most real deer canines were placed in male graves. This suggests that these were all canines which had been accumulated during the lifetime of the deceased and that some had been worn by him/her for many years.

The imitation beads were found only in female graves. They were assembled in necklaces and other complex jewelry (Fig. 26). What is curious is that within a single necklace composed of many beads clustered together and mixed with marble and spondylus beads of various shapes and sizes, some of the beads could be well worn while others seem to have been newly made for the funeral to put on the deceased as part of the visual impact of the ceremony.

As mentioned above, the propeller-shaped beads first wore through in the middle, finally breaking in half with the two halves re-shaped and re-drilled. Even these secondary holes can sometimes display heavy wear (Fig. 27). This process of transformation from the original propeller shape to a single bead with almost-worn-through

holes must have taken many years and may even have been trans-generational. An experiment is currently underway to establish how quickly wear develops on these beads when they are worn continuously. After more than two years, the beads, strung together in a necklace with drilled dog and coyote canines, only exhibit a faint polish, especially where the beads touch the skin (Duffy personal communication, January 2008). Nevertheless, in this Late Neolithic context when the beads were finally buried as parts of complex ornaments for deceased women and girls they were effectively taken out of circulation. At that point, connecting living members of the community and the deceased beginning their journey into another spiritual realm must have been of overriding importance at the moment of burial. Elsewhere (Choyke 2001), it has been suggested that the beads may have come from members of the family group of the dead girl or woman, assembled to create these special burial ornaments. The copy beads would thus have been employed as a direct way of linking the living with the dead, establishing direct ties between the ancestors, people who were still in the present world and these newly dead members of the community. The fact that these "old" beads were associated with still-living community members and perhaps their immediate ancestors must have added to the value of these burial ornaments.

Conclusions

Time is a relative concept. On the one hand, people experience it as individuals and relive it as memories of events. On the other hand, collective group memories may be experienced in constructed memories of the past that can be expressed in the intensive, habitual use of particular, familiar objects over long periods of time. For whole societies or social collectivities this could mean the perseverance over hundreds of years of manufacturing and use traditions of particular tool and ornament types, extending deep into a mythological past. For individuals within those social collectivities, old familiar objects and ornaments used by them or even their immediate descendents over a lifetime of accumulated experiences were material expressions of past memories. Conkey (1993) has talked about the power of the tangible to materialize the intangible cultural principles, beliefs, and values that make humans both materialists and symbolists.

Particular types of prehistoric bone tools had the potential to be exploited over the lifetimes of individuals because bone is such a tough, durable material. Such objects would have embodied the memory of both the recent and far-distant constructed past for the groups who traditionally used them. Intensively used tools and ornaments made of osseous materials would have represented the experience and *savoir faire* of the practitioners closely associated with them. Some tools and ornaments may even have been employed across generations, linking the more immediate past and present with the expected, comfortably predictable future. Examples of the various ways the long-term use of traditional bone objects worked to sustain social memory are presented here connected with descriptions of two types of recent traditional bone objects where the individual biographies are available

In this paper, I have tried to show how the fate of two kinds of objects deriving from the remnants of traditional society in Central and Eastern Europe reflects their users' attempts to maintain their former identities with reference to familiar objects that were regularly used in the recent past. The first case, bone combs formerly used all over the region, were still being used by older and middle-aged women from Transylvanian villages until quite recently. Their use took on special meaning to the age-cohorts of women forced by economic circumstance to live outside the village as domestic workers in Hungary. The combs were part of their traditional dress and were conserved as a way of showing that these individuals still adhered to the old, traditional values of their childhood. These combs were meant to last a lifetime and these women continued to use them as a sign of thrift even after many of the teeth had broken. There are even examples of combs, broken beyond use but carefully preserved in attics, from a time when these combs were used communally within the family over four decades. Combs, thus, were also intimately associated with the living, present memory of a past family grouping. As this older generation dies out and the middle-aged women and their children move into the modern world these symbols of the traditional past have lost their value and are being ruthlessly thrown away or forgotten, replaced by modern plastic combs.

Another modern example of the way the potential longevity of bone tools can be used to negotiate identity within a closed circle of people comes from Sofia in Bulgaria. Here, a group of old shoemakers are still making shoes and repairing them as they were taught in their youth. The tools they employ are even older than they are. The bone leather burnishers discussed in this paper were owned by master shoemakers living before the advent of World War II. The three shoemakers using these burnishers live in a modern apartment enclave and their small business is fighting a losing battle to survive beside cheap stylish shoe stores. Rather they cling to their traditional way of working for the sake of each other and as an expression of their profession in the face of the hostile world outside the doors of their little workshop. Once they are gone their knowledge of shoe-making and the tools they used will lose all value for subsequent generations. Their past will become irrelevant to the present.

The fact is that with such ethnographic examples it is possible to get the histories of individual objects and actually ask their users how they use the tool, for how long and in what social contexts. Clearly, tools made from bone are resilient and can be used for decades, over several generations even. To the people still using them these bone objects have become much more than merely insignificant objects made in a cheap, readily available raw material. By taking histories of how these "modern" tools functioned, who used them, and the social meaning or subsequent loss of value behind it, it becomes evident that studying the condition, in particular the raw material and site context as well as the form of objects, may give us insight into the various ways social relations might have been negotiated in the past using coeval material culture. Bringing all these variables together is new in the study of archaeological bone tools.

In this paper a variety of characteristic bone tools and ornaments were reviewed from the Neolithic and Bronze Age of Hungary. The pieces described are meant to represent examples of the way special objects displaying intensive wear or outstanding in terms of their raw material, form or the way they were disposed of may be interpreted. The three characteristic, carefully manufactured bone tools – a metapodial awl, a spoon and a hook from the Early Neolithic site of Ecsegfalva 23 – are all tools that were manufactured throughout the 600 years of the existence of the Körös Culture on the Great Hungarian Plain. In other words, these objects were all familiar parts of the material culture of the Körös people, object types that had a very, very long tradition of manufacture in the region. In addition, all three of the individual objects found at the Ecsegfalva 23 site display intensive signs of wear that most likely took longer to develop than the length of time the small hamlets where they were used were occupied. Thus, each of these objects, when it was finally discarded, had a remembered past that might have spanned decades of family memory concerning events and individuals associated with the object.

Although bone tools remained very important in the Middle Bronze Age, they are either very simply made or quite elaborate objects, possibly produced by specialists. Even the simplest of tools, however, such as the rib scrapers from the large Transdanubian tell site of Százhallombatta-Földvár were sturdy enough to have been used for extended periods of time although it is difficult to say how long because nothing is known about the intensity of the work or even what kinds of materials they were used to scrape. Some of them evidently had active edges that were continuously renewed and that display a very highly polished surface. Other elaborate bone and antler objects from Middle Bronze Age sites were mostly related to controlling the movements of animals and displaying the special status of riding horses. Most of these decorative and complex objects show signs of intensive wear that would have taken some considerable time to develop. Of particular interest in this regard is a pair of handles discovered close to each other at Száz-hallombatta-Földvár and carved from sheep metatarsals with holes and pins to fix inside what must have been a soft, pliable material like leather for reins. The wear on these pieces is so extreme that it must have taken several decades to develop, potentially allowing these objects to pass through the hands of more than one generation.

The final category of archaeological object that consistently displays intensive wear and continuous curation on these prehistoric Hungarian sites are pendants and beads made from the teeth of various wild animals, especially wild boar and bear, and domestic animals, particularly dog canines. Such teeth may well have had both an apotropaic role and been identity markers related to gender, age or perhaps even clan affiliation. Many such beads were drilled through the roots and when they wore through at the hole, the teeth were carefully conserved and re-drilled, in spite of the fact that dog canines at least would have been easily available. In contrast, perforated pig incisors display only slight wear and only rarely the same kind of extreme wear and curation behavior seen on dog teeth or the teeth from wild animals.

Of particular interest are a series of burials at the Late Neolithic site of Polgár 6, where women and girls were buried with elaborate headdresses, necklaces, and belts put together for the burial ritual from propeller-shaped beads meant to imitate red deer canines. Based on the variable degrees of wear, these special beads seem to have been worn for varying extended amounts of time and, at least in the case of the young girls, not by the deceased person who eventually received them. Some individual beads may have been worn, broken and repaired over the course of many years. An on-going experiment where such beads have been worn continuously in a necklace for over a year shows that these beads develop visible wear only very slowly. These imitation red deer beads with a few real red deer canine beads scattered among them thus could have been used by funeral participants to make reference to their personal remembered past and a constructed, mythological past connecting the living and the dead. They were worn by the living and given to the dead, linking generations through this kind of material memory.

Clearly there is a disparity between the social and contextual detail available for the ethnographic and archaeological examples presented here. Furthermore, it must be acknowledged that the modern bone objects were used in complex traditional societies under intense pressure for change. Far less background information is available for objects used in the pre-literate societies from the distant past. This does not mean, however, that some of the general principles related to the ways these "modern" tools were used and manipulated cannot be used to model the way analogous objects were employed in less complex, prehistoric societies. Explicit recognition of relative length of use has not previously been

attempted on objects clearly exhibiting heavy wear and repeatedly repaired. More objective ways of identifying morphological traits characteristic of long-time utilization need to be developed. For now, it is only possible to identify objects at the two extreme ends of the time-use continuum: short-lived ad hoc objects and objects used over very long periods. Here, the argument has been made for why it would be important to try to develop such a methodology, lifting studies of worked osseous objects beyond intuitively interpreted macro-features and avoiding their subjective interpretation.

Bibliography

Beldiman, C. 1999-2000. L'industrie matières dures animales dans le site Néolithique ancien de Dudeşt II Vechi, Dép. De Timiş. *Anales du Banat* 7-8, pp. 75-92.

Beldiman, C. 2000. Objets de parure en matières dures animales du Néolithique ancien de Roumanie: Bracelets en bois de cerf. *Bulletin du Musée Départemental "Teohari Antonescu"* 5-7, pp. 31-45.

Beldiman, C. 2002. Sur la typologie des outils en matières dures animales du Néolithique Ancien de Roumanie: Le poinçon sur demi-métapode perforé. In: *Ateliers et Techniques Artisanales. Contributions Archéologiques.* C. Gaiu (ed.). Bistriţa: Musée Départemental.

Beldiman, C. and Popuşoi, E. 2001. L'industrie des matières dures animals dans le site néothlique ancien (culture de Starčevo-Criş) de Trestiana, dép. de Vaslui, Roumanie: Aiguilles à chas. *Acta Musei Petrodavensis Memoria Antiquitatis* 22, pp. 351-402.

Birtalan, A. 2003. Ritualistic use of livestock bones in the Mongolian belief systems and customs. In: *Proceedings of the 45th Permanent International Altaistic Conference (PIAC).* Alice Sárközi and Attila Rákos (eds.). Altaica Budapestinensia MMII. Budapest: Research Group for Altaic Studies, Hungarian Academy of Sciences, Department of Inner Asian Studies, Eötvös Loránd University, pp. 34-59.

Bourdieu, P. 1977. *Outline of a Theory of Practice.* Cambridge: Cambridge University Press.

Bökönyi, S. 1960. Reconstruction des mors en bois de cerf et en os. *Acta Archaeologica Academiae Scientiarum Hungaricae* 12, pp. 113–122.

Chapman, J. 2000. *Fragmentation in Archaeology: People, Places, and Broken Objects in the Prehistory of South Eastern Europe.* London: Routledge.

Choyke, A. M. 1979. A Classification of the Bone and Antler Tools from the Bronze Age Hill-fortress of Pákozdvár. *Alba Regia* 17, pp. 9–21.

Choyke, A. M. 1983. "An Analysis of Bone, Antler, and Tooth Tools from Bronze Age Hungary." PhD dissertation, State University of New York at Binghamton.

Choyke, A. M. 1997. The Bone Manufacturing Continuum. *Anthropozoologica* 25-26, pp. 65-72.

Choyke, A. M. 2001. Late Neolithic Red Deer Canine Beads and their Imitations. In: *Crafting Bone – Skeletal Technologies through Time and Space*. A. M. Choyke and L. Bartosiewicz (eds.). British Archaeological Reports, International Series 937. Oxford: BAR Publishing, pp. 251-266.

Choyke, A. M. 2001. A Qantitative Approach to the Concept of Quality in Prehistoric Bone mManufacturing. In: *Animals and Man in the Past*. H. Buitenhuis and W. Prummel (eds). Publicatie 41. Groningen: Centre for Archeological Research and Consultancy (ARC), pp. 59-66.

Choyke, A. M. 2005. Bronze Age Bone and Antler Working at the Jászdózsa–Kápolnahalom Tell. In: *From Hooves to Horns, from Mollusk to Mammoth: Manufacture and Use of Bone Artifacts from Prehistoric Times to the Present*. H. Luik, A. Choyke, C. Batey and L. Lõugas (eds.). Proceedings of the 4th meeting of the ICAZ Worked Bone Research Group in Tallinn (26-31 August 2003). Muinasaja Teadus/Research into Ancient Times 15, pp. 129-156.

Choyke, A. M. in press. Continuity and Discontinuity at Győr-Szabdrét-domb: *Bone Tools from a Chalcolithic Settlement in Northwest Hungary. In: Bone, Antler, Teeth. Raw Material for Tool Production in Prehistoric and Historic Periods*. Jörg Schibler (ed.). Proceedings of the 3rd meeting of the ICAZ Worked Bone Research Group in Basel (4-8 September 2001). Internationale Archäologie/International Archaeology Arbeitgemeinschaft, Symposium, Taging, Kongress, Rahden/Westfalen, Germany: Verlag Maria Leidorf GmbH.

Choyke, A.M. 2007. Objects for a Lifetime – Tools for a Season: The Worked Osseous Material from Ecsegfalva 23. In: *The Early Neolithic on the Great Hungarian Plain. Investigations of the Körös Culture Site of Ecsegfalva 23, County Békés*. A. Whittle (ed.). Vol. 2. Varia Archaeologica Hungarica 21, Budapest: Institute of Archaeology of the Hungarian Academy of Sciences, pp. 641-666.

Choyke, A. M., Vretemark, M., and Sten, S. 2003. Levels of Social Identity Expressed in the Refuse and Worked Bone from the Middle Bronze Age Százhalombatta-Földvár, Vatya Culture, Hungary. In: *Behaviour Behind Bones. The Zooarchaeology of Ritual, Religion. Status and Identity*. S. Jones O'Day, W. van Neer and A. Ervynck (eds.). Oxford: Oxbow Books, pp. 177-189.

Conkey, M. 1993. Humans as Materialists and Symbolists: Image-making in the Upper Paleolithic of Europe. In: *Origins of Humans and Humanne*. David Tab Rasmussen (ed.). Boston: Jones & Bartle, pp. 95-118.

Cristidou, R. and Legrand, A. 2005. Hide Working and Bone Tools: Experimentation Design and Application. In: *From Hooves to Horns, from Mollusc to Mammoth: Manufacture and Use of Bone Artifacts from Prehistoric Times to the Present*. H. Luik, A. Choyke and

C. Batey (eds.). Proceedings of the 4th meeting of the ICAZ Worked Bone Research Group in Tallinn (26-31 August 2003). Muinasaja Teadus/Research into Ancient Times 15, pp. 385-396.

Currey, J. D. 1979. Mechanical Properties of Bone Tissues with Widely Differing Functions. *Journal of Biometrics* 12, pp. 313-319.

David, N. and Kramer, C. 2001. *Ethnoarchaeology in Action*. Cambridge: Cambridge University Press.

Foltiny, S. 1965. Bronze- und urnenfelderzeitliche Hirshhorn- und Knochentrensen aus Neiderösterreich. *Mitteilungen des Instituts für österreichische Geschichtsforschung* 95, pp. 243-249.

Hardy, K. and Sillitoe, P. 2003. Material Perspectives: Stone Tool Use and Material Culture in Papua New Guinea. *Internet Archaeology* 14 (summer). http://int-arch.ac. uk/journal/issue14/hardy_index.html.

Hüttel, H.-G. 1981. Bronzezeitliche Trensen in Mittel- und Osteuropa. Grundzüge ihrer Entwicklung. *Prähistorische Bronzefunde* 16(2).

Ingold, T. 1990. Society, Nature, and the Concept of Technology. *Archaeological Review from Cambridge* 9(1), pp. 5-17.

Jones, A. 2003. Technologies of remembrance. In: *Archaeologies of Remembrance: Death and Memory in Past Societies*. Howard Williams (ed.). New York: Kluwer Academic/Plenum Publishers, 1983, pp. 65-88.

Kisléghi Nagy Gy. 1911. Az óbessenyői Őstelep (The Óbessenyő prehistoric settlement). *Archaeologiai Értesítő* 31(1), pp. 147-161.

Kovács, T. 1969. A százhalombatta bronzkori telep (The Bronze Age settlement at Százhalombatta). *Archeológiai Értesítő* 96, pp. 161-169.

Kwint, M. 1999. Introduction: The Physical Past. In: *Material Memories: Design and Evocation*. M. Kwint, C. Breward and J. Aynsley (eds.). Oxford: Berg Press, pp. 1-16.

LeMoine, G. 1997. *Use Wear Analysis on Bone and Antler Tools of the Mackenzie Inuit*. BAR International Series 679. Oxford: BAR Publishing.

MacGregor, A. 1985. *Bone, Antler, Ivory and Horn: The Technology of Skeletal Materials since the Roman Period*. London: Croom Helm.

Malinowski, B. 1939. The Group and the Individual in Functional Analysis. *American Journal of Sociology* 44, pp. 938-964.

Makkay, J. 1990. Knochen, Geweih und Eberzahngegenstände der frühneolithischen Körös-Kultur. *Communicationes Archaeologicae Hungariae* (1990), pp. 23-58.

Marinescu-Bâlcu, L., and C. Beldiman 1997. L'industrie des matières dures animales appartenant à la civilisation Néolithique de Starčevo-Criş en Roumanie. Le site de Grumâzeşti, Dép. de Neamt. *Acta Musei Petrodavensis. Memoria Antiquitatis* 21, pp. 273-296.

McCabe, Richard E. 1982. Elk and Indian: Historical Values and Perspectives. In: *Elk of North America: Eco-*

logy and Management. J. W. Thomas and D. E. Toweill (eds.). Harrisburg, PA: Stackpole Books, pp. 61-123.

Middleton, D. and D. Edwards. 1997. Introduction: Memory, Cognition and Image Production. In: *Collective Remembering*. D. Middleton and D. Edwards (eds.). London: Sage, pp. 1-23.

Mozsolics, A. 1960. Die Herkunftfragen der ältesten Hirshgeweihtrensen. *Acta Archaeologcia Academiae Scientiarum Hungaricae* 12, pp. 125–135.

Murray, C. 1979. Les techniques de débitage de métapodes de petits ruminants a Auvernier-Port. In: *L' Industrie en Os et Bois de Cervidé durant le Néolithique et l'Âge des Métaux.* H. Camps-Fabrer (ed). Paris: Editions CNRS, pp. 27-35.

Nandris, J. 1972. Bos primigenius and the Bone Spoon. London: University of London, Institute of Archaeology, *Bulletin* 10, pp. 63-83.

Perišić, S. 1984. *Predmeti od Kosti, Roga i Kamena* (Objects of bone, antler, and stone)., Katalog 13. Belgrade: Muzej Grada Beograda.

Pétrequin, A-M. and P. Pétrequin. 2006. *Objects de Pouvoir en Nouvelle-Guinée.* Catalogue de la donation Anne-Marie Pétrequin and Pierre Pétrequin, Paris: Musée d'Archéologie Nationale de Saint-Germain-en-Laye.

Pfaffenberger, B. 1988. Fetishized Objects and Humanized Nature: Towards an Anthropology of Technology. *Man* 23, pp. 236-252.

Pfaffenberger, B. 1992. Social Anthropology of Technology. *Annual Review of Anthropology* 21, pp. 491-516.

Popuşoi, E. and C. Beldiman. 1993-1998. L'industrie des matières dures animals dans le site de la cvilization Starčevo-Criş Trestiana, dép. De Vaslui. Un example d'étude: les spatules. *Acta Moldaviae Meridoalis* 15-20(1), pp. 82-115.

Poroszlai, I. 2000. Excavation Campaigns at the Bronze Age Tell Site at Százhalombatta–Földvár I: 1989-1991; II. 1991-1993. In: *Százhalombatta Archaeological Expedition, Annual Report* 1. I. Poroszlai, and M. Vicze (eds.). Százhalombatta: Matrica Museum, pp. 13-74.

Russell, N. 1998. Cattle as Wealth in Neolithic Europe: Where's the Beef ? In: *The Archaeology of Value.* D. Bailey (ed.). BAR International Series 730. Oxford: Archeo-press, pp. 42- 54.

Radley, A. 1997. Artefacts, Memory and a Sense of the Past. In: *Collective Remembering.* D. Middleton and D. Edwards (eds.). London: Sage, pp. 46-60.

Schibler, J. 1981. *Typologische Untersuchungen der cortaillodzeitlichen Knochenartefakte. Die neolithischen Ufersiedlungen von Twann.* Band 17. Schriftenreihe der Erziehungsdirektion des Kantons Bern, Bern: Archäologischen Dienst des Kantons Bern, Staatlicher Lehrmittelverlag.

Sillar, B. 1996. The Dead and the Dying. *Journal of Material Culture* 1, No. 3, pp. 250-289.

Spector, J. 1991. What this Awl Means: Toward a Feminist Archaeology. In: *Engendering Archaeology.* J. Gero and M. Conkey (eds.). Oxford: Blackwell Publishers, pp. 388-406.

Stark, M. 1999. Social Dimensions of Technical Choice in Kalinga Ceramic Traditions. In: *Material Meanings.* E. Chilton (ed.). Salt Lake City: University of Utah Press, pp. 24-43.

Taborin, Y. 2004. *Language sans parole. La parure aux temp préhistoriques.* Paris: La maison des roches.

Taylor, A. and A. Cohen Kiel. 2003. *Recovering the Social Life of Things.* PDF file on Internet site: http://www.cs.cornell.edu/People/Sengers/DomesticTech03/Taylor (last accessed June 2009).

Wobst, M. 1997. Towards an "Appropriate Metrology" of Human Action. In: *Time, Process, and Structured Transformation in Archaeology.* S. van der Leeuw and J. Mcglade (eds.). London: Routledge, 426-448.

THE RE-GENERATION OF THE NEOLITHIC: SOCIAL MEMORY, MONUMENTS AND GENERATIONS

Liam Kilmurray

Abstract

In recent years archaeologists have begun to address the role of social memory in the past. There has been an accompanying increase in the use of constructs taken from the cognitive sciences. Monuments have been at the forefront of such interpretations, and the site of the importation of cognitive science constructs into archaeology. The purposes of this paper are two-fold; firstly, to argue that archaeologists have not fully demonstrated the mnemonic characteristics of monuments, and secondly, to show how archaeologists have not paid sufficient attention to the prehistoric specificity of demographic realities. The important link between past population structures and the transmission of social memory through time has been glossed over. Crucially, in terms of social memory, Neolithic life spans have been misunderstood. As a result, the "timing," duration, and overlap of generations in prehistory has been missread. This has resulted in a distortion of the role of social memory in prehistory. Prehistorians have thought of a generation in today's terms, that is, one that begins at 25 years of age – at the one-third mark of a person's life. In reality, Neolithic people lived on average for 30-35 years and a generational "cohort" matured at perhaps age 15, the point at which a person's life was half way over. There was little grand-parentage overlap; this had important ramifications for the storage, reactivation and transmission of social memory.

The emergence of a wide variety of monuments is one of the defining characteristics of the Neolithic. In this period, a new conception of temporality was occasioned, a new ontology emerged, and a new understanding of the past came about. Archaeologists have recognized the role of monuments as mnemonic devices, but they have not explained the mechanisms behind this mnemonic role. I will demonstrate specifically how passage graves acted as mnemonic devices by examining the contexts of memory that they contain. This mnemonic analysis will be coupled with a newer understanding of the specific characteristics of Neolithic demography, such as shorter generations. By placing the time line of Neolithic generations into a proper perspective, archaeology can offer a new reading of the importance of social memory and gain a better understanding of the importance of collective architectural mnemonics.

Keywords: Neolithic, demography, generations, passage graves, mnemonic devices

***

1. Introduction

Over the past decade or so, archaeologists have sought to examine the role of social memory in past societies (Rowlands 1993; Holtorf 1997, 1998; Bradley 1998, 2002; Thomas 2000). The inclusion of social memory studies into prehistory is still in its infancy. Social memory is a complex issue, its definitions are myriad,[1] and even advocates have noted problems associated with its study. Social memory, it is said, remains "a non-paradigmatic, transdisciplinary, centreless enterprise" (Olick and Robbins 1998:106). In prehistoric studies, further problems stem from the manner in which prehistorians have inadequately addressed generations in terms of memory and demography.

While they may have adopted some of the constructs and tenets of the cognitive sciences, archaeologists have not paid sufficient attention to the prehistoric specificity of the demographic realities of the Neolithic. In particular, the generational span (including its "maturation point," duration, and timing) has been misunderstood, and this has resulted in a distortion of the role of social memory in prehistory. This is due, in part, to the over-estimation of the duration of a generation, which is usually thought of in contemporary terms – 25 years – as opposed to the more accurate figure of 15 years per generation in the Neolithic. Scholars speak of a Neolithic that

---

1. The succinct definition followed here is that social memory is the memory that individuals hold of the collective; they are memories of such importance as to be remembered socially. This does not mean that they are not individual, on the contrary, they are memories that individuals share, memories of history, of more or less common thought concerning the way things were in the past, and are in the present. It is less important to know the content of such memories than to understand the mechanisms for their transmission.

lasted 80 generations, or the building of Stonehenge lasting 55 generations. But these figures stem from the length of today's generations. Neolithic people lived shorter lives. There were fewer years in which grandparents overlapped with grandchildren, or even parents with children. This had a profound impact on the role of memory and mnemonics in prehistoric communities. There must, then, be a re-thinking of the Neolithic in terms of the shorter life-spans that were characteristic of the period. This will reveal the significance of monument building and its relationship to social memory.

Memory is practice; it must be maintained and transmitted. Neolithic monuments did this: they were richly imbued with mnemonic characteristics. They kept social memory alive, and provided a means for its transmission. Many Neolithic monuments, such as Newgrange and Stonehenge, were built and rebuilt over centuries, with the involvement of many different generations. Indeed, I will argue that there were specific demographic patterns in the Neolithic which *required* that an emphasis be placed on the persistence of social memory. Neolithic demographic patterns were characterized by lower overall population sizes, dispersed communities, lower life spans, and the truncation of the grandparent-child-grandchild pattern with which we are familiar today.[2]

The fact that Neolithic people may have lived a maximum of some 30 or 35 years placed an onus upon the transmission of memory. This is why the demographic profiles of the Neolithic were intimately related to the use of monuments as mnemonic devices. Misunderstanding the impact of shorter generations in the Neolithic is an important oversight given the intrinsic importance of generations in areas of archaeological interest such as the transmission of culture, monuments, and social memory. In an attempt to correct this misunderstanding, I will demonstrate the relationship between monuments and social memory. I will argue that both the widespread occurrence and persistence of monuments such as passage graves are attributable to their mnemonic characteristics. I will show that although cognitive scientists have constructed valuable approaches to studying memory – through their application of generational memory – these constructs are not directly applicable to prehistoric studies of social memory.

The specific demographic patterns of the Neolithic necessitated the use of mnemonic devices to transmit information across generations. Thus, there are serious problems in the use of constructs taken from the cognitive sciences and applied to the generational realities of the Neolithic. I will conclude by making the case for a "regenerating" of the Neolithic, arguing that once it is understood that generations were, on average, shorter in

the Neolithic, then the statistics that archaeologists routinely employ have underestimated both the "duration" of the Neolithic period and the significance of social memory and monuments.

2. The Neolithic: Monuments and Memory

[E]very process of action is a production of something new, a fresh act; but at the same time, all action exists in continuity with the past, which supplies the means of its initiation (Giddens 1979:70).

Since the 1990s, monuments have become a rich source of data for examining social memory. A diverse range of approaches has sought to understand monuments in a mnemonic light. Places such as Newgrange or Stonehenge are frequently seen as repositories of social memory (Bender 1993, 1998). More recently, Mayan temples (Joyce 2003) and Byzantine walls (Papalexandrou 2003) have joined the ranks of megaliths (Bradley 2002) and earthen mounds (Pauketat and Alt 2003) – all analyzed as markers of the human desire to commemorate. This is a testament to the fruition of the post-processualist critique (Shanks and Tilley 1987; Hodder 1992) and the turn to cognition and meaning in the social sciences in general. Collective architectural projects, it is now accepted, were intimately connected with memory. In the Neolithic, monuments were involved in the making, storage and transmission of social memory.

At one time the Neolithic period in temperate Europe was thought to have lasted just 500 years, roughly from 3000 to 2500 BC (Whittle 1980a, 1980b). This Neolithic, defined variously as a "package" (domestication, monuments, polished stone, etc.) had rushed in on a "wave of advance" (Ammerman and Cavalli-Sforza 1973). But, with the emergence of radiocarbon dating, the duration of the Neolithic in Europe was extended to 3000 years – from 5000 to 2000 BC (Renfrew 1973). Despite the enlargement of the Neolithic it was still generally perceived to consist of only some 80 generations (Bender 1993). However, in order to interpret the longevity of Neolithic monuments and their role in the transmission of social memory, a more accurate understanding of Neolithic demographics is important.

The passage graves of temperate Europe illustrate both points – they were very long lived, and they were mnemonic devices. Passage graves were first constructed in Brittany around 5000 BC (Lecornec 1994). In Britain they are found at around 3400 BC, and in Ireland they were first built ca. 3300 BC, with construction finally terminating[3] around 2000 BC. All told, this represents

---

2. Western notions of generations and life spans are the default here. It is recognized that there are vast differences in life span throughout the globe and through different periods. However, for the sake of both consistency and to address specifically Western literature, Western notions of age structures are used.

3. The cessation of monument construction, remodeling or even acts of deposition does not signal the end of the monument in terms of its centrality to social memory. See Holtorf (1997, 1998) for a discussion of the afterlife of monuments. See Last (1998) for a discussion of the re-use of monuments.

an impressive span of some 3000 years. Yet archaeologists, among others, have been slow to address this enormous continuity. Perhaps this is because acknowledging this continuity requires an analysis of the way prehistoric people remembered their own distant pasts. Despite being the subject of some of the most recent discussions (Bradley 2002), the "past in the past" has traditionally been a muted issue (but see Bloch 1977). Yet monuments provide us with an opportunity to examine the materiality of the past. The past was a resource drawn upon by the community; and some monuments, by the time of their "completion," were already *of* the past.

For example, the communal construction at Silbury Hill is estimated to have taken a century to construct[4] (Richards and Thomas 1984). Along with this continuity, further pasts were created, as it is notable that there were recurrent constructions at many other monuments (Bradley 1998:17; Harding 1997; Hodder 1990). Therefore, monuments not only came from the past, but they lasted so long that they created more pasts. They also consumed the past as well. In the ditches at Stonehenge, there were deposits of cattle bones that were already hundreds of years old at the time of their deposition (Bayliss et al. 1997). Neolithic people were not only fully cognizant of the past, but, in fact, they actively curated the past. Many other monuments were repeatedly visited, new depositions were made at them, and alterations to their form and even location were made. This "continuity" was not solely a matter of revisiting or re-modeling monuments, but one of sustaining the practices of memory. This is crucial: people would have *experienced* the reworking of their landscapes.

The significance of monuments, and particularly their significance to social memory, lies not only in their longevity, but also in the fact that they span many 'generations'. For the period under consideration (5000 to 2000 BC), monuments were *the* source of information for inter-generational transmission of memory on a social scale. This involvement of enormous numbers of Neolithic generations in the commemoration of the past was something more pronounced than we are perhaps able to contemplate today. But it does explain the many mnemonic characteristics of Neolithic monuments.

The mnemonic characteristics and contexts of monuments

Archaeology has begun to focus on the mnemonic aspects of Neolithic monuments, and research has suggested that monuments were collective mnemonics, but the mechanics of *how* monuments acted as mnemonics has not been fully addressed. It must also be acknowledged that there were many other mnemonics in the Neolithic, such as oral histories,[5] the deposition of hoards, and the fragmentation of materials (Chapman 2000). Yet our focus is

on monuments, which themselves were mnemonic devices in a wide variety of ways. Indeed, the aura of monumentalism itself is a mnemonic (Holtorf 1997). The erection of a monument required the marshalling of significant resources. The monument was a testament to coordination and cooperation, it was more than the sum of its mnemonic characteristics and practices – the aura of the monumental project sanctioned and created new social worlds. In addition, at monuments, the atmosphere engendered through burial, through the deposition of exclusive artifacts, and occasionally of already ancient bones, created a rich fabric of meaning by which to impress memory. These mnemonic contexts have rarely been examined by archaeologists, but they are profuse and, I suggest, can be read mnemonically.

The cognitive theorist Parkman noted that there is an intricate connection between colouring, light and dark, and remembering (1993:101). We can see the utility of this analysis for archaeology in the characteristics of passage graves, which, for one, took advantage of these contexts and cues. Cognitive studies also tell us that a "context," in the mnemonic sense, is that which surrounds a target, that which is spatial, temporal, or meaningful in nature (Smith 1994). Context affects the recall, delivery, and intake of memory (Davies and Alonso-Quecuty 1997). Events are remembered better when there is contextual cueing (Smith 1994:169).

There are some generic shapes that are so deeply embedded in a culture that they almost inevitably start a train of associations, reminding us of other places, other cultures, or, more simply, the presence of other people. To carry such associative force, these shapes must in turn be either ubiquitous – found again and again so that they become thoroughly familiar – or so intensely, so engagingly particular that they are emblazoned in our minds (Lyndon and Moore 1994:235).

Another one of the key factors in remembering is redundancy – that is, repetition – a mnemonic aid that is encountered frequently on the passage graves. The same range of motifs is found over and over again. The ubiquitous chevrons, cup-marks and spirals were frequently placed in the same positions. The art at Newgrange is an excellent example of the deployment of such mnemonic motifs (Fig. 1). In fact, repetition is found at these monuments in two ways: both in memory and in ritual, which share the concept of invariance, and although monuments each have their own peculiarities, there are also many invariances. For example, the otherwise profuse "tunnel" motif is never found on monuments that contain an actual "tunnel," such as the passage of the passage graves (Bradley 1997). There is, moreover, an invariant absence of utilitarian items such as tools or plain ceramics. Instead, only the finest "ornamental" tool types and the most elaborate ceramics are found inside the passage graves (O'Kelly 1982).

---

4. Or three million work-hours (Barrett 1994:29).

5. Neolithic words are "lost" to us, and our mnemonic search must be limited to the context in which such utterings took place. Words and sounds would have been vital components of mnemonic ceremony, as

Joyce notes, "visual perception decays more rapidly than auditory sense information, which persists up to ten times longer" (2003:106-7).

Fig. 1. Newgrange, kerbstone. (Photo: L. Kilmurray).

On a broader scale of contextual cueing, the vast majority of passage graves were situated on hills and ridges, of which and from which there were often quite striking views (Ruggles 1999; Cummings 2003). A further consistency is witnessed in the orientation of many passage graves to the southeast. The mnemonic characteristics of light were also put to good use. Monuments such as Calanais, Stonehenge, and Newgrange, are oriented upon celestial events. There are also many monuments, particularly in Ireland and Scotland, at which quartz pebbles have been deposited (Jones and Bradley 1999). The front façade of Newgrange is constructed of quartz and grandolite rock, making the monument gleam in moonlight and sunlight. This widespread use of quartz seems particularly oriented toward moonlight, and indeed it may have acted as a synecdoche for the moon, and been connected to special astronomical events. Further mnemonic significance is found in the art on many megalithic monuments. The redundancy of the art has been noted, but there are also rules of placement to much of this art. At the Knowth passage grave there is a higher placement of the curvilinear art and lower placement of the rectilinear art (Eogan 1986:184). Also, there are rules of inclusion and exclusion of various art styles at many monuments, and an internal/external placement to various motifs. This suggests that the art was used to communicate ideas – to transmit information.

The reasoning behind these social memory prompts may have been more immediate. Rault suggests that the megalithic art at Fourknocks (Fig. 2), Le Petit Mont, and Ses Kilgreen were, in fact, blueprints for the building of the monument of La Ville Picard (Rault 1997:6). Furthermore, the "plan" of Newgrange, it is argued, is reflected in the rock art on the chambered monument of Anneville, Jersey (Rault 1997). The many mnemonic characteristics of Neolithic monuments strongly suggest that the congregations at monuments were participat-

ing in events designed to secure social memory. All of these mnemonic functions were aimed at an audience, with the purpose of transmitting information between generations. To this end, ritual was used as a delivery system.

The rituals attending the placement of the dead inside passage graves were notable for their powerful mnemonic significance. One type of ritual was a threefold process: isolation – liminality – incorporation. Passage graves can be understood to be marked by this triad also. The isolation of the dead (or living) took place outside the blocked chambers, sometimes in areas demarcated by standing stones or a cursus. The long dark passages were the areas of suspended liminality (the two passages at Knowth, for example, are 34.2 and 40 meters long, respectively) through which the living (and the dead) progressed. The inner space of the recessed chambers themselves were the incorporative areas, in which multiple cremations were often placed. The morphology of the monument can be linked to different phases of ritual, and it can also be extended to different types of memory. For instance, short-term memory aides are found at the external areas of the tombs (which could be marked by the art on the kerb stones or some other mnemonic). The repeated visits and deposits at tombs or the seasonal penetration of celestial bodies inside the chambers represent a "working memory."[6] Finally, the presence of the dead and the integrity of the monument itself signify long-term memory, and the long-term storage of social memory. The architecture of the monuments, ritually infused, embodies the mechanisms of human memory. They served not only to represent memories but were also instruments for creating and sustaining memories. But why did such complex and richly infused mnemonic practices and materials emerge precisely at this time?

---

6. This refers to immediate memories that are 'sustained' in working memory, on their way perhaps to becoming long-term memories.

Fig. 2. Fourknocks,
decorated lintel.
(Photo: L. Kilmurray)

Neolithic Social Change

The emergence of mnemonic institutions seems to have been due to the dramatic and far-reaching changes in Neolithic sociality. The very first long-lived congregational activities begin in the Neolithic of temperate Europe. Whether these groups practiced radiating mobility (Hassan 1981:92) or some form of tethered mobility (Whittle 1996), the monumental "project" drew together people from scattered bands into more durable settlements. These initial congregations were the glue that bound together the new communities of the Neolithic. Continuity blossomed *in situ*, leading to a new settlement pattern and the development of novel inter-generational connections. It was at this time that a cohesive social memory and social identity – formed through a durable set of practices that outlasted the temporary congregation itself – were created and sustained. This can be opposed to the congregations of the Mesolithic, which were less durable. Hunter-gatherers were kept together in large part through exchange (Woodburn 1982). Neolithic monuments occasioned broader and more sustained social contact, communities became larger, they lasted longer, and they experienced sustained inter-generational contacts.

3. Generations

The generations referred to in the archaeological literature, however, are misunderstood. Archaeologists do recognize the critical importance of demographics (Cohen 1977; Buikstra 1997), but few have made *generations* a feature of Neolithic study (see Jennbert 1998:34). How archaeologists understand generations is important because we are constantly making (implicit) statements about generations, statements using constructs that draw upon longevity, continuity, durability, and transmission. This is the very stuff that interpretations of prehistory rest upon, but there are problems with how generations are seen.

A variety of social memory researchers have recognized the crucial nature of generations in the transmission of social memory (Schuman and Scott 1989; Schuman et al. 1994). Mannheim's seminal research (1952) highlighted the role of generations in the "solidification" of social memory. Zerubavel states that our links with the past are often couched in terms of biology (2003:56), that is, in terms of the dead and living generations that precede us, and that generational overlap contributes to the stability of cultural institutions (Zerubavel 2003:60). Perhaps most importantly, generations are a bridge between individual and collective memory. Generations are also a link in the intersection of individual and collective *identity*. Changes made in one generation act to limit *and* facilitate the actions of the following generations. Further, they are seen as a rebuff to those who claim that the malleability of memory makes it impossible to study (Olick and Robbins 1998:128). The transmissions between generations keep social memory alive, albeit altered; social memory nonetheless persists through generations *if* mechanisms for its transmission are in place. One such mechanism was the building of a monument and its continued upkeep by successive and overlapping generations. Generations are thus important, not simply as a heuristic device, but in actuality. Yet, what is a generation?

A generation is comprised of people born roughly at the same time, forming an age cohort. The coming of age of the generation is placed at the age when children are ready to take the place of their parents. Today this is usually thought to be around 25 years of age, at roughly one-third of the parental life span. However, archaeologists and anthropologists have extended this current, Western, definition of a generation to prehistory. It is held that each generation lasted between 20 and 25 years. Rappaport, for instance, argues that in non-literate societies, the limits of living memory will be exhausted after five generations, or 100 years (1999:258). Zerubavel describes a generation as "the twenty-five year legs of our imaginary historical relay

	Quanterness		Isbister	
	Number	*% of pop.*	*Number*	*% of pop.*
Adults	85	54	185	54
Teenagers	36	23	62	18
Children	26	17	70	20
Infants	10	6	24	7
Total	157	100	342	100

Table 1. Breakdown of age profiles from Isbister and Quanterness. (Rounded decimals account for the 'missing' one percent.)
From this data Hedges (1982) was able to highlight 4 major points:
1. There was a high incidence of infant deaths
2. The bulk of deaths fell between the ages of 15–29 years
3. The highest incidence of deaths occurred between 20–24 years
4. There was a small incidence of deaths over 30 years (restricted to 30–49)

race" (2003:58). But, this figure is incorrect and has led to many erroneous interpretations of Neolithic society.

Using this 25-year figure, archaeologists consider the Neolithic to have lasted 80 generations, from 3500 to 1500 BC (e.g. Bender 1993). Elsewhere, the classic figure of 55 generations at work on Stonehenge between 2600 BC and 1400 BC (Chippendale 1979:205) implies that in 1200 years each generation lasted 21.8 years.

In terms of the construction of monuments, the "over-extended" generations that archaeologists have been working with have painted an incorrect or at least incomplete picture. Because, if a generation is almost 25 years, and this is one third of the parental life span, then Neolithic people would need to have an approximately 75-year life span, too. This was simply not the case in the Neolithic. To refute, then, this widespread importation of the 25-year generation into prehistory, we must consider the demographic profiles that the remains of Neolithic people reflect.

4. Neolithic Demography

To judge from the bodies found in the graves of the third and second millennia life expectancy of the period was considerably shorter than today. A crude death rate of about 40 per 1,000 per annum has been suggested, far higher than the 14 per 1,000 which is now the average for Western Europe, but comparable with the figures still found in much of the Third World. Put another way, and not including the victims of an undoubtedly high infant mortality rate, perhaps 10 per cent of the population had a life expectancy of only 10 years, as much as 60

per cent could reach only 25 years, and only 30 per cent could expect to live to 40 (Burgess 1980:161-2).

Physical remains from two Neolithic sites in Scotland provide us with a chance to examine Neolithic life spans (see Table 1). At the chambered tomb of Isbister, South Ronaldsy, Orkney, the remains of 341 individuals were discovered: 185 adults, 62 teenagers, 70 children, and 24 infants. At Quanterness the figures are comparable to those from Isbister. From a recovered population of 157 there were: 85 adults, 36 teenagers, 26 children, and 10 infants. If we add the two Orkney sites together, we get a total of 499 individuals, and a breakdown as follows: 270 adults, 98 teenagers, 96 children, and 34 infants.

People could not expect a long life: 19 years 11 months, at birth, was the average life expectancy (Burgess 1980:11). Those who survived their teenage years could expect another 9 years, giving them a life expectancy of 29 years of age. What emerges from Hedges' analysis is the fact that "those under 20 would have outnumbered those over 20 by 3-1, and only 1.5% would have been over 40. Whereas today, those under 20 are outnumbered 3-1 by those over, and 45% of the population today are over 40" (Burgess 1980:14).[7]

At the passage grave of Newgrange, the dental remains of two individuals (possibly a male and female) revealed two ages: 25 and 40 years respectively (O'Kelly 1982:107). At Neo Nikomedia, comparable results are witnessed: males 31, females 30. Beyond Europe, a similar pattern is witnessed. At Catal Höyük, an analysis of 268 bodies demonstrates that the average "death age" was 34.3 for males and 29.8 for females (Hassan 1981). Those who did live to 50 or above constituted only 2.13 % of the population (*ibid*:111).

In the Neolithic our evidence strongly points to a shorter life span (Hassan 1981; Hedges 1982, 1984), despite the odd rarity of skeletal remains that indicate an older person, such as that of the 50 to 60 year-old man of Skateholm (Larson 1985:372). That this was exceptional is witnessed by the fact that the "old man's" burial rite contrasted with that of everyone else: cremation rather than inhumation (Tilley 1996:35). There are other examples of prehistoric remains that have been attributed an age of 70 or even in some cases 80 (J. Chapman pers. comm. 2004). However, on average, most people in the Neolithic, regardless of whether there is a slight difference between biological years and actual years (Hedges 1984), lived "only" around 30 years, very few saw 40 years, and even fewer 50 years. As we would read it today, a generation begins at the one-third point of a person's life. Therefore, a Neolithic generation began at about 15 years of age, but was over within 15 years. Thus, 100 years for five generations is not accurate.

7. Hedges' approach has been questioned on the grounds of permanence of residency and osteological interpretation (Fraser 1982). However, the physical analyses of numerous Neolithic remains reveal an average age at death of around 30 years.

Period	Years	Life Expectancy
1. Paleolithic	50,0000 BC – 10,000 BC	19.9
2. Mesolithic	10,000 BC – 6,000 BC	31.4
3. Neolithic	6,000 BC – 2,500 BC	26.9
4. Bronze Age	2,500 BC – 1,500 BC	32.1
5. Iron Age	1,500 BC – AD 500	27.3
6. Roman Empire	AD 1 – 400	27.8

Table 2. Life expectancy at birth from ancient times to AD 400.

It is, moreover, not just to the earlier Neolithic that these demographic structures apply. Similar life spans are found in the Late Neolithic rock-cut shelter at Loise-en-Brie (Boquet-Appel and Noel 1997). Analysis of 170 Neolithic skeletons from this site revealed a life expectancy of between 25 and 28 years. It appears that the pattern is clear: that of early death as compared to our 21st century standards (see Table 2).

These figures are static estimates, both the nature of the archaeological record and the ambiguity of Neolithic burial rite present great interpretative difficulties. What we can say with some certainty is that compared to today there were far fewer adults in a community – given low population densities[8] – and also that they died at a much younger age. Life, then, although far from "nasty, brutish, and short," was indeed shorter. What is significant for our purposes is that the memory span was therefore shorter. The generational gap was truncated, and the grandparent-grandchild overlap minimal if it existed at all.

Humans alive today are usually in touch with three generations of other members of their lineage: grandparents, parents, and siblings (including children this would make 4). Today a 15-year-old has, with two "contiguous" generations (omitting siblings), a much larger store of memory to draw upon. A crude measurement of this is to view an individual at 15, parents at 40, (one set of) grandparents at 65, totaling 210 years of a "memory store" from these relatives to draw upon. In stark contrast, a 15-year-old Neolithic inhabitant of say, the Boyne Valley, had perhaps[9] parents aged 30, with no grandparents, totaling a generational "bridging" of 60 years. This is a substantial, world-view-altering difference, and is important for understanding both the trans-

mission of social memory and the use of data from the cognitive sciences.

5. Cognitive Science Constructs

We have seen that there were profound differences in Neolithic life spans, and that this was reflected in social memory structures. The domains of memory were of a keener significance in the Neolithic. Revisiting the dead at the passage graves or re-incising the spirals on the Knowth kerbstones were events charged with mnemonic significance. Therefore, for archaeology, our current understandings of Neolithic communities, their elders, their transmissions, and their social relations, must be re-considered. Taking age estimates from today, or from historical ethnography, is not sufficient; it simply dresses the Neolithic in the robes of modernity. The cognitive schemes archaeologists routinely draw upon in discussing prehistory or anthropologists in their ethnographic accounts are based on specific age profiles that bear little resemblance to the Neolithic situation.

Two issues in particular are of great interest to Neolithic analyses. Firstly, it is widely held within memory studies that the age bracket of 17 to 25 is a definitive period both in the formation of individual memory and definition of the self (Mannheim 1952; Schuman et al. 1997; Pennebaker et al.1997; Schuman and Scott 1989). That is, by the age of 25 the process of absorption of particular types of knowledge and memory is almost complete (Conway 1997:21). Importantly, the generation of people who fit within this bracket will form the collective memory of the group in following years. Manheim states:

[The] inventory of experience which is absorbed ... from the environment in early youth often becomes the historically oldest stratum of consciousness, which tends to stabilise itself as the natural view of the world (Manheim 1952:328).

A second important area for Neolithic consideration is the idea in cognitive studies which refers to the reiteration of a collective memory after a period of some 25 years (Schuman et al. 1994). In roughly 25 year periods,

---

8. Demographic structure is intimately linked with generational structure. The size and the age-structures of Neolithic communities are difficult to uncover. Estimates for the population of the Boyne Valley ca. 3000 BC range from 1200 (O'Kelly 1982:107), to 3000 or 5000 (Herity 1974). The entire population of the country in 3000 BC is estimated to have been close to the region of 150,000 - 200,000 (Cooney and Grogan 1994:69).

9. Our understanding of family structure in the Neolithic is based in large part on assumptions.

Memory "store"	Parents	Grandparents	Total
Contemporary 15-year-old	80 years	130 years	210 years
Neolithic 15-year-old	60 years	0 years	60 years
Difference	20 years	130 years	150 years

Table 3. Memory stores compared.

many 'explosions' of particular generational importance are witnessed. The 25th anniversary of the Vietnam War, of the student riots in Paris or a silver wedding anniversary are all cited as examples of this 25-year reactivation phenomenon.

These two issues are of the utmost importance in the analysis of Neolithic population structures. They imply fundamental differences between modern concepts of social memory and the realities of prehistory. Put bluntly, most Neolithic people would have been dead by the age of 30 or 35; and there would have been few survivors around to attend a reunion of "Newgrange: 25 years on" - perhaps no one at all. In all likelihood, we are talking of a period where "teenagers" and those in their early 20s may have largely organized the construction of Neolithic monuments. Whether it is made explicit or not, the "25th" is a pervasive idea within prehistoric interpretations. It manifests itself explicitly in constructs surrounding the length of generations, and it is frequently implicit in terms of how archaeologists view the significance of age, aging, anniversaries, and the longevity of monuments (see Table 3).

Crucially, the builders of Neolithic monuments would have been within the 17- to 25-year-old bracket – which is the most important formative stage for social memory. This is an important point: people wove different narratives of the past into their present, and they were formed partly through the narratives of the past that existed at the time of their upbringing. It is important that we understand the formative years of this age "cohort." The "inventory of experience" that Manheim discusses was characterized in part by the construction of monuments. The "stratum of consciousness" which became the "natural view of the world" was a consciousness in which tradition, and the need to reiterate and commemorate social memory, was paramount. The continuance of social memory is revealed through monument building. Failure to pay attention to this aspect of the Neolithic means that we misunderstand the full significance of monuments and their role in transmitting social memory.

6. Conclusion: Re-Generating the Neolithic

Why is this important? Why is the construction of generational profiles that do not match the prehistoric reality such a problem? The answer is that the old generational profiles do not cater to the shorter life spans and the more rapid generational turnovers of the Neolithic. The all-important age bracket of 17-25 years has been either misunderstood, "misplaced," or its significance downplayed. A more contextual and historically particular understanding of the demographic realities of Neolithic society will affect our interpretations in many ways. It will substantially alter the analysis of the significance of monuments as places of memory, revealing the importance of their mnemonic characteristics. It will also cast some light on the interpretation of Neolithic social structures because, as Hedges notes, "shorter life-expectancy poses problems for the passing on of specialist knowledge, while it makes the idea of its possession in the hands of an elite rather doubtful" (1982:19). The Neolithic is frequently depicted as a stratified society in which there was steady progress towards the Bronze and Iron Ages and towards modernity. But the Neolithic was a far different place than the "Wave of Advance" model or the Early–Middle–Late chronological constructs make it out to be.

The implications for our understanding of the Neolithic, not least of social memory, are enormous (see Table 4). If each person lived on average for 30 years, then a given generation would be substantially shorter, lasting around 15 years. This would produce a figure of about 133 generations throughout the Neolithic – significantly more than the aforementioned 80 generations. The bloodlines between those who built Silbury Hill becomes a figure of eight or so generations, not the figure of four or five previously adhered to. Similarly, the 55 generations at work on the many phases of Stonehenge becomes around 90 generations. Understanding this is crucial for the development of Neolithic studies, as many monuments involved almost twice as many generations as previously envisioned.

This is an important lacuna in archaeological explanations, concerned as we are with the trajectory of people and materials though time. Shorter life spans and generations imply profound social differences in the past. Modern society gives death the "imprint of meaninglessness" (Olick and Robbins 1998), but the ontological reality of the Neolithic differed radically. Genealogies are strung out in shorter succession, age sets become elders quickly, and places become ancient

Duration	Old Generations	New Generations	Change
Stonehenge	55	90	35
Neolithic	80	133	53
Passage graves	120	200	80

Table 4. Regenerating the Neolithic.

sooner. With lengthy genealogies came the need to re-think the world and to recognize a distant past – with all the social implications that this entails. The past itself became a potent force, and commemoration gained the status of an institution. It is from this perspective that monuments as mnemonic devices may best be seen. Indeed, the lengthy duration of passage grave construction and the widespread occurrence of many other types of monuments are best explained in this light. Monuments were an answer to the demands of demography and the resultant challenges and limitations on social memory. The spectacular constructions of Newgrange, Stonehenge, and other, more modest, monuments, were mnemonic devices writ large on the landscape. They were arenas of social memory for communities whose elders rarely saw their forties.

In order to trowel away at the barriers to the past, archaeologists have constructed a tentative liaison with cognitive studies. One goal of such cooperation should be to enable a closer and more accurate reading of some of the temporal and mnemonic characteristics of Neolithic social life. Yet what is argued in this paper is that we must not hastily import external constructs, but tailor them accordingly. There is little value in archaeologists taking in the data and the conclusions of memory researchers if it does not profit us, if it does not speak directly to a prehistoric past. We should, in other words, contextualize these constructs to our own data and our own specific needs. By doing this, a clearer understanding of the role of social memory can emerge. Just as the quartz-speckled façade of Newgrange enabled the monument to be seen clearly from afar, understanding Neolithic life spans can allow us to see the importance of monuments, social memory, and generations, from a better vantage point.

Bibliography

Ammerman, A. J. and Cavalli-Sforza, L. L. 1971. Measuring the Rate of Spread of Early Farming in Europe. *Man* 6, pp. 674-88.

Ammerman, A. J. and Cavalli-Sforza, L. L. 1973. A Population Model for the Diffusion of Early Farmers in Europe. In: *The Explanation of Culture Change: Models in Prehistory*. C. Renfrew (ed.). London: Duckworth, pp. 343-358.

Bayliss, A., Bronk Ramsey, C. and McCormac, G. 1997. Dating Stonehenge. In: *Science and Stonehenge*. B. Cunliffe and C. Renfrew (eds.). Oxford: Oxford University Press, pp. 39-59.

Barrett, J. 1994. *Fragments from Antiquity*. Oxford: Blackwell.

Bender, B. 1993. Stonehenge – Contested Landscapes (Medieval to Present Day)? In: *Landscapes: Politics and Perspectives*. B. Bender (ed). Oxford: Berg, pp. 245-279.

Bloch, M. 1977. The Past and the Present in the Present. *Man* 12, pp. 278-292.

Bogin, B. 2001. *The Growth of Humanity*. Toronto: Wiley-Liss.

Bocquet-Appel, J. P., Bacro, J. N. 1997. Brief Communication: Estimates of Some Demographic Parameters in a Neolithic Rock-Cut Chamber (Approximately 2000 BC) Using Iterative Techniques for Aging and Demographic Estimators. *American Journal of Physical Anthropology* 102, pp. 569-575.

Bradley, R. 1997. *Rock Art and the Prehistory of Atlantic Europe*. London: Routledge.

Bradley, R. 1998. *The Significance of Monuments*. London: Routledge.

Bradley, R. 2002. *The Past in Prehistoric Societies*. London: Routledge.

Buikstra, J. E. 1997. Paleodemography: Context and Promise. In: *Integrating Archaeological Demography:Multidisciplinary Approaches to Prehistoric Population*. R. R. Paine (ed.). Carbondale, IL: Centre for Archaeological Investigations, pp. 367-380.

Burl, A. 1995. *A Guide to the Stone Circles of Britain, Ireland and Brittany*. New Haven: Yale University Press.

Burgess, C. 1980. *The Age of Stonehenge*. London: Dent.

Burgess, C. 1984. *The Age of Stonehenge*. London: Sterling.

Chapman, J. 2000. *Fragmentation in Archaeology: People, Places, and Broken Objects in the Prehistory of Southeastern Europe*. London: Routledge.

Chippendale, C. 1994. *Stonehenge Complete*. London: Thames and Hudson.

Cohen, M. 1977. *The Food Crises in Prehistory: Overpopulation and the Origins of Agriculture*. New Haven: Yale University Press.

Cole, J. 1998. The Work of Memory in Madagascar. *American Ethnologist* 25, No. 4, pp. 610-633.

Cooney, G. and Grogan, E. 1994. *Irish Prehistory: A Social Perspective*. Dublin: Wordwell.

Conway, M. A. 1997 (ed.). *Cognitive Models of Memory*. Cambridge: MIT Press.

Cummings, V. 2003. Building from Memory: Remembering the Past at Neolithic Monuments in Western Britain. In: *Archaeologies of Remembrance: Death and Memory in Past Societies*. H. Williams (ed.). London: Kluwer Plenum, pp. 25-44.

Davies, G. and Alonso-Quecuty, M. 1997. Cultural Factors in the Recall of a Witnessed Event. *Memory* 5, pp. 601-614.

Eogan, G. 1986. *Knowth and the Passage-Tombs of Ireland*. London: Thames and Hudson.

Fraser, D. 1982. Correspondence (Reply to Hedges 1982). *Scottish Archaeological Review* Vol.1, Part 1, pp. 144-145.

Giddens, A. 1979. *Central Problems in Social Theory*. London: MacMillan.

Harding, J. 1997. Interpreting the Neolithic: The Monuments of North Yorkshire. *Oxford Journal of Archaeology* 16, No. 3, pp. 279-295.

Hassan, F. A. 1981. *Demographic Archaeology*. Toronto: Academic Press.

Hedges, J. W. 1982. An Archaeological Perspective on Isbister. *Scottish Archaeological Review* Vol.1, Part 1, pp. 5-20.

Hedges, J. W. 1984. *Tomb of the Eagles*. London: John Murray.

Herity, M. 1974. *Irish Passage Graves*. Dublin: Irish University Press.

Hodder, I. 1990. *The Domestication of Europe*. Oxford: Blackwell.

Hodder, I. 1992. *Theory and Practice in Archaeology*. London: Routledge.

Holtorf, C. 1997. Megaliths, Monumentality, and Memory. *Archaeological Review from Cambridge* 14, No. 2 (for 1995), pp. 45-46.

Holtorf, C. 1998. The Life-histories of Megaliths in Mecklenburg-Vorpommern (Germany). *World Archaeology* 30, No. 1, pp. 23-38.

Jenbert, K. 1998. From the Inside. A Contribution to the Debate about the Introduction of Agriculture in Southern Scandinavia. In: *Harvesting the Sea, Farming the Forest*. M. Zvelebil, L. Domanska, R. Dennell (eds.). Sheffield: Sheffield Academic Press, pp. 31-35.

Jones, A. and Bradley, R. 1999. The Significance of Colour in European Archaeology. *Cambridge Archaeological Journal* 9, No. 1, pp. 112-114.

Joyce, R. A. 2003. Concrete Memories: Fragments of the Past in the Classic Maya Present. In: *Archaeologies of Memory*. R. M. Van Dyke and S. E. Alcock (eds.), Oxford: Blackwell Publishers, pp. 104-125.

Kilmurray, L. 2004. "Social Memory and Archaeology: A Consideration of the Mnemonic Characteristics of the Monuments of the Neolithic in Ireland and Britain." University of Sheffield: unpublished doctoral dissertation.

Larsson, L. 1985. Late Mesolithic Settlements and Cemeteries at Skateholm, Southern Sweden. In: *The Mesolithic in Europe*. C. Bonsall (ed.). Edinburgh: John Donald Publishers, pp. 367-378.

Last, J. 1998. Books of Life: Biography and Memory in a Bronze Age Barrow. *Oxford Journal of Archaeology* 17, No. 1, pp. 43-53.

Lecornec, J. 1994. *Le Petit Mont, Arzon, Morbihan*. Rennes : Documents Archeologiques de l'Ouest.

Lyndon, D. and Moore, C. W. 1994. *Chambers for a Memory Palace*. Cambridge: The MIT Press.

Manheim, K. 1952. The Problem of Generation. In: *Essays on the Sociology of Knowledge*. P. Kecskemeti (ed.). New York: Oxford University Press, pp. 276-320.

O'Kelly, M. J. 1982. *Newgrange*. London: Thames and Hudson.

Olick, J. K. and Robbins, J. 1998. Social Memory Studies: 'From "Collective Memory" to the Historical Sociology of Mnemonic Practices'. *Annual Review of Sociology* 34, pp.105-140.

Papalexandrou, A. 2003. Memory Tattered and Torn: Spolia in the Heartland of Byzantine Hellenism. In: *Archaeologies of Memory*. R. M. Van Dyke and S. E. Alcock (eds.). Oxford: Blackwell Publishers, pp. 56-80.

Parkman, A. J. 1993. *Memory: Phenomena, Experiment and Theory*. Oxford: Blackwell.

Pauketat, T. R. and Alt, S. M. 2003. Mounds, Memory, and Contested Mississippian History. In: *Archaeologies of Memory*. R. M. Van Dyke and S. E. Alcock (eds). Oxford: Blackwell Publishers, pp. 151-179.

Pennebaker, J. W., Paez, D. and Rime, B. (eds.) 1997. *Collective Memory of Political Events: Social Psychological Perspectives*. Mahwah, NJ: Lawrence Erlbaum Associates.

Rappaport, R. A. 1999. *Ritual and Religion in the Making of Humanity*. Cambridge: Cambridge University Press.

Rault, S. 1997. *From Anneville to Zedes: A Ritual Seascape? Megaliths and long-distance contacts in Western Europe*. British Archaeological Reports International Series 661. Oxford: BAR Publishing, pp. 5-16.

Renfrew, C. 1973. *Before Civilization*. London: Pimlico.

Richards, C. and Thomas, J. 1984. *Ritual activity and structured deposition in Later Neolithic Wessex*. British Archaeological Reports, British Series 133. Oxford: BAR Publishing, pp. 189-218.

Rowlands, M. 1993. The Role of Memory in the Transmission of Culture. *World Archaeology* 25, No. 2, pp. 141-151.

Ruggles, C. 1999. *Astronomy in Prehistoric Britain and Ireland*. New Haven: Yale University Press.

Schuman, H. and Scott, J. 1989. Generations and Collective Memories. *American Sociological Review* 53, pp. 785-793.

Schuman, H., Belli, R. and Bischoping, K. 1997. The Generational Basis of Historical Knowledge. In: *Collective Memories of Political Events: Social Psychological Perspectives. J.W. Pennebaker, D. Paez and B. Rime (eds.). Mahwah, NJ: Lawrence Erlbaum Associates, pp. 47-77.

Shanks, M. and Tilley, C. 1987. Social Theory and Archaeology. Cambridge: Polity Press.

Smith, S. M. 1994. Theoretical Principles of Context – Dependent Memory. In: Theoretical Aspects of Memory. P. Morris and M. Gruneberg (eds.). London: Routledge, pp. 168-191.

Thomas, J. 2000. Death, Identity and the Body in Neolithic Britain. Journal of the Royal Anthropological Institute 6, pp. 653-668.

Tilley, C. 1996. Ethnography of the Neolithic. Cambridge: Cambridge University Press.

Woodburn, J. 1982. Egalitarian Societies. Man 17, No. 3, pp. 431-451.

Whittle, A. 1980a. Two Neolithics? Part One. Current Archaeology 70, pp. 329-334.

Whittle, A. 1980b. Two Neolithics? Part Two. Current Archaeology 71, pp. 371-373.

Whittle, A. 1996. Europe in the Neolithic. Cambridge: Cambridge University Press.

Zerubavel, E. 2003. Time Maps: Collective Memory and the Social Shape of the Past. Chicago: University of Chicago Press.

REMEMBERANCE PRACTICES IN AQUINCUM: MEMORY IN THE ROMAN CAPITAL OF PANNONIA INFERIOR – TODAY'S BUDAPEST

Paula Zsidi

Abstract

This paper is concerned with material remains that were intentionally left for posterity by the Roman citizens of Aquincum, the capital of Pannonia Inferior. The Roman occupation, which lasted for over four centuries from the middle of the AD 1st century, brought to this region – besides oral remembrance – the custom of the lasting remembrance of people and events, especially with the introduction of stone carving and literacy. There is a rich find material from excavations in and around the Roman town and its cemeteries. Three different levels or categories of remains have been differentiated here according to the significance of certain events whose memory they were intended to perpetuate. The first category, concerned with monuments commemorating events of imperial importance was aimed at the population as a whole. The second category encompasses remains of local significance of special importance to the local elite, while the greatest numbers of remains had personal relevance to families and individuals, most of them tomb steles and sepulchers raised in honor of deceased inhabitants of the town by their immediate descendents. These monuments in particular were also aimed at commemorating the fame of local families relative to each other and to enlighten visitors to the town about which families were most prominent in the town. The third category of remains come from private acts of memory revolving around burial rites at the grave side of the deceased involving the ritual communications of the immediate family with the recently deceased.

Keywords: Late Roman Aquincum, imperial events, local power structures, individual commemoration

***

Introduction

Various branches of science deal with human remembrance, naturally from different points of view. Besides medical science, psychology, and philosophy, human remembrance has been the central topic of a number of literary works (such as works by Proust, Remarque, and Bellow) and works of fine art (Dali and many contemporary American artists, summarized in Schacter 1996, e.g.). There is, however, only a single branch of science that deals exclusively with human remembrance and the objects of remembrance, that is, the objectified past. This branch of science is archaeology. The buried and forgotten historical relics that resurface, either consciously bequeathed to descendants or preserved by chance, so-called flashbulb memories, an expression borrowed from psychology (Schacter 1996, 269-277), offer a glimpse into the life of human societies and cultures and how they viewed and manipulated the past for the immediate benefit of their present. The history of empires reconstructed from these objects comprises the history, the past of communities, both small and large. The role and significance of objects changed as literacy appeared and spread in parallel with oral remembrance, although not even written documents could replace the use of material remains as aids to memory. (Just remember that most of us bring some tangible souvenirs, perhaps only a piece of stone or a shell from a journey even when we keep a diary or take photos and videos). This fact luckily comprises a long-term justification for archaeology, still a relatively young branch of science.

This paper will be concerned with material remains that were intentionally left for posterity by the Roman citizens of Aquincum, the capital of Pannonia Inferior (Fig. 1). The Roman occupation, which lasted for over four centuries from the middle of the AD 1st century, brought to this region – besides oral remembrance – the custom of the lasting remembrance of people and events, especially with the introduction of stone carving and literacy. The rich find material comes from the Roman town and the cemeteries that surrounded it. These areas occupied about one fourth of the territory of what is today modern Budapest. Excavations have yielded a multitude of objects, especially inscriptions carved in stone that were prepared with the intention of creating a monument commemorating both individuals and events and aimed at various sectors of both the local population and visitors to the town who might not have been familiar with local power structures. (For the latest summaries of research at Aquincum see Zsidi 2003, 2004.) It is not possible to describe all of them here; only a group of the main types of such memorial remains will be introduced. These objects and features offer insights into why certain monuments were raised as practiced by a range of inhabitants living in Aquincum.

Barrett discusses "different practices of social memory" (1993, 246). Three different levels or categories of remains have been differentiated here according to the significance of certain events whose memory they were intended to perpetuate. The first category contains relatively few remains, reporting on events of imperial importance, aimed at the population as a whole. The second category encompasses remains of local significance, especially of importance to the local elite, while the greatest numbers of remains were of personal relevance, most of them tomb steles and sepulchres raised in honor of deceased inhabitants of the town by their immediate descendents. These monuments in particular were also aimed at commemorating the fame of local families relative to each other and to enlighten visitors to the town about which families were most prominent. The third category of remains come from private acts of memory revolving around burial rites at the grave side of the deceased involving the ritual communications of the immediate family with the recently deceased.

Remembrance of events of imperial importance

Aquincum was the capital of a strategically important border province of the Roman Empire so it is no wonder that the few remains that recorded events of imperial significance were mostly connected with the military. Some of the memorials were intended to publicize the loyalty of the individual who had the monument raised to the ruler (and therefore their family or sphere of influence); see examples in Barrett (1993, 236-247). This was the function of the inscription offered to Herennius Etruscus, Emperor Messius Decius's son and co-ruler (Facsády 2003), which expressed the fealty of the *legio II Adiutrix* of Aquincum to the emperor (Fig. 2). The stone is a tangible material memory of the strong link between the Pannonian legions and this pair of rulers, the existence of this connection is also known from historiography.

Another group of remains in this category was intended to record imperial events for local people on the level of propaganda. Examples of such objects from Aquincum include the honey-cake molds that were found in large numbers in one of the largest pottery works in the town (Kuzsinszky 1932, 55ff). The molds depict events in Marcus Aurelius' rule that were the most important for the citizens of Aquincum – the Markomann wars, which threatened the town and events connected with it. The clearly recognisable figure of the ruler, dressed in ornamental armor, dominates one of the honey-cake

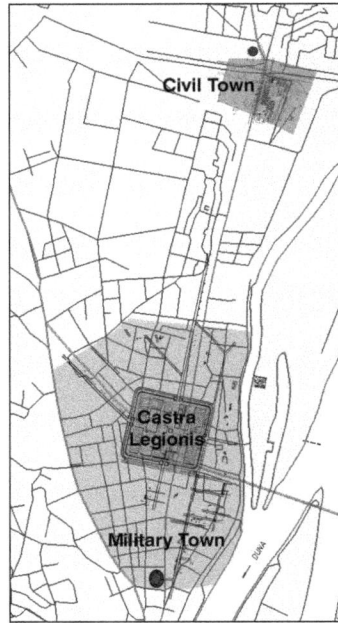

Fig. 1.
Topography of
Aquincum

molds as he holds a triumphal parade over the defeated barbarians (Facsády 1993, 264; Facsády 1996, 24) (Fig. 3). On another mould, the emperor, who protected the peace of the empire, shakes hands with his brother, the co-ruler Lucius Verus (Facsády 1993, 263; Facsády 1996, 21) (Fig. 4). The potters depicted events that determined the fate of the empire by copying the depictions on coins, although at the level of folk art. The audience was clearly the public-at-large and the honey-cake molds were intended to remind them of the source of peace, political stability, and power in their daily lives.

The inscriptions that recorded the visit of the emperors to Aquincum occupy a transitional place between the remains of imperial and local importance. Nearly every emperor paid a visit to the center of this province on the Danube (summarized in Németh, 2000, 19-22; Póczy, 215-231). Some of the monuments were officially raised on the occasion of such visits, reflecting the relationship to central power desired by the person raising the monument. For example, a fragmentary inscription found in the Military Town of Aquincum says that L. Baebius Caecilianus, proconsul, had the memorial put up on the occasion of Emperor Septimus Severus' visit to Aquincum in AD 202 (Németh 1976, 193-196). Another group of inscriptions was carved in connection with the typically large-scale construction and reconstruction works that took place in parallel with the coming of any imperial presence. These inscriptions name the occasion and the construction itself and also the person or institution that financed the investment, with the contribution recorded in a building inscription. Most of the inscriptions of this kind in Aquincum were linked to visits of the emperors of the Severus dynasty (Zsidi 2002a, 132-149). Such monuments served to remind the local populace of the links their local rulers and families had with

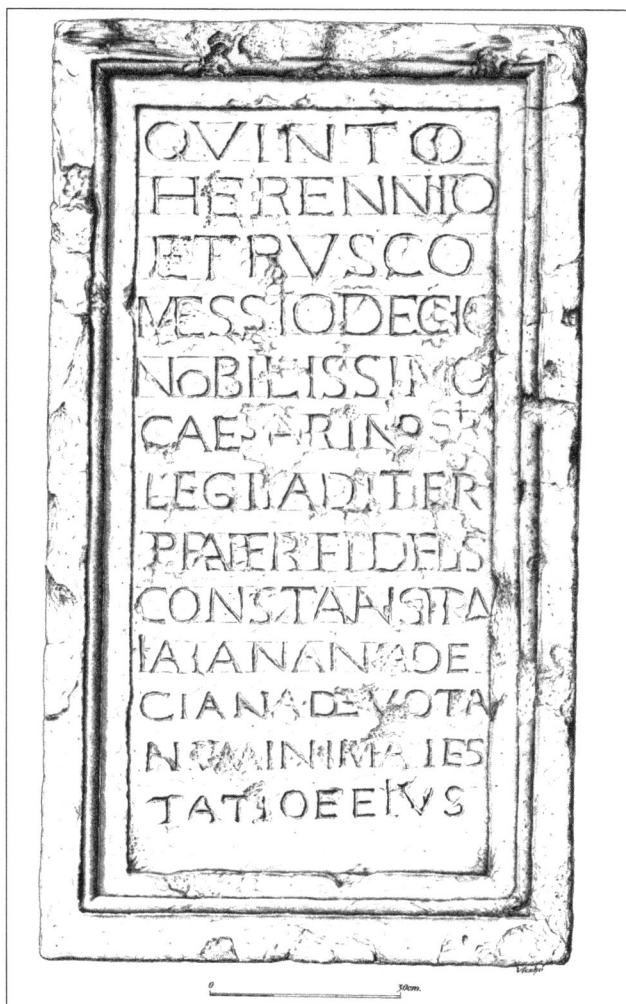

QVINTO
HERENNIO
ETRVSCO
MESSIODECI
NOBILISSIMO
CAESARINOSR
LEGIIADITER
PPAERFIDELIS
CONSTANSITA
IAIANANADE
CIANADEVOTA
NVMINIMAIES
TATIOEEIVS

Fig. 2. Inscription offered to Herennius Etruscus
(Aquincum, Military Town cemetery)

Fig. 4. Honey-cake molds, Marcus Aurelius shaking hands
with Lucius Verus (Budapest, 'Gázgyár' pottery workshop)
Altar stone of C. Cornelius Corinthus' dedicated to Silvanus
Terracotta model created by the potter Hilarus (Intercisa,
Dunaújváros)

Fig. 3. Honey-cake molds with triumphal scene (Budapest,
'Gázgyár' pottery workshop)

SILVANO
SILVSERI
SACRVM
CORINTHVSN
VMMVLAR
IVSVSLM

Fig. 5. Altar stone of C. Cornelius Corinthus' dedicated to
Silvanus

the imperial center with the intent of strengthening the position of these families through linking memories.

Remembrance of events of local significance

After the Marcomann wars, the province of Pannonia Inferior enjoyed the favor of the new imperial dynasty, and, similarly to other towns of the province, a large wave of construction was undertaken in Aquincum in which private individuals also took part. The constructions of the Severus period were linked with its heyday as a power center in the Province, the town's reconstruction and were certainly financed by the state. Remains of smaller architectural reconstructions, executed to meet local political demands, can be found in every part of this urban settlement. Most of these constructions can be dated based on building inscriptions, especially those built during the rule of Severus Alexander, the last emperor of the dynasty. Besides on-going events in the empire, also reported on by Classical historiographers and authors, local upper-class inhabitants wished to record events of local importance that were significant in the smaller political world of Aquincum and its *territorium*. Not incidentally, inscriptions raised by private persons were also fashionable in the Severus period (Gabler 1966, 20-35; Zsidi 2002a, 143-146). The numerous stone monuments from this period show that the wealthy and economically influential class in society played a major part in donating the funds for these construction works. The commissioners liked to advertise and perpetuate their generosity in inscriptions. During the period of Emperor Alexander Severus in Carnuntum, the capital of Pannonia Superior and not far distant from Aquincum, the number of the building inscriptions is much lower than in Aquincum. Most of the inscriptions found in Carnuntum date from the beginning of the Severus period, although the construction boom can clearly be documented from the preserved architectural remains (Kandler 2000, 43-45). The monuments with inscriptions suggest that the building boom in Aquincum must have been a protracted process which reached its peak at the end of the period. The wealthy civilian classes, which had grown in size, expanded its influence within the municipal administration and increased their economic weight, taking over a major part of these construction expenses from the state. They commemorated their contributions in inscriptions on the buildings they paid for (Zsidi 2002a, 146).

We know the names of a number of the important Aquincum citizens who contributed to the development of the architectural townscape. C. Titius Antoninus Peculiaris, a member of the municipal council of Aquincum (*decurio*) and high priest of the emperor cult, financed the decoration of the forum of the Military Town of Aquincum and had a *nymphaeum* built (CIL III 10495; Póczy, 1983, 259; CIL III 10496=6452, Fitz 1982, 32).

His name also appears on a customs stamp from Savaria (in Pannonia Superior province), where he is mentioned as a tax-collector in the provincial customs administration (Tóth 1998, 25-26, 259). This fact indicates that he had significant economic influence extending well beyond the borders of the town of Aquincum.

C. Cornelius Corinthus' name is found on an inscription that records the reconstruction of a temple in Aquincum. An altar stone dedicated to Silvanus he raised has also been preserved (CIL III 3500; Ürögdi 1964, 239-245; Zsidi 1995, 31, 56) (Fig. 5). The latter inscription reveals that C. Cornelius Corinthus was a banker (*nummularius*), while his legal status was that of a liberated slave.

Searching for traces of acts of remembrance, one usually looks for objects, yet the scenes of that remembrance may also be very revealing. When the monument inscriptions recorded imperial events they were usually placed in the busy central areas of the town, on public buildings, shrines, temples or on the construction itself where they could be seen by the greatest number and variety of people. By their positioning and architectural design they were designed to convey the recorded event to the greater public. A good example is offered by a terracotta model (Fig 6) which probably represented one of the gates of the Civil Town of Aquincum (Zsidi 2002b, 59, 138 note 291). (The model possibly represents the eastern gate of the legionary fortress; Visy and Hainzmann 1991,101, Cat. No.122). Above the arched gateway of the model where the building inscription should be, the self-important potter, Hilarus, commemorated himself. Probably C. Iulius Sextinus, tenant (*conductor*), had the original inscription placed above the town gate (T. Nagy 1973, 134; Zsidi 1995, 31,63) (Fig. 7). The fragmentary inscription on a relief-decorated stone plaque found in the Civil Town near the town gate, probably carved during the rule of Septimius Severus, contains the names of the goddesses Baltis and Dea Syria. The inscription reveals that a citizen of Aquincum of eastern origin was responsible for funding the construction of an ornamented arched gateway. All these forms of memory are associated with members of the ruling class displaying the wealth of individuals and their families relative to each other and the local people they ruled.

Remembrances of personal relevance

The most numerous remains in Aquincum are the objects that preserve the memory of individuals. Within this group the most common finds are the depictions and inscriptions on sepulchres, sarcophagi, and tomb steles, all of which would have been visible above the ground. This group of remains would actually merit several papers and it this group which is discussed most frequently in the archaeological literature of Aquincum, most recently by Szirmai (2003, 233-234), with further

Fig. 6. Terracotta model created by the potter Hilarus (Intercisa, Dunaújváros)

Fig. 7. Inscription of C. Iulius Sextinus tenant (conductor) (Aquincum, Civil Town)

Fig. 8. Grave stele of Claudius Severus with T.M.P. inscription (Budapest, Víziváros)

Fig. 9. Collegian grave stele with a characteristic carved funeral wreath (Aquincum, Civil Town, eastern cemetery) The rhyming inscription on the sarcophagus of Aelia Sabina (Aquincum, Mititary Town, northern cemetery)

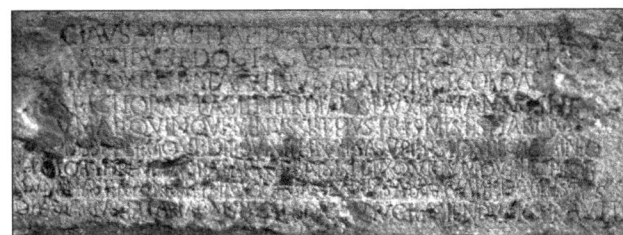

Fig. 10. The rhyming inscription on the sarcophagus of Aelia Sabina (Aquincum, Mititary Town, northern cemetery)

literature, e.g. Németh 1999). Therefore, only a few characteristic representatives of the more than 500 sepulchral monuments recovered to date in Aquincum and its surroundings will be discussed here.

The contents of inscriptions on both the sepulchres and the sarcophagi were generally carved following prescribed patterns. Beside the personal data (name, age, origin, and profession of the deceased and the family) the inscription contained stereotypic formulae. One such formula was characteristic of Aquincum and its environs: *titulum memoriae posuit*, which means that the inscription was meant to commemorate, (for example, see Németh 1999; 16, No. 21; Fitz 1961/62, 33-48 has more to say about this type of inscription) (Fig. 8). Often the person who paid for having the sepulchre carved was noted but may not actually have been a member of the family of the deceased. Thus, an artisan college (*collegium fabrum et centonariorum*) operated an entire stone-carving workshop (Sz. Burger 1959, 9-26; T. Nagy 1971, 122-124) intended to secure appropriate burial for the members of the college and keep alive the memory of the dead. A carved funeral wreath was one characteristic element on these tomb steles (Fig. 9). In other cases, the public organization(s) and societies (*collegium*) who ordered the memorial inscription added the sum they paid for the monument in the monument inscription itself. The nicest example is an inscription that states that citizens from Cologne (*cives Agrippinenses*) had the particular sepulchre raised for the price of 72 denars (L. Nagy 1942, 467).

Sometimes one can find more personal inscriptions as well, especially on sarcophagi. A characteristic phenomenon in Aquincum was writing rhymed inscriptions on sarcophagi, although similar ones occurred in other parts of the province as well. A touching example can be found on the sarcophagus of a woman named Aelia Sabina (Fig. 10). The rhyming inscription on the apparently simple sarcophagus reflects the sorrow of the grieving husband. It tells us that the 25 year-old musician played the water organ and was popular among the inhabitants of the town as well (Németh 1999, 64-65). The parents of a young girl, Cassia, who died at the age of four years and five months, ordered another similarly touching inscription in verse. In the rhymed inscription the little girl, bereft of the care of the parents, took sorrowful farewell from her parents, whom as the inscription says, she would never have offended in any way (Németh and Topál 1991, 73-84).

The depictions of the deceased on the burial monuments were usually not intended to be real portraits. Differences in the features probably reflect the skill and training of the carver or fashions of the day (T. Nagy 1971, 113). Nevertheless, personal aspects can be recognized on the representations, obviously ordered by the commissioners. In this respect, the figures of two soldiers serving in the legion at Aquincum are character-

istic. One of them was Castricius Victor from Como in northern Italy, whose military paraphernalia – and therefore individual property – depicts the characteristic costume of the AD 1st century (T. Nagy 1943, 463; Németh 1999, 19) (Fig. 11). One can see a belt characteristic of the AD 3rd century (Németh 1999, 137; Ubl, 2002, 281, Taf. III) on the tomb stele of Aurelius Bitus, a trumpeter in the legion in Aquincum. The trumpeter was depicted together with his son who had died quite young (Fig. 12).

The local population, the Celtic Eraviscans, adopted the need and practice of preserving personal memory from their Roman masters (Mócsy 1975, 145-152). The tomb steles provide a glimpse of the "folk costume" of the Celtic women, which, based on how they appear on the tomb steles, they even continued to wear more than one hundred years after the beginning Roman occupation in the AD 1st century (Fig. 13). The fact that they found that the ruling Eraviscan found it important to depict the deceased in this traditional costume speaks to the power of memory and nostalgia in subtly resisting social change in the domestic sphere. (Some additions to the traditional costume of the Celtic woman are discussed in Bíró 2003, 89-102) and Csontos 2003, 103-110). Such traditional depictions must have been aimed at other upper class Celtic-Roman families, reinforcing appropriate behavior for women in these social circles. Men, more closely tied to the central power, are almost immediately depicted in Roman style clothing on tomb steles. Traditional dress memory, thus, played no role in male self-identity in these native high-class circles.

Objects placed in the grave comprised a smaller group of objects related to even more personal, less public, remembrance compared to the carvings on the sepulchres, meant to be seen by a wider public. Usually "uncommon" objects or "irregularities" reflect an addition to the usual grave furniture (food, drink, and articles of clothing) in this group of remains; an example of such an object is the rattle found in the grave of a child in the Military Town (Bertin 1998, 44-45, fig. 17). Objects kept in the pouch hanging from the belt, old and worn belt mounts and fragments of coins, which often mirror centuries-older fashions, frequently occur in the graves of men (for example, Zsidi 1987, 68, 72). The most touching example is perhaps that of a woman from Aquincum who "took" the portrait of her husband along with her to the grave, or rather the man, presumably her husband, placed his portrait in this woman's grave to accompany her on her long journey as a remembrance (Póczy 1968, 331-336) (Fig. 14). This painted portrait of a man is unique in Aquincum, not only in terms of its portrait genre, but also as concerns its painting technique. The picture was painted on a thin plank of oak cut far from Aquincum, perhaps in an Eastern or North African province of the empire. The characteristic features of a black-haired and bearded man with an oval face also attest to his East-

Fig. 11. Grave stele of Castricius Victor (Budapest, Víziváros)

Fig. 12. Grave stele of Aurelius Bitus (Aquincum, Military Town, western cemetery)

Fig. 13. The "traditional costume" of the Celtic women on a grave stele (Aquincum, Military Town, western cemetery)

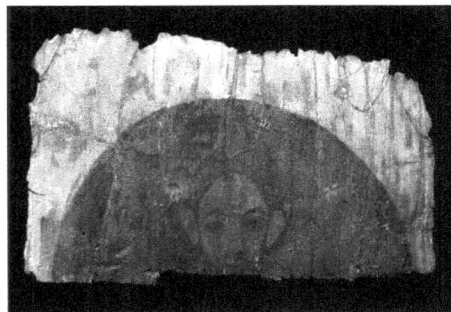

Fig. 14. Painted portrait of a man from a Late Roman grave (District III, Budapest, Jablonka Street)

ern origins. Such objects reflect acts of very individual remembrance restricted to the immediate family who would have been present at the burial itself.

The most important scenes of personal remembrance were the cemeteries where the families regularly kept the memory of recently deceased family members alive. The designation of the ultimate resting place of the dead had been set out centuries before in the 12-table laws in the 5th century BC. Based on these laws, the first cemeteries were also established in Aquincum at set distances along the roads running out of the town (Topál 2003, 161-167). In addition it was considered important that cemeteries be located in peaceful and beautiful locations as part of the roles they played as scenes of remembrance and advertisement (Curk 1997: 67-72) (Fig. 15). People entering the town were first confronted with a view of the sepulchers so that even before they arrived in the town they would be apprised which of the wealthy families had significant political influence in the town at that moment. It is very likely that once families died out or ceased to be influential their sepulchers were cannibalized for their stone for use in other monuments as shown by regulations prohibiting people to steal tomb steles.

Based on a plethora of textual sources, numerous scholars have described how the cult of the dead was practiced (e.g. Marquardt 1886, 341-385). The internal organization of graves and the grave furniture may also reveal a great deal about the nature of this cult. It is evident that an "industry" evolved to serve the cult of the dead. As previously mentioned there were colleges in Aquincum that concerned themselves with the burial of their members and some that were actually specialized in this exact field (collegia funeratica). A few stone carving workshops and pottery works producing funeral lamps have been uncovered in the vicinity of cemeteries, for example, a pottery workshop specializing in lamps, the most common grave offering, was also found in the vicinity of the earliest cemetery of Aquincum Civil Town (Póczy and Zsidi 2003, 191-192).

Some of the first cemeteries established along the roads in Aquincum ceased to function as the town began to develop at the end of the AD 2nd and beginning of the 3rd century when more outlying districts farther from the main roads were used for burials, for example, the southern cemetery of the Civil Town (Zsidi 2002c, 145). The abandonment of the cemeteries – places of remembrance – was the result of a single administrative decision aimed at changing the urban structure of the town. In a way this also represented a decision to erase the memory of the people buried there as well. Sepulchers were pulled down, local temporary stone carving workshops were set up and the usable stones were transported to construction works or used for new graves in the new grave parcels (Zsidi 1997a, 250). Probably these cemeteries were no longer being used for burial at the time of their elimination and somehow the need to remember

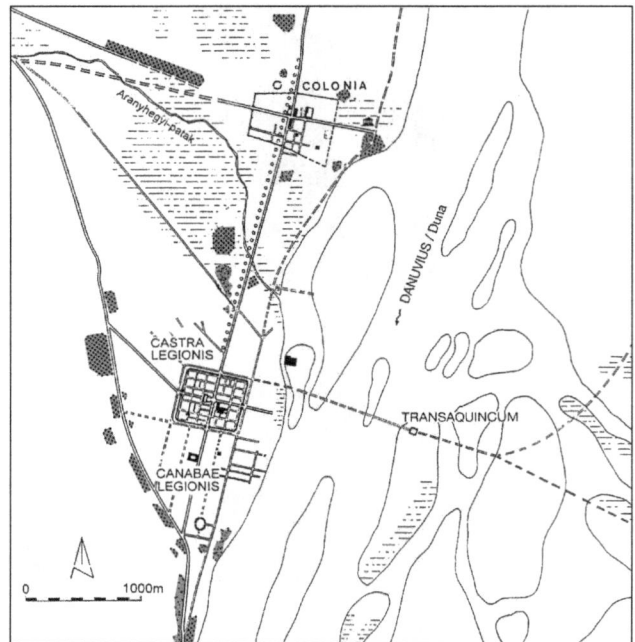

Fig. 15. Roman Period cemeteries in Aquincum

those buried there was no longer important suggesting the possibility that no direct relatives remained to honor the dead buried there.

A particular phenomenon occurred in the large public cemeteries of Aquincum (Fig. 15) which has also been observed elsewhere; the so-called layer of find material found between the graves. The fill of the graves also tends to contain large numbers of pottery shards (Zsidi 1997b, 144-145, among others). Sources mention that the family members of the dead met regularly at the grave side (Marquardt, 1886, 378-385). Researchers agree that the pottery fragments must be the remains of funeral feasts that were held regularly at the grave of a deceased family member (here you can see a reconstruction) which often included the ritual smashing of vessels, for example in Carnuntum (Bad Deutsch-Altenburg-Austrich) (Elter et al. 1999, 92, 102, 106-108). The funeral feast held on the ninth day after the burial and on certain feast days (e.g. Parentalia) is depicted on some of the grave steles. Usually, a small table (tripus) covered with food is placed in the center of the image field while a servant or maid standing next to the deceased is shown ready to serve the food (for more on this topic see: Walde 2001, 236) (see Fig. 12).

Another custom found in Aquincum (Zsidi and Ujvári 2002, 530-531; Lassanyi and Bechtold 2006, 76-78) helped maintain constant contact with the dead. A terracotta tube may sometimes be found, usually made from imbrex (ceramic tile) or a hollow brick was placed in a vertical position on top of the grave. The custom (profusio), which came from Italy where its execution was more elaborate with finely built tubes placed on top of a funeral construction (Spadoni 2003, 28-29), made it easier for family members to feel they were in direct contact with the dead. It was important in the Roman belief system that the dead did not feel closed out from or alienated from their family. In preventing this, the family aimed to gain the goodwill of the spirit of the deceased. The existence of such "communication channels" can be observed even in early Christian times (L. Nagy 1938, 132).

Similar customs linking the living with the dead may be found even today. On a visit to rural Transylvania, my hostess, who was a widow, told me that she was preparing to go to the cemetery because it would have been her husband's 60th birthday. This was a so-called "even" anniversary, which meant that the family and her husband's contemporaries in the village would gather at the grave and offer brandy, refreshments and fresh homemade milk-loaf to their deceased relative. This story reveals that people have the impulse to celebrate the memory of the dead in similar ways and for similar reasons irrespective of the society they live in and despite differences of thousands of years.

Conclusions

Material culture was manipulated consciously by Roman citizens during the 400 year span of their occupation at Aquincum to express three kinds of memory in Roman Aquincum. Material remains were intentionally left for posterity by the Roman citizens of Aquincum. The Roman occupation, which lasted for over four centuries from the middle of the AD 1st century, brought to this region – besides oral remembrance – the custom of using material culture to create lasting memorials to people and events mostly through stone carving and inscriptions. Three different levels or categories of remains were singled out in this paper based on the kinds of events being commemorated and remembered.

The first kind of memorializing is represented by a few monuments related to the central imperial power. The construction of these monuments was funded by officials in the local administration and various organizations and fraternities in the town. These monuments were constructed or added on to as a way of commemorating events of imperial importance. Inscriptions placed on these major, centrally located, constructions aimed at informing the masses in Aquincum about the long-term connections of individuals in the local administration about their good connections with the central powers. Since these monuments stood for many years, the inscriptions and fame of the buildings themselves would have served as a continuous reminder of the significance of the families responsible for raising them. The creation of honey-cake molds memorializing important imperial events also served as easily distrib-

uted subtle pieces of material propaganda aimed at all sectors of the population supporting a picture of central power and success.

The second category is represented by remains of local significance, especially to the Aquincum elite. Although the greatest number of archaeological finds had a personal relevance to local wealthy families who could afford to raise elaborate tomb steles and sepulchral monuments constructed in honor of deceased town dwellers by the various guilds-societies they belonged to as well as their immediate descendents. These monuments in particular were also aimed at commemorating the fame of the locally important groups and families who competed socially with each other over decades and generations. These cemeteries were located along the roads leading into the town so they also served the purpose of memorializing the social elite in Aquincum for visitors to the town since these burial structures would have been among the first structures travelers would encounter as they came into the provincial capital. These structures stood as long as the societies operated and the families were present in the area. Eventually, as the families lost importance and their memory faded away the monuments were often quarried for their stone material.

The third category of remains come from private acts of memory revolving around burial rites at the grave side of the deceased involving the ritual communications of the immediate family with the recently deceased. Families of the deceased would return on the anniversary of their relatives death to hold feasts and communicate directly with the dead through ceramic tubes or hollow bricks stuck vertically into the graves. Vessels holding the food were ritually smashed and left between the graves. These are the remains of ritual remembering by private citizens with no aspect of the public memorializing characteristic of the first two categories.

As excavations continue in the area of the Military and Civil Towns of Aquincum, ever more objects and buildings used by important social groups and citizens to materialize public memories of power and importance will come to light. On a more personal level, the many new discoveries of the graves of average citizens will also bring new information about the way more common folk tried to memorialized the dead of their families over the four centuries of Roman occupation at Aquincum.

Bibliography

Barrett, J. C. 1993. Chronologies of Remembrance: The Interpretation of Some Roman Inscriptions. Conceptions of Time and Ancient Society. *World Archaeology* 25, No. 2, pp. 236-247.

Bertin, P. 1998. Előzetes jelentés a Bécsi út 44. sz. alatt végzett leletmentésről (Preliminary report on the rescue excavations carried out at Bécsi Street 44). *Aquincumi füzetek* 4, pp. 44-45, fig. 17.

Bíró, M. T. 2003. Ein neurerer Beitrag zur pannonischen einheimischen Frauentracht. In: *Pannonica Provincialia et Archaeologica Evgenio Fitz Octogenario dedicata.* Á. Szabó and E. Tóth (eds.). *Libelli Archaeologici*, n.s. 1. Budapest: Magyar Nemzeti Muzeum, pp. 89-102.

Csontos, K. 2003. Cicada brooches on Pannonian Stone Monuments. In: *Pannonica Provincialia et Archaeologcia Evgenio Fitz Octogenario dedicata.* Á. Szabó and E. Tóth (eds.). Libelli Archaeologici, n.s. 1. Budapest: Magyar Nemzeti Muzeum, pp. 103-110.

Curk, I. Mikl. 1997. Ästhetik und römische Grabanlagen. Ein Versuch am Material von Slowenien. Akten des IV. Internationalen Kolloquiums über Probleme des provinzialrömischen Kunstschaffens. *Situla* 36, pp. 67-72.

Ertel, Christine, Gassner, V., Jilek, S. and Stiglitz, H. 1999. Untersuchungen zu den Gräberfeldern in Carnuntum. Vol. 1. *Der archäologische Befund.* Vienna: Austrian Academy of Sciences, pp. 92, 102, 106-108.

Facsády, A. 1993. Aquincumi terrakotta ábrázolások (La representation des empereurs en terre cuite au Musée d'Aquincum). *Budapest Régiségei* 30, pp. 263-272.

Facsády, A. 1996. Kaiserdarstellungen aus Terracotta im Museum von Aquincum. In: G. Bauchhenss (ed.), *Akten des 3. Internationalen Kolloquiums über Probleme des Provinzialrömischen Kunstschaffens.* Cologne: Rheinland-Verlag, pp. 21-25.

Facsády, A. 2003. Herennius Etruscus basis in Budaújlak. In: *Pannonica Provincialia et Archaeologcia Evgenio Fitz Octogenario dedicata.* Á. Szabó and E. Tóth (eds.). *Libelli Archaeologici*, n.s., No.1. Budapest: Magyar Nemzeti Muzeum, pp. 243-248.

Fitz, J. 1961/62. Titulum memoriae posuit. *Alba Regia* 2/3, pp. 33-48.

Fitz, J. 1982. *Pannonok évszázada. Pannonia 193-284* (The great age of Pannonia AD 193-284). Budapest: Corvina.

Gabler, D. 1966. Munera Pannonica. Magánszemélyek közcélú adományai Pannoniában (Munera Pannonica. Public donations by private persons in Pannonia). *Archaeológiai Értesítő* 93, pp. 20-35.

Kandler, M. 2000. Zur Bautätigkeit in Carnuntum unter den Severer. In: *Gentes, Reges und Rom.* J. Bourzek, H. Friesinger, K. Pieta, B. Komoróczy (eds.). Brno: Spisy Archeologického ústavu Akademie věd České Republiky 16, pp. 43-52.

Kuzsinszky, B. 1932. *A gázgyári római fazekastelep Aquincumban* (Das grosse römische Töpferviertel in Aquincum). Budapest Régiségei 11.

Marquardt, J. 1886. *Das Privatleben der Römer. Das Begräbniss.* Leipzig, 1886.

Mócsy, A. 1975. *Pannonia a korai császárság idején* (Pannonia in the early imperial period) Budapest: Akadémiai Kiadó.

Nagy, L. 1938. Pannonia Sacra. Emlékkönyv Szent István király halálának 900. évfordulóján I (Pannonia Sacra. Memorial book on the 900th anniversary of Saint Stephan's death). Budapest: Magyar Tudományos Akadémia.

Nagy, L. 1942. Budapest az Ókorban. Temetők és Temetkezes (Budapest in Antiquity. Cemeteries and). In: *Budapest Története* 1-2. K. Szendy (ed.). Budapest: Király Magyar Egyetemi, pp. 464-485.

Nagy, T. 1943. A Castricius sztélé kora (The period of the Castricus stele). *Budapest Régiségei* 13, pp. 463-470.

Nagy, T. 1971. Kőfaragás és szobrászat Aquincumban (Taille de pierre et sculpture à Aquincum). *Budapest Régiségei* 22, pp. 122-124.

Nagy, T. 1973. *Budapest története* 1. *Római kor* (The history of Budapest 1. The Roman age). Budapest: Föv. Tanácsa.

Németh, M. 1976. Septimius Severus 202. évi látogatásának újabb feliratos emléke Aquincumból (A further epigraphic monument from Aquincum of the visit of Septimius Severus in the year AD 202). *Budapest Régiségei* 24, pp. 193-199.

Németh, M. 1999. Vezető az Aquincumi Múzeum kőtárában (Directory of the Aquincum museum lapidary). Vol. 16, No. 21, Budapest: Budapest History Museum.

Németh, M. 2000. Pannonien und die römischen Kaiser. In: *Von Augustus bis Attila. Leben am ungarischen Donaulimes.* Schriften des Limesmuseums Aalen 53. Stuttgart: Konrad Theiss Verlag, pp. 19-22.

Németh, M. and Topál, J. 1991. Verses szarkofág mumifikált temetkezéssel a Bécsi úti sírmezőből (Beschrifteter Sarcophag mit mumifizierter Bestattung von Gräberfeld an der Bécsi Strasse). *Budapest Régiségei* 27, pp. 73-84.

Póczy, K. 1968. Gemaltes Männerporträt aus einem Mumiengrab in Aquincum. In: *Studien zur Geschichte und Philosophie des Altertums.* J. Harmatta (ed.). Budapest: Akadémia, pp. 331-337.

Póczy, K. 1983. Az aquincumi katonaváros utcahálózata és fontosabb épületei a II. és a III. században (Das Srassennetz und die wichtigere Gebäude der Militärstadt von Aquincum im 2. und 3. Jahrhundert). *Archaeológiai Értesítő* 110 (1983), pp. 252-273.

Póczy, K. 2004. *Aquincum, Budapest római kori történelmi városmagja* (Aquincum, Budapest's Roman period historical town magic). Budapest: Enciklopédia.

Póczy, K. and Zsidi, P. 2003. Lokales Gewerbe und Handel. In: *Forschungen in Aquincum 1969-2002.* P. Zsidi (ed.). Budapest: Aquincum Nostrum Vol. 2, No. 2, pp. 185-206.

Schacter, D. L. 1996. Emlékeink nyomában. Az agy az elme és a múlt (Searching for memory. The brain, the mind, and the past). New York: Basic Books. [Háttér Kiadó Lélek]

Spadoni, D. 2003. I riti funerari. In: *Aspetti di vita quotidiana dalle necropoli della Via Latina località Osteria* del Curato. R. Edigi, P. Catalano, D. Spadoni (eds.). Rome: Istituto Arti Grafiche Mengarelli, pp. 23-29.

Szirmai, K. 2003. Die Steinbearbeitung in Aquincum. In: Forschungen in Aquincum 1969-2002. P. Zsidi (ed.). Budapest: Aquincum Nostrum II.3, No. 2, pp. 233-244.

Sz. Burger, A. 1959. Collégiumi kőfaragó műhelyek Aquincumban (Marbreries collegiales à Aquincum). Budapest Régiségei 19, pp. 9-26.

Topál, J. 2003. Die Gräberfelder von Aquincum. In: Forschungen in Aquincum 1969-2002. P. Zsidi (ed.). Budapest: Aquincum Nostrum II.2, No. 2, pp. 161-167.

Tóth, E., 1998. Savaria az Ókorban. In: Savaria – Szombathely története a város alapításától 1526-ig (Savaria – the history of Szombathely from the town's foundation to 1526). Pál Engel (ed.). Szombathely: Szombathely Megyei Jogú Város Önkormányzata, pp. 7-67.

Ubl, H. J. 2002. Ein "Ringschnallencingulum" aus Lauriacum. In: M. Buora (ed.), Miles Romanus dal Po al Danubio nel Tardoantico. Convegno internazionale Pordenone-Concordia Sagittaria, March 2000. Pordenone: Consorzio universitario Pordenone.

Ürögdi, Gy. 1964. A bankélet nyoma Aquincumban (Spuren von Bankgeschäften in Aquincum). Budapest Régiségei 21, pp. 239-245.

Visy, Zs and Hainzmann, M. 1991. Instrumenta Inscripta Latina. Das römische Leben im Spiegel der Kleininschriften. Pécs, Ausstellungskatalog 101, Cat. No. 22.

Walde, E. 2001. Die Dienerinnen auf den römischen Grabreliefa in der Provinz Noricum. In: T. Panhuysen (ed.), Die Maastrichter Akten des 5. Internationalen Kolloquiums über das provinzialrömische Kunstschaffen – im Rahmen des CSIR. Maastricht: Stichting Willem Goossens, pp. 235-243.

Zsidi, P. 1987. Budapest XI. kerületi Gazdagréten feltárrt 4-5. századi temető (Das auf dem Gazdagrét (Budapest XI. Bez.) freigelegte Gräberfeld aus dem 4-5. Jahrhundert). Communicationes Archaeologicae Hungariae 1987, pp. 68, 72.

Zsidi, P. (ed.), 1995. Gods, Soldiers, Citizens in Aquincum. Guide to the Exhibition. Budapest: Budapest History Museum.

Zsidi, P. 1997a. Ein in Aquincum neugefundenes Grabmal. Akten des IV. Internationalen Kolloquiums über Probleme des provinzialrömischen Kunstschaffens. Situla 36, pp. 247-255.

Zsidi, P. 1997b. Grabummauerungen am nördlichen Rand der Canabae von Aquincum (Budapest III, Ladik St.). Communicationes Archaeologicae Hungaricae 1997, pp. 144-145.

Zsidi, P. 2002a. Transformation of the town structure in the Civil Town of Aquincum during the Severi (A. D. 193-235). Acta Archaeologica Academiae Scientiarum Hungaricae 53, pp. 132-149.

Zsidi, P. 2002b. Aquincum polgárvárosa az Antoninusok és a Severusok korában (Aquincum Civil Town during the Antoninus and Severus periods). Budapest: Enciklopédia.

Zsidi, P. 2002c. Az aquincumi polgárváros délkeleti előtere az újabb kutatások tükrében (Der südöstliche Vorraum der Zivilstadt von Aquincum im Spiegel der neueren Forschung). Budapest Régiségei 35, No. 1, pp. 143-157.

Zsidi, P. (ed.), 2003. Forschungen in Aquincum 1969-2002. Budapest: Aquincum Nostrum 2.2, No. 2.

Zsidi, P. 2004. Aquincum. Ergebnisse der topographischen und siedlungshistorischen Forschungen in den Jahren 1969-1999. Situla 42, pp. 209- 230.

Zsidi, P. and Ujvári, G. 2002. Ein Bronzekästchen aus Aquincum. In: A. Giumlia-Mair (ed.), I Bronzi Antichi: Produzione e technologia. Atti del XV Congresso Internazionale sui Bronzi Antichi. Monographies instrumentum 21. Montagnac: Ed. Monique Mergoil, pp. 530-538.

MEMORY OF A BETTER DEATH: CONVENTIONAL AND EXCEPTIONAL BURIAL RITES IN CENTRAL EUROPEAN CEMETERIES OF THE AD 6th AND 7th CENTURIES

Irene Barbiera

Abstract

In this work the meaning of some complex and lavish assemblages in graves dated to the Lombard period (AD 6th and 7th centuries) will be explored. Assemblages of this type have traditionally been interpreted as expressions of ethnicity or rank. Reconstruction of ethnic Lombard dress traditions and women's dress in particular was based on them. The low occurrence of these assemblages among the graves considered here shows that they do not represent a traditional costume. Their chronological distribution and relation to gender, age, and cemetery construction, however, reveals some interesting aspects of these special assemblages, indicating that they were not merely a passive reflection of ethnicity or rank, but could be employed actively within different funerary systems. It is evident that different communities, using similar types of so-called "Lombard" artifacts, developed different strategies for remembering the deceased and expressing their identity in the power structure. Some explanations for these different behaviors are considered.

Key words: Early Middle Ages, Lombards, burial rites, memory, gender

***

Introduction

Significant changes in the ways deaths were commemorated occurred between Late Antiquity and the Early Middle Ages in Europe. In fact, from the AD 5th century on, certain new trends in funerary customs begin to appear. The tradition of funerary inscriptions and stone monuments with inscriptions, typical for the Roman period, decreased noticeably in the archaeological records in most areas, although there are some exceptions to this trend (for the case of southern Italy, see De Rubeis 2005 and for the case of Pavia see Majocchi in this volume). Besides, more stress was given to grave goods, which become wealthier and more lavish, at least in some graves. Weapons and brooches are the most characteristic funerary artifacts deposited in this period, but the majority of graves contained simpler artifacts like combs, buckles, pots and so on.

If the Roman monuments, with their written text and stone markers, preserved the memories "that have been created for us, not those that have been accidentally preserved" (Hope 2003, p. 136), Early Medieval graves, with their non textual symbols, are open to different interpretations. Grave goods were possibly chosen by mourners according to some criteria. Objects themselves can have a long and complex history and can evoke memories of the peoples who owned them or through whose hands they have passed in successive exchange (Eckardt and Williams 2003, van Houts 1999; for the case of Early Medieval sword depositions in graves and their history see Theuws and Alkemande 2000). Also, the association of different objects in graves might have been related to the desire to preserve and transmit a certain memory of the death. Among the different identities that individuals have in their life, like gender, age, rank, social position within the family or ethnic affiliation, some were chosen to be remembered, some others to be forgotten. In the context of funerary rituals all symbols of remembering and forgetting were displayed in front of the community and grave goods were simply the final result of such a ceremony. We have no idea whether some kind of monuments in perishable material were built on graves. What archaeologists can work on now is a set of grave goods, which, after the funeral, remained hidden under the earth. Their loss from circulation and their presence in graves, next to the ancestors, could thus only be transmitted to generations by the process of remembering, since they were no longer visible.

Moreover, space and position of graves in the cemeteries might have been employed to emphasize social relations. A constructed space implies a known order and the precise memory of the ancestors already buried there. This means that the community recorded topographies of cemeteries, through monuments, inscriptions or oral transmission.

For the use of objects and space to symbolize the memory of the deaths, different interpretations have been offered in the last decades. Grave goods sought to represent different identities of the dead. For some scholars grave goods were meant to transmit an ethnic memory of the deceased, while for others it was instead related to rank. Recently new identities have started to be recognized.

In this study, I will try to explore some of the possible reasons behind the development of these funerary trends to see what kind of identity or identities were symbolized through the grave goods and attempt to explain why grave good depositions started to be used as a way of negotiating new social roles.

Ethic identity and grave goods

Traditionally, the custom of grave good deposition during this period has been interpreted as a way of expressing the ethnic identity of the individuals. In particular, German groups would have deposited weapons and brooches to differentiate their origins from the Romans, who would have buried their dead with fewer and simpler artifact types. Also, different types of graves and burials are considered expressions of different ethnic traditions. Romans were buried in graves with subterranean stone constructions, while Germans interred their dead directly into the ground. This idea was introduced and developed between the two World Wars and was largely used by German archaeologists during the Second War World to legitimize the expansion of the *Reich* towards the east and west. Using these archaeological studies, it was in fact possible to claim that those were regions of ancient German origin (Feher 2002; Hessmann 2002). During the 1980s, new meanings were given to these theories, which are still in use today. Several attempts were, in fact, made to define the typical funerary traditions of the Germanic peoples versus the Romans (Bierbrauer1984; Brozzi 1989) and to distinguish the different types of Germanic groups mentioned in the sources, on the basis of different kinds and styles of brooches and weapons. Germanic traditions penetrated the Roman *limes* together with the invading Germanic groups, and were gradually abandoned according to a process which has been defined as "acculturation" to indicate the assimilation of Roman traditions by the barbarians (Bierbrauer 1984). In the specific case of Italy, for instance, weapons and certain types of brooches are assumed to have been deposited in graves from AD 569, when the 'Lombards' invaded the peninsula, until about the end of the seventh century, when the barbarians' conversion to Catholicism and integration with the indigenous populations was completed.

Scholars have suggested that grave goods found in the graves of this period were expression of the *tracht*, the traditional costume of each group (for a study on the origin of such ideas see Fehr [2002]). This means that each group could be identified by a set of traditions, one of which included the manner of dressing, visible in the way the dead were dressed on the day of their funerals. For instance, the costume of 'Lombard' women in Pannonia was suggested by Menghin (Menghin 1985). 'Lombards' moved from Germany to Italy through Pannonia (Lower Austria and Hungary), where they ruled for about 50 years during the first half of the AD 6th century. We know this from Procopius of Cesarea and other later sources (*Origo Gentis Langobardorum* and Paulus Diaconus, *Historia Langobardorum*),

A group of cemeteries excavated in Hungary and dated to the first half of the AD 6th century was attributed to the Lombards on the basis of grave good types. In this case, some similarities were found with artifacts excavated in Italy. However, it should be stressed here that these were mainly brooches (thus, only one type of artifact), while other types of objects like weapons were not so similar between the two areas. Weapons from Pannonian 'Lombard' graves were more similar to weapons from the area east of the Danube, where another group was settled, the Gepids (Curta 2001). The same can be said for decorated pots. A type of pot decoration which is considered a typical Lombard production is actually disseminated in areas where the Lombards never moved, like eastern Hungary for instance (Curta 2001). Thus, only brooches could be claimed to represent the ethnic identity of the 'Lombards' in Pannonia. However, this idea can also be discarded because of the fact that some types of brooches found in Hungary can be found in the Danubian region of present-day Germany and in Merovingian areas. Consequently, it does not seem possible to identify the route of the Lombards, as described by the documentary sources, with a line of coherent and ethnically characterized material culture (on the problem of migration and material culture see Anthony [1997]; on the problem of Lombard migration between Hungary and Italy, see Barbiera [2005]). If we were to follow the "diffusion" of ethnic objects we would have, as a result, very strange migration movements, including Lombard men moving to the east, and their wives, with a few other men, moving to the west! On the basis of artifact types and styles it was even possible to claim that groups of Lombard women moved from northern Italy to Alemannia around the year AD 600 (Graenert 2000), a migration movement not documented by any of the sources. Following the object distribution is confusing and could lead one to suppose a strange migration phenomenon, because "people move and not culture" (Anthony 1997). Trade in luxury goods can easily explain the distribution of at least some types of objects (for a study on trade between Anglo-Saxon England and North Sea countries see Hills [1999]).

The ethnic interpretation of grave goods is also problematic because typical elements of the "Roman" and

"German" traditions have been found mixed in the same graves; the number of graves with weapons and brooches is generally limited compared to the percentage of graves containing simpler artifacts, as we shall see below. Further, it has been revealed recently that in some cases areas of production of "ethnic" objects do not correspond to the areas of their deposition in graves (Daim 2001). The most interesting case comes from Rome, where a workshop has been excavated in which the types of objects produced were those found in the graves from the Lombard territories (Ricci 1995). This is the only documented case of such a workshop in Italy and it is interesting that it was found in a non-Lombard area.

The ethnic interpretation of grave goods has been addressed because it has been seen as a reflection of modern thoughts on the interpretation of the past. In particular, early medieval migrating groups have been seen as the founders of modern nations and thus characteristics typical of modern nationalism have been applied to their understanding, including language and cultural unity and ethnic cohesion (Diaz-Andreu, Champion 1996). Rather, from a historical point of view, the Germanic groups described by the sources were not coherent ethnic units, but rather mixed groups probably comprised of warriors (Geary 1983; Pohl 1991). Their cohesion was guaranteed by powerful chieftains and the belief in a common origin (Wolfram 1979).

Women's costume

As mentioned above, artifacts from female graves excavated in Hungary have been used to reconstruct the costume of Lombard women. This would have been a traditional costume of the Lombards, transmitted from one generation to the next to preserve the memory of ethnic belonging during migration. This type of dressing tradition would have been finally abandoned after the Lombards settled in Italy. What has not been taken into consideration is the fact that traditional costume was reconstructed from graves, which represent a special place for the construction, invention and manipulation of identities and do not necessarily reflect reality.

According to Menghin's reconstruction, the Lombard female traditional costume was characterized by certain dress elements and a few tools hanging from the dress (Menghin 1985, Fig. 1). If we observe the percentage of graves containing the objects considered typical of the 'Lombard' women's costume, it becomes apparent that most are rather rare, representing the exception rather than the rule (Fig. 2, the table is based on the artifacts excavated in four Hungarian cemeteries, Hegykő, Szentendre, Tamási and Kajdacs, all excavated by Istvan Bóna, between the 1950s and 1970s). The percentages are calculated on the number of female graves only. Only beads were present in the majority of female graves. Different types of brooches, considered together, were also

rather common (they are found in 30% of female graves), but the disk brooch, considered by Menghin to be the typical Pannonian brooch of the Lombards, is the rarest among the three types found. There was never more than one hairpin in these graves; the chain, the sword and the silver plaques decorating the dress were quite rare. The bag or pouch, which according to Menghin hung from the belt, is not documented in any of these female graves. This was rather a typical male dress element. It was made of leather, and fit directly on the belt, in the same way as present day pouches for men in Hungary. It contained small tools such as strike-a-lights, flints, tweezers, small knives, awls, and so on.

From these observations, it follows that the reconstructed traditional costume does not reflect a trend and in some cases the artistic reconstruction even included purely imaginary details. Actually, there was a group of artifacts representing exceptions, while other artifacts occurred more commonly in the graves. Reconstructing the costume from burials is even more problematic if we consider male graves. It is not a coincidence that no typical 'Lombard' male costume was suggested by archaeologists. In fact, males were not buried with dress accessories, like females, but mainly with tools or weapons, so a different concept or rather a different kind of memory was created for men as opposed to women.

If not the "typical Lombards," who were, then, these ladies with unconventional grave goods? In the following paragraphs I will consider in further detail the distribution patterns of exceptional and conventional grave goods in male and female graves to see which memory of the dead they were meant to evoke.

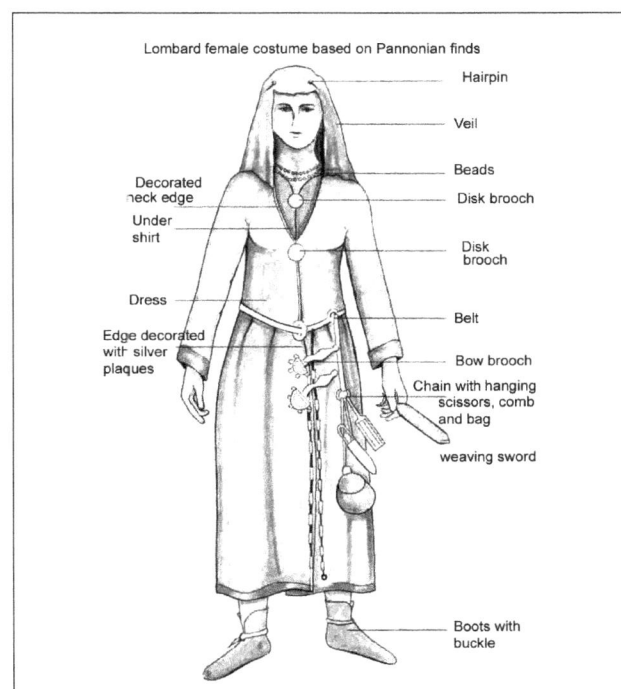

Fig. 1. Costume of Lombard woman from Pannonia (After Menghin, 1985)

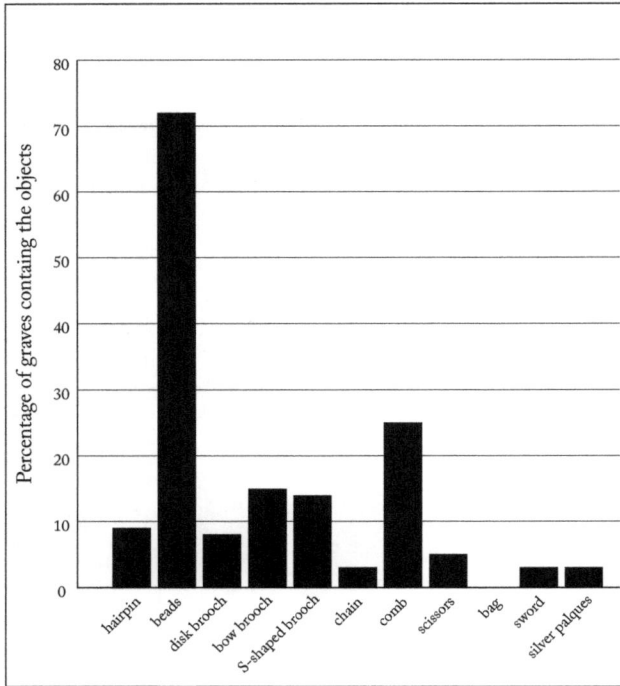

Fig. 2. Frequency of Menghin's female costume elements in female graves from Hungary (Hegykő, Szentendre, Tamási and Kajdacs). Percentages are calculated on the number of female graves only.

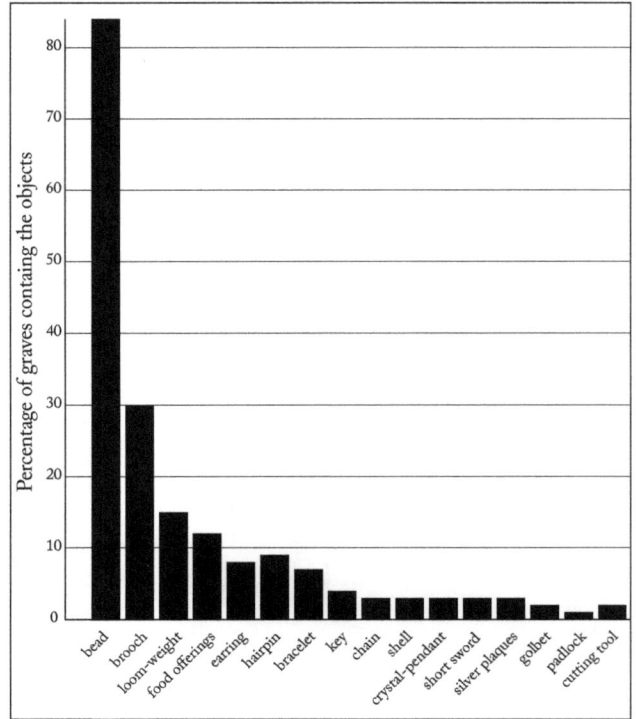

Fig. 3. Frequency of 'female' artifact types in the graves from Hegykő, Szentendre, Tamási and Kajdacs. The percentages are calculated on the number of female graves only.

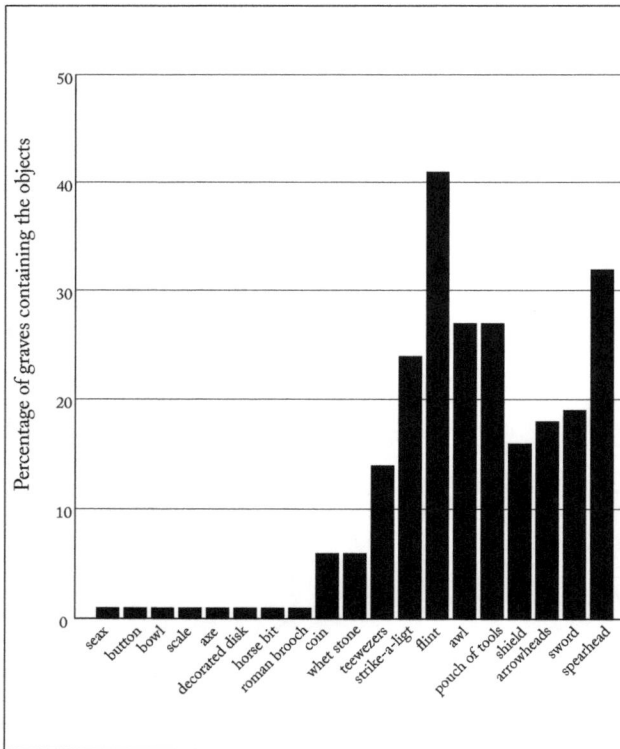

Fig. 4. Frequency of 'male' artifact types in the graves from Hegykő, Szentendre, Tamási and Kajdacs. The percentages are calculated on the number of male graves only.

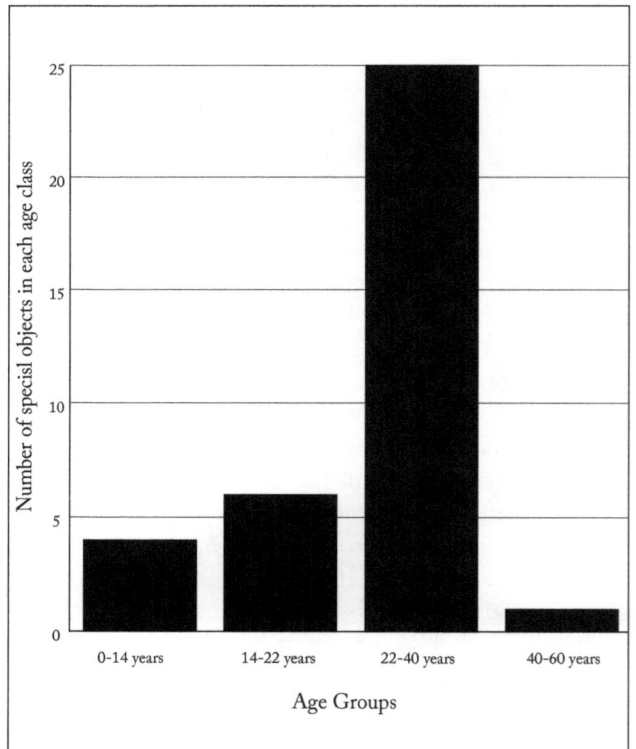

Fig. 5. Distribution of 'special objects' in female graves from Hegykő, Szentendre, Tamási and Kajdacs.

Special grave goods and gender

As has been shown recently, grave goods, present in the cemeteries studied from the Early Middle Ages, were related to gender, and genderized grave goods were related to age at death (Halsall 1995; Barbiera 2005). In particular, an analysis of cemeteries excavated in Hungary and dated to the 'Lombard' occupation (the same cemeteries used to reconstruct the costume of Lombard women) showed, analogously to contemporary cemeteries in the area of Metz in France (Halsall 1995; Halsall 1996), that grave goods could be classified into three groups. One group can be defined as "male" and included weapons and other artifacts. They were never found in graves together with "female" artifacts, which included jewelry or dress ornaments. A third group of artifacts was found associated with both "male" and "female" assemblage types, this can be called "neutral" since it included a group of artifacts, which could be deposited both in male and female graves. This group was therefore not used to symbolize gender roles. It was also possible to show that "male" and "female" artifact types were related to age at death. In particular, "female" types were given to women who died while still in their fertile years. Brooches were of the "female" type, symbolized this status better, since it was given mainly to young and adult women and in only a few cases to mature ones. Beads were the most widespread type in female graves; they were found in female graves of all ages and also in a few male graves, usually in very small numbers. Weapons were the typical "male" type related to age; in fact they were given to adults and mature males only (Barbiera 2005). The "male," "female" and "neutral" groups each included both elements of the dress and tools, but in general, females were characterized by personal elements, while males had weapons or tools. Knives, combs, pots, scissors, buckles and belt elements were 'neutral' and could be found in all age groups, though combs were rare in children's graves (an interesting work on the symbolic meaning of comb depositions in graves can be found in Williams [2003]). Therefore, in these cemeteries different assemblages were chosen to acknowledge or ignore gender roles, according to the age at death of the individuals.

Space was also used to symbolize gender and age groups. In fact, graves tended to be arranged in clusters of males, females and children. In some cases, older peoples were also grouped together (Barbiera 2005).

Thus, the graves containing objects traditionally considered by scholars to be expressions of "Lombardness" rather turned out to be expressions of maleness or femaleness, and this was related to age at death. In fact, different values were ascribed to life phases of males and females, with seniority the most important factor for males, and fertility for females.

However, there were a few males who seem to have been more male then others and some females who seem to have been more female than others. These graves contained the highest number of the most common gender-characterized artifact types, but also a number of exceptional objects (with a frequency below 5%, calculated on the total number of 94 female graves, identified on the basis of anthropological analyses and graves with female artifact types). A few such graves were found in each cemetery studied. Only bracelets and earrings were found in the cemetery of Hegykő where they were quite common considering the number of graves in the cemetery. Thus, they do not represent an exception, but rather a trend in this particular community. In the case of female graves, exceptional objects (as can be seen from Fig. 3) were represented by silver or bronze keys, a chain hanging from the belt like the one drawn by Menghin, a sea shell, mainly found in children's graves, a crystal pendant, a short sword, decorated silver plaques sewn onto the dress or leather belt, a glass goblet, a padlock (documented in one grave only), and a type of cutting tool. Some of these objects were interpreted as domestic tools, used by women in the kitchen or in textile production (such as the short sword or the cutting tool) or were employed to symbolize the role of housewife (like the keys). Some of them seem to have had a practical function, but not all of them, like the keys, which were in some cases functional, in others only decorative. It is difficult to believe, as has been claimed, that swords were employed in textile production as weaving swords because of their shape and weight (Bank-Burgess 1997). Also, in one of the graves brought to light in Kajdacs, a sword was deposited in a special and symbolic way: thrown into the soil next to the coffin, in the same way spears were usually treated in male graves, showing that it might have been perceived, at least in this case, as a weapon.

In the case of males (Fig. 4), there were few special objects and these occurred only once in the graves considered here (there are a total of 89 male graves, defined as male on the basis of anthropological analyses and presence of male artifact types). These types include a seax, bone buttons, a bronze bowl, a scale, an axe, a decorated bone disk (whose function might have been decorative), a horse bit and a Roman brooch. As opposed to females, male graves contained a lower number of exceptional objects and the highest number of more common artifacts, showing that male assemblages were more consistent than those of females. Also, the number of male graves containing special objects is very low; in total there are only six graves (one of an adolescent, three adults and two mature individuals). However, this distribution conforms to the construction of male-seniority observed through the distribution of male artifact types (Barbiera 2005).

In the case of females as well, special objects reflect age-based status. As can be seen in Fig. 5, the most special objects were given to adults, while they were given very rarely to mature individuals. In most cases, children received sea shells or chain belts. Adolescents occurred, in general, in low numbers since mortality was lowest at this age. Thus, the death of a young woman would have represented, in social terms, a greater loss, since for the family it would have meant the loss of a possible link with other families through her marriage or the opportunity to have new heirs (Halsall 1996). In the case of males, maturity and the role of family leader might have been stressed through a larger display of goods in graves.

Therefore, it seems that such objects were only deposited in some cases to further emphasize femininity or masculinity within a system of grave-good depositions related to gender and age roles. While male assemblages among mature individuals and adults were quite homogeneous, greater differences in wealth and the number of grave goods are apparent among female graves.

Graves with special objects, for which a chronology was established, come mainly from the middle and second half of the 6th century (see Fig. 6), which corresponds to the last phase of cemetery use, at least according to the suggested chronology (Bòna 1990).

Thus, in a system of age-based status, in which different objects were expressions of gender roles, there was a period, possibly corresponding to the final phase of cemetery use, in which more special objects were deposited in some of the graves. These were mainly graves of young and early adult females as well as a few mature males.

Objects of this type have often been interpreted as a way of expressing the ethnic status of the ruling 'Lombards', and the wealthiest graves have been seen as expressions of rank for preeminent warriors and their wives. However, a re-examination of grave goods here demonstrated that they were chosen to remember or to further emphasize the gender of some individuals. Brides, young wives, mothers-to-be and mothers tended to have richer burials than others; does this variability relate to differences in rank? If so, why is this not so evident in male graves? Do differences actually reflect something about the gender of the mourners? Or about marriage alliances? Or about the conditions of war? Interestingly, the change in the kind of objects deposited in graves becomes apparent in one particular chronological phase; does this imply that society was starting to grow in complexity? It is quite difficult to answer these questions. To better clarify this matter we should try to see what happened to both usual and exceptional grave goods in other areas occupied by the Lombards.

Kin groups and ancestors

Similar grave goods were deposited in graves dated to the Lombard period in cemeteries in Slovenia (Kranj) and the Friuli-Venezia-Giulia region in Italy (S. Stefano, Cividale, Udine and Romans d'Isonzo, Gorizia), but they seem to express completely different identities. These cemeteries were found in areas occupied by the Lombards in phases later than the Hungarian ones. In particular, it is probable that the area of Kranj was occupied after AD 547-548; we know from written evidence (Procopius of Cesare is again our source) that in this period the Emperor Justinian gave the *Polis Norikum* to the Lombards. What is not certain is whether Kranj belonged to this area or to the Friuli region (for a discussion of this matter see Barbiera, 2007), however, Kranj is considered here together with Friulian cemeteries since it presents the same cemetery construction. The Friuli region was occupied just after AD 569. These steps in the Lombard migration, however, are still quite controversial, since the historical sources presented this migration as a mass movement, whereas it would seem that the population movement actually took the form of a slower wave of migration.

If we observe the percentage of graves containing "neutral", "male", and "female" objects in these areas, quite striking differences are observable compared to the results obtained in the Hungarian cemeteries. "Female" types are not very common compared to what was found in Hungarian burials (Fig. 7). It should be stressed here that the percentages in the Hungarian sample were calculated on the number of female graves only, while a calculation of this type was not possible in this case because the gender of individuals identified from bones, in Kranj, which is a very large cemetery, has not yet been identified. However, when considering all the graves from the four Hungarian cemeteries, 36% of the graves contained beads and 13.5% contained brooches, while loom weights, food offerings, earrings, hairpins, and bracelets had frequencies of occurrence ranging between 5% and 15%. In Italian cemeteries, beads were found in less than 7% of the graves and brooches in little more than 6% of the graves. All other artifacts occur less than 3% of the time. This means that in Italy almost all the "female" artifacts represent exceptions, while the norm was represented by "neutral" graves or graves without grave goods.

Percentages are even lower in the case of males (Fig. 8). All artifacts have a frequency under 4%. The most common artifact is a belt, sometimes richly decorated as in the graves of the cemetery of Santo Stefano at Cividale, or as in most cases, special belts to hang the sword from. Swords are the most common weapon type, found in 2.7% of the graves. In Hungarian cemeteries, spearheads were found in 14.4% of the graves, when all excavated graves are considered, and swords in 8.5% of the graves. Clearly, also in the case of male burials, graves with weapons are scarce. Very few men received "male" grave goods compared to women.

Graves containing non-gendered artifact types or no grave goods at all prevailed in these cemeteries. Thus,

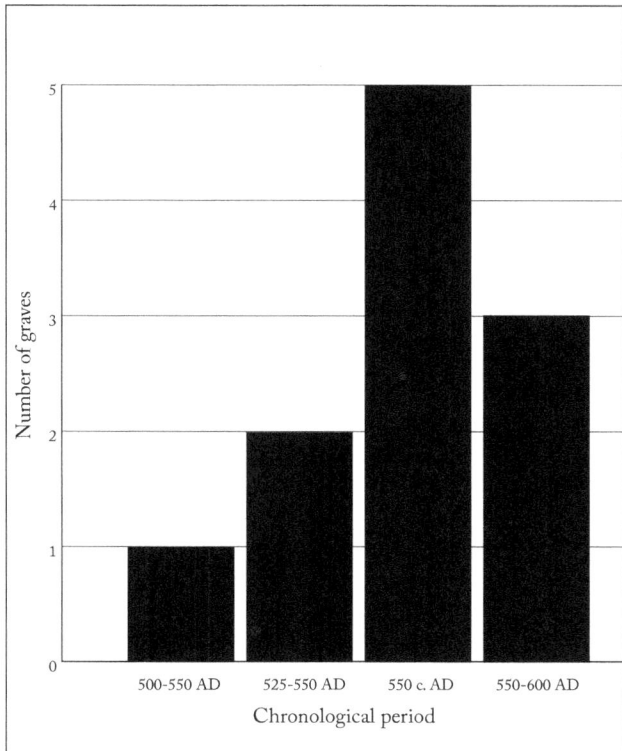

Fig. 6. Chronological distribution of male and female graves with 'special objects' (for which a precise chronology has been suggested) from Hegykő, Szentendre, Tamási and Kajdacs.

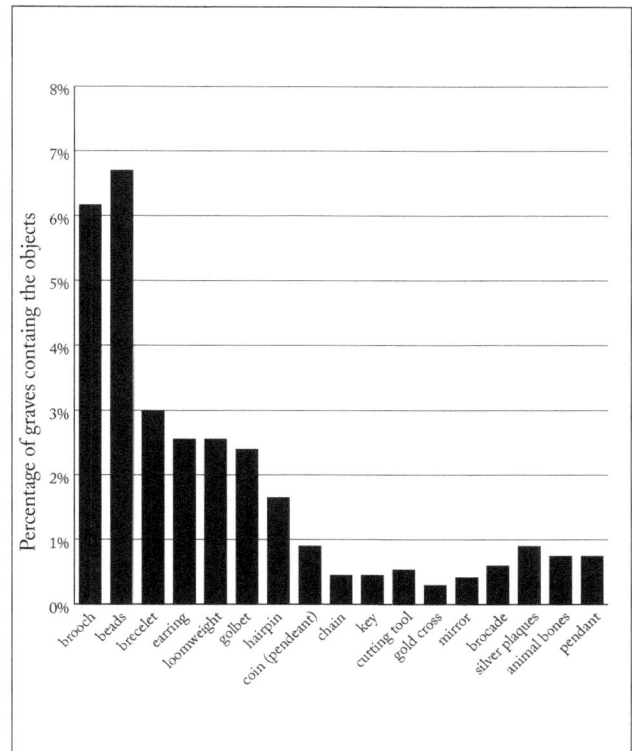

Fig. 7. Frequency of 'female' objects from S. Stefano, Romans and Kranj. Percentages are calculated on the total number of graves.

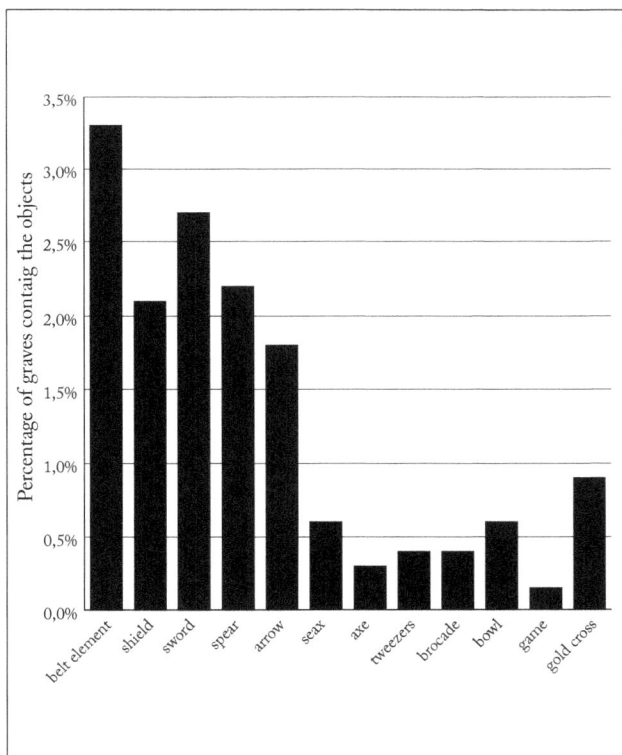

Fig. 8. Frequency of 'male' objects from S. Stefano, Romans and Kranj. Percentages are calculated on the total number of graves.

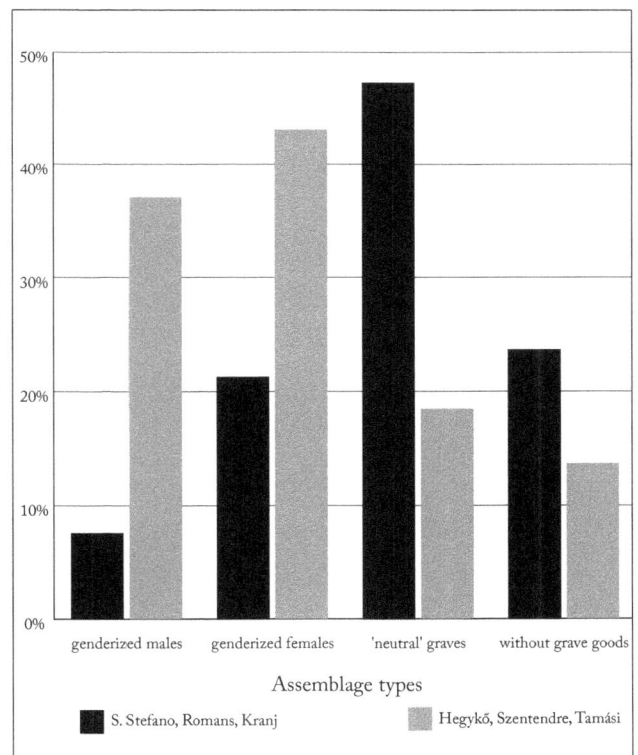

Fig. 9. Frequency of 'male', 'female', 'neutral' assemblages and of graves without grave goods in S. Stefano, Romans and Kranj, considered together and in Hegykő, Szentendre and Tamási considered together.

the situation seems reversed in Italy compared to the slightly earlier Hungarian sample. All "male" and "female" artifact types are exceptions, while the norm is neutrality or no grave goods (Fig. 9). The case of males with swords therefore represents an exceptional occurrence, since few individuals were buried in this way, whereas in Hungary this practice was normal for mature male individuals and adults. "Female" artifact types were more common, so compared to males, female assemblages appear slightly more consistent in the Italian context.

This distribution of grave goods in Italian cemeteries also reflects cemetery construction. As has already been demonstrated (Barbiera 2005), the few graves with weapons or brooches were scattered in the cemeteries and surrounded by graves with simpler grave goods. Graves with more elaborate artifact types are chronologically dated to the second half of the AD 6th century-beginning of the AD 7th century. This period corresponds to the first phases of cemetery use in S. Stefano and Romans. While Kranj started to be used from the beginning of the AD 6th century, it was only in the middle of this period that grave goods became more elaborate in this cemetery. Therefore, it seems that at a certain point, and for a short period, grave goods were more lavish. Later graves started to be neutral or did not contain grave goods, but spatially surrounded more complex graves. Separate grave groups, with a core of graves containing weapons and female types, were clearly visible in S. Stefano, possibly in Romans and in one area of Kranj. Some other cemeteries recently excavated in the Friuli-Venezia-Giulia region also showed a distribution of graves in groups separated by empty areas (these are Lovaria and Pradamano, in Buora [1988] and Buora [1994]). This also seems to have been a tradition at Aquileia in the AD 2nd- and 3rd- century cemeteries. There, funerary walls were employed to create separate burial areas for different families and monuments constructed to stress the graves of the ancestors (Hope 2001); according to a similar principle, in later phases this was expressed through use of space and grave goods. This construction principal was also documented in the AD 3rd-4th century cemetery of Iutizzo (Udine, in Buora 1996). Although the documentation is scanty, this use of space may show that an old tradition was maintained for centuries in these areas, even though the means of expressing it changed. At this time, this theory cannot be demonstrated with certainty.

My hypothesis is that in the cemeteries analyzed here, grave goods were employed to create the figure of venerated ancestors around which descendants were willing, even anxious, to be buried. In later phases, grave goods become rare and simpler or were no longer deposited although proximity to wealthy ancestors might have been seen as a marker of prestige (Barbiera 2005).

Instability and the deaths

Although grave goods in the two study areas (Hungary on the one side and Italy and Slovenia on the other) are displayed in the graves to construct two different memories of the deceased, there was a period in both areas in which social roles were emphasized more than at other times. Chronology is crucial at this point to understand this shift in the number and richness of grave goods depositions. Unfortunately, traditional chronology is based on a circular argument and is not of great help. Since the sources mentioned a Lombard migration in AD 568, 'Lombard' graves from Hungarian cemeteries are assumed to have stopped being used in this year (even if there are some elements showing that this was not actually the case, such as the presence in some graves of later-dated artifacts and a C14 date on one of the graves, see Barbiera [2005]) and, conversely, it is claimed that Italian cemeteries began to be used from AD 568-569.

If we accept this traditional chronology and the idea that these cemeteries belonged to communities touched by the 'Lombard' migration, the two models would represent different steps in the evolution from conventional assemblages expressing gender to the emergence of exceptional assemblages characterized by more complex grave goods in Hungary. Later, a completely different meaning for grave goods deposition meant to create venerated ancestors (males with weapons and females with brooches) would emerge, and finally a phase in which the custom of depositing grave goods was abandoned, and space and proximity to the ancestors played an important role in the expression of identities. It is, however, hard to believe that a migrating group adopted new funerary traditions so suddenly. It is more probable that such changes evolved in slower phases. In this case, the date of AD 568 does not represent a real *caesura* in cemetery use and burial costume. Possibly the phases for the depositions of exceptional objects in the two areas correspond to the same chronological phase, the middle and second half of the AD 6th century in Hungary and the second half of the AD 6th and beginning of the AD 7th century in Italy. This phase may correspond to greater changes in the two areas related to wars and migration.

It is also possible that the two types of cemetery construction reflected two different social organizations and funerary traditions in the two areas and had little to do with the migration of the 'Lombards'. It could be argued that deposition of grave goods, which spread as a custom in Europe during this period, meant various things reflecting variable parameters in these two different areas, roughly during the same chronological period.

What we know for sure from written sources is that in this period people lived in these areas in situations of war (Procopius of Cesarea, *Wars*) and great changes were taking place during this phase, particularly after the Gothic Wars, in land possession and aristocratic composition (Gasparri 2002; Wickham 2002). As has been previously noted, the large estates of Roman times were drastically damaged in all the areas within the *limes*. Concomitantly, on a regional scale, small properties survived and become the model of ownership. While during late Roman times, military and political power were separated, in this period of wars and instability, warriors started to infiltrate the landowning elite and to hold political power (Harrison 2002). Therefore, a new leading class arose during this period, comprising both Romans and barbarians. At this moment in history, belonging to this new class became the most important point to be stressed, rather than ethnic identity (Gasparri 2002).

In this period of changes and instability, new ways to remember the past and display power were developed as expressions of a new political mentality (This process has been well illustrated in Headeger 2000). The transmission of origin myths took on particular importance, including the one narrating the Lombard migration from the mythical land of 'Scandinavia' to Italy. This story, first orally transmitted, was finally written as a way to legitimize and affirm the power of the Lombards in Italy (Pohl 2002). Also, rituals started having a special function to legitimize and clarify positions of power (see Fiano in this volume and Le Jan 2000) and the giving of weapons played a special role in this sense. Belongings and wealth were symbols of power and status and as such were displayed on public occasions (La Rocca 2004). Layser (1994) has explained the attitude of kings, aristocrats, and bishops, towards bringing precious belongings such as silver and gold vessels, belt fittings, and luxury clothing back to camp after battles as a way of deifying their status and office. Objects were thus actively used to define social and political roles by the ruling elite. Some pieces of written evidence clearly testify to such attitudes. One text, written by Theophylatus Simokates was analyzed by Walter Pohl (1999). In this text, a Gepid soldier steals a golden belt from an emperor's guard and kills him. When the soldier is captured, he is immediately suspected of having stolen it, since it was not normal for a simple soldier to possess such a belt. A later case was described by Liutprand of Cremona (analyzed in La Rocca 2004), in which Marquis Adalbert of Cremona, not wanting to be recognized during the Hungarian invasions, threw away his golden belt and all his *preciosum apparatum* which would have immediately identified him. In fact, he was subsequently taken for a common soldier and thus, succeeded in escaping.

The absence of written documents in this period has in the past been attributed to the "barbarization" of the Roman world. Germans invading the Roman Empire and becoming the leading class were illiterate, while ecclesiastics, coming from the Roman world, preserved this faculty. It has been shown recently that this was not the case (Harrison 2002); it is not clear whether documents written during the AD 6th and 7th centuries were not produced for some reason or were lost. What is interesting is that, besides written and non-written documents, verbal and symbolic memory took on a particular role in social communication.

The display of objects in the graves of this period at the moment of burial can be understood in this context. During the funeral, social roles were emphasized, created, and negotiated through the grave goods as a way of establishing social boundaries for the living (Härke 2001). Surely, graves had some sort of markers that have since perished, otherwise they could not have been found by the relatives of the dead or community members; what cannot be proven is whether or not these markers bore some sort of inscription. In any case, the identity of the dead was expressed during the funeral through a non-written code, grave goods, and remembered by the community orally. In this phase of great changes and confusion, when inscriptions were for some reasons lacking, symbolic codes were employed to be impressed on the minds of the living. Memory, and in particular orally transmitted memory, played an important role in the transmission and preservation of social order and individual roles as displayed in cemeteries.

Grave goods associations and complexity could be used in this context to express different kinds of social identities in different areas, as has been shown here. Norms and exceptions could be produced through different systems of values, rather than as passive manifestations of rank or ethnicity.

It is possible that a period of special stress and instability meant that the elite made greater investments in grave goods to better clarify social relations or to emphasize new power positions attained by the families of the deceased. Old powerful kin groups might have had less need to clarify their role in society than those starting to emerge or which were competing to emerge. Such new positions might have been gained through the advent of migrating groups or the integration of newly arriving families or even during the turmoil caused by wars. In a context of great confusion of this kind, more complex assemblages might have been buried according to different funerary systems to better clarify special and political positions and mark the lines of social relations among the living.

Conclusions

In this study, I have tried to consider some aspects of burial deposition during the AD 6th and 7th centuries. What has emerged is that during a period in which the custom of depositing objects in graves was spreading, various communities used objects to express different social identities and to mediate social relations in different forms and levels. Variable degrees of complexity might have had different meanings to participants in the funeral even if they seem to be connected to a particular chronological period. In particular, two different cemetery constructions registered in Hungary and Italy, the first based on gender and life span categories, the second on kin-group membership, might represent two different funerary traditions used to express different social constructions and political needs (Barbiera 2005). The custom of grave good depositions might have been appropriated and elaborated depending on these two funerary traditions in the study areas. When instability, wars, and migration affected the two areas there might have been a stronger need for clarifying positions of power through rituals and symbols, transmitted from generation to generation by the memory of those participating to the funerals, rather than relying on written words. This might have been reflected in more complex assemblages emphasizing wealthy ancestors or richer relatives within systems in which kinship membership on the one side and the role in family construction on the other were the aspects to be displayed in a funeral. In this context, the process of remembering and forgetting relied on symbols, which were malleable and fluid and therefore are often difficult to understand in retrospective.

Acknowledgements

I would like to thank Alice Choyke for involving me in this project of organizing a session on Memory at the 10th EEA Meeting and in the editing of this volume, and for her suggestions on the elaboration of this work and for her English corrections. I also would like to thank John Chapman for his valuable suggestions and Judith Rasson for her help in correcting the English in this paper.

Bibliography

Anthony, D. 1997. Prehistoric Migration as Social Process. In: *Migrations and Invasions in Archaeological Explanation.* J. Chapman and H. Hamerow (eds.), British Archaeological Reports, International Series 664. Oxford: BAR Publishing, pp. 21-32.

Bank-Burgess, J. 1997. An Webstuhl und Webrahmen. In: *Die Alemannen.* R. Herzog and A. Koller (eds.). Stuttgart: Archäologisches Landmuseums, pp. 372-378.

Barbiera, I. 2005. *Changing Lands in Changing Memories. Migration and Identity during the Lombard Invasions.* Documenti di Archeologia 19. Florence: Edizioni all'Insegna del Giglio.

Barbiera, I. 2007. Il sesso svelato degli antenati. Strategie funerarie di rappresentazione dei generi a Kranj Lajh e Iskra in Slovenia (VI-XI sec.). In: *Agire da donna. Modelli e pratiche di rappresentazione (secoli VI-X).* C. La Rocca (ed.). Collection Haut Moyen Age 3. Turnhout: Brepols, pp. 23-52.

Bierbrauer, V. 1984. Aspetti archeologici di Goti, Alamanni e Longobardi. In: *Magistra Barbaritas. I barbari in Italia.* Milan: Libri Scheiwiller, pp. 445-508.

Bóna, I. 1990. I longobardi in Pannonia. In: *I Longobardi.* Gian Carlo Menis (ed.). Milan: Electa, pp. 14-73.

Brozzi, M. 1989. *La popolazione romana del Friuli longobardo.* Udine: Deputazione di Storia Patria per il Friuli.

Buora, M. 1988. Pradamano. Scavo di necropoli rurale del periodo alto medievale. *Aquileia Nostra* 59, pp. 387-388.

Buora, M. 1994. Lovaria. Comune di Pradamano del Friuli. Campagne di scavo 1992-1994. *Aquileia Nostra* 65, pp. 368-374.

Buora, M. 1996. *I Soldati di Magnenzo. Scavi nella necropoli romana di Iutizzo, Codroipo.* Archeologia di Frontiera 1. Trieste: Società Friulana di Archeologia.

Cracco Ruggini, L. 1989. La città imperiale. In: *Storia di Roma.* vol. 4, E. Schiavone and E. Gabba (eds.). Turin: Einaudi, pp. 201-266.

Curta, F. 2001. *The Making of the Slavs: History and Archaeology of the Lower Danube Region ca. 500-700.* Cambridge: Cambridge University Press.

Daim, F. 2001. Byzantine Belts and Avar Birds. Diplomacy, Trade and Cultural Transfer in the Eighth Century. In: *The Transformation of Frontiers from Late Antiquity to the Carolingians.* W. Pohl, I. Wood and H. Reimitz (eds.). The Transformation of the Roman World 10. Leiden: Brill, pp. 143-188.

De Rubeis, F. 2005. Scritture epigrafiche e scritture librarie in Italia meridionale. In: *Die Langobarden. Herrchaft und Identität.* W. Pohl and P. Erhart (eds.), Forshungen zur Geschichte des Mittelalters 9. Vienna: Verlag der Österreichischen Akademie der Wissenschaften, pp. 525-531.

Diaz-Andreu, M. and Champion, T. 1996. Nationalism and Archaeology in Europe: An Introduction. In: *Nationalism and Archaeology in Europe.* M. Diaz-Andreu and T. Champion, (eds.). London: UCL Press, pp. 1-23.

Eckardt, H. and Williams, H. 2003. Objects without a Past? The Use of Roman Objects in Early Anglo-Saxon Graves. In: *Archaeologies of Remembrance. Death and Memory in Past Societies.* H. Williams (ed.). New York: Kluwer Academic/Plenum Publishers, pp. 141-192.

Fehr, H. 2002. Volkstum as Paradigm: Germanic People and Gallo-Romans in Early Medieval Archaeology since the 1930s. In: *On Barbarian Identity. Critical Approaches to Ethnicity in the Early Middle Ages.* A. Gillett, (ed.) Studies in the Early Middle Ages 4. Turnhout: Brepols, pp. 177-200.

Gasparri, S. 2002. The Aristocracy. In: *Italy in the Early Middle Ages 476-1000.* C. La Rocca, (ed.). The Short Oxford History of Italy. Oxford: Oxford University Press, p. 59-84.

Geary, P. 1983. Ethnic Identity as a Situational Construction in the Early Middle Ages. *Mitteilungen der Anthropologischen Gesellschaft in Wien* 113, pp. 15-26.

Graenert, G. 2000. Langobardinnen in Alamannien. *Germania* 78, pp. 418-446.

Halsall, G. 1995. *Settlement and Social Organisation. The Merovingian region of Metz.* Cambridge: Cambridge University Press.

Halsall, G. 1996. Female Status and Power in Early Merovingian Central Austrasia: the Burial Evidence. *Early Medieval Europe* 5, pp. 1-24.

Härke, H. 2001. Cemeteries as Places of Power. In: *Topographies of Power in the Early Middle Ages.* M. de Jong, F. Theuws with C. van Rhijn (eds.). The Transformation of the Roman World 6. Leiden: Brill, pp. 9-30.

Harrison, D. 2002. The Development of Elites: from Roman Bureaucrats to Medieval Warlords. In: *Integration und Herrschaft. Etnische Identitäten und soziale Organisation im Frühmittelalter,* W. Pohl, M. Diesenberger (eds.). Forschungen zur Geschichte des Mittelalters 3. Vienna: Verlag der Österreichischen Akademie der Wissenschaften, p. 289-300.

Hedeager, L. 2000. Migration Period Europe: the formation of a political mentality. In: *Rituals of Power.* F. Theuws and J. L. Nelson, (eds.). The Transformation of the Roman World 8. Leiden: Brill, pp. 15-58.

Hessmann, H. 2002. Archaeology in the "Third Reich". In: *Archaeology, Ideology and Society. The German Experience.* H. Härke, (ed.). Berlin: Peter Lang, pp. 67-142.

Hills, C. 1999. Spong Hill and the Adventum Saxonum. In: *Spaces of the Living and the Dead: An Archaeological Dialogue.* C. Karkow, K. M. Wickham-Crowley and B. K. Young, (eds.). American Early Medieval Studies 3. Oxford: Oxbow Books, pp. 15-26.

Hope, V. 2001. *Constructing Identity: The Roman Funerary Monuments of Aquileia, Mainz and Nimes.* British Archaeological Reports, International Series 960. Oxford: BAR Publishing, pp. 74-76.

Hope, V. 2003. Remembering Rome. Memory, Funerary Monuments and the Roman Soldier. In: *Archaeologies of Remembrance. Death and Memory in Past Societies.* H. Williams (ed.). New York Kluwer Academic/Plenum Publishers, pp. 113-140.

Laser, K. 1994. Early Medieval Warfare. In: *Communication and Power in Medieval Europe: The Carolingian and Ottonian Centuries.* T. Reuter, (ed.). London: Hambledon Press, pp. 29-50.

La Rocca, C. 2004. Tesori terrestri, tesori celesti. In: *Tesori. Forme di accumulazione della ricchezza nell'alto medioevo (secoli V-XI).* S. Gelichi and C. La Rocca, (eds.). Rome: Viella, pp. 123-141.

Le Jan, R. 2000. Frankish Giving of Arms and Rituals of Power: Continuity and Change in the Carolingian Period. In: *Rituals of Power.* F. Theuws and J. L. Nelson, (eds.). The Transformation of the Roman World 8. Leiden: Brill, pp. 281-309.

Menghin, W. 1985. *Die Langobarden. Archäologie und Geschichte.* Theiss: Stuttgart.

Pohl, W. 1991. Concepts of Ethnicity in the Early Medieval Studies. *Archaeologia Polona* 29, pp. 39-49.

Pohl, W. 1999. Social Language, Identities and the Control of Discourse. In: *East and West: Modes of Communication.* E. Chrysos and I. Wood, (eds.). The Transformation of the Roman World 5. Leiden: Brill, pp. 127-141.

Pohl, W. 2002. La costruzione di una memoria storica: il caso dei Longobardi. In: *Studi sulle società e le culture del Medioevo per Girolamo Araldi.* L. Gatto and P. Supino Martini, (eds.). Florence: Edizioni All'Insegna del Giglio, pp. 563-580.

Ricci, M. 1995. Relazioni culturali e scambi commerciali nell'Italia centrale romano-longobarda alla luce della Crypta Balbi in Roma. In: *L'Italia Centro Settentrionale in età longobarda.* L. Paroli, (ed.). Florence: Edizioni All'Insegna del Giglio, pp. 239-274.

Theuws, F. and Alkemande, M. 2000. A Kind of Mirror for Men: Sword Deposition in Late Antique Northern Gaul. In: *Rituals of Power.* F. Theuws and J. L. Nelson (eds.). Leiden: Brill, pp. 401-476.

van Houts, E. 1999. *Memory and Gender in Medieval Europe, 900-1200.* Toronto, University of Toronto Press.

Williams, H. 2003. Material Culture as Memory: Combs and Cremation in Early Medieval Britain. *Early Medieval Europe* 12, pp. 89-128.

Wickham, C. 2002. Rural Economy and Society. In: *Italy in the Early Middle Ages.* C. La Rocca, (ed.). Short Oxford History of Italy. Oxford: Oxford University Press, pp.118-143.

Wolfram, H. 1979. *Die Goten.* Munich: Beck.

RITUAL MEMORY AND THE RITUALS OF MEMORY: CAROLINGIAN AND POST-CAROLINGIAN KINGSHIP

Maria Fiano

Abstract

Although death is universally perceived as a moment of fracture and crisis, funerary rituals suprisingly are almost completely absent from the rituals of Carolingian kingship between the ninth and eleventh centuries. Following K. F. Werner (1985), according to whom the period of a *mutatio regni* is one of extreme political frailty, we would expect – as a consequence of the nature of the period analyzed – the heavy exploitation and staging of suitable rituals concerning death and its aftermath. Contemporary sources, however, do not report episodes linked to funerary rituals comparable to those that were staged in later times (Kantorowicz 1957). This may be explained by a sharp shift of attention from the importance given to the moments/events of death and burial – resulting in rich grave goods found in burials well into the eighth century – to remembrance. Memory of the past, as a matter of fact, legitimated the present power, guaranteed the power to come, and offered salvation for the soul. If, on the one hand, this process can be considered a generalized one not only employed by kings, then it is in the rituals of kingship, on the other hand, where it should be most easily detected, thanks to the wealth of documentation related to them. Analyzing the death of several kings it has been possible to outline the strategies used in the management of memory, namely: a) rituals, which include prayers to save the soul, special masses, donations and remembrance banquets, and the bestowal of the symbols of power on the successor; b) the choice of the places of burial, which can be seen as a sign of continuity or break with tradition; c) practices of re-use, in which gestures and objects are re-used in a clear process of *imitatio regni*.

The management of remembrance strategies, moreover, leads to the analysis of women's roles as keepers of memory, corresponding to two diverging and conflicting models, as has been clearly shown (Geary 1994 a-b). In addition, writing down the rituals of remembrance allowed those in control of the writing processes to also control the memory of the past and, therefore, the interpretation of the present.

Keywords: Early Middle Ages, Carolingian Europe, rituals of memory, funerary rituals.

***

Introduction: ritual memory

In February 874, Louis the German travelled to Frankfurt, where he consulted his retainers on "the harmony and the state of the kingdom." Louis spent Lent in prayer. One night, his father, Emperor Louis the Pious, appeared to him in a dream, suffering and tormented, *in angustiis*; speaking Latin, his father asked to be freed from these torments. Louis woke up, shaken by that vision, and immediately sent out letters to every monastery in his kingdom, asking the monks to pray for the salvation of the deceased emperor's soul. On Easter day, Louis himself visited Fulda monastery in order to pray and commemorate his father. The sufferings tormenting the late emperor would have been not so much due to his remorse for a particular sin as to his lack of authority, to the fact that he had not been able to act against the evils spreading across his empire. The vision is reported in the annals of Fulda and is not unique in its kind.[1] A whole series of royal visions were presented during this period, in which both kings and emperors were seen suffering unspeakable torments in the Otherworld as a consequence of their sins or deficiencies. Prayers, fasts, and acts of charity were deemed necessary, not only to remember them but also to deliver them from those pains (Février, 1981; MacGuire, 1989; Wollasch, 1990; McLaughlin, 1994; Lawers, 1996; Treffort, 1996).

---

1. *Annales Fuldenses*, year 874: "Venit enim virca Kalendas Februar ad Franconofurt ibique de concordia et statu regni cum fidelibus suis consiliatus est. Diebus autem quadragesimuae cum negotiis secularium rerum depositis orationi vacaret., vidit quadam nocte in somnis genitorem suum Hludowicum imperatorem in angustiis constitutum, qui eum hoc modo latino affatus est eloquio: «Adiuro te per dominum nostrum Iseu Christum et per trinam maiestatem, ut me eripias ab his tormentis, in quibus detineor, ut tandem aliquando vitam possim habere aeternam». Hac ergo visione perterritus epistolas per cuncta regni sui monasteria destinavit, obnixe postulans, ut animae in tormentis positae suis apud Dominum precibus intervenirent. Rex autem Hludowicus in ebdomada paschali Fuldense monasterium (causa orationis) petiit et inde reversus generalem habuit conventum in villa Tribure".

The importance these prayers had for the salvation of the soul in this period – often in conjunction with donations to support and pay for them – is remarkable, even for those who practised pre-Purgatory. We see here the staging of actual rituals related to the remembrance of the dead that ensured the survival of memory, and, at the same time, the legitimacy of the present, rooted in that memory and in that tradition. To analyse this kind of memory, therefore, seems to be fruitful, especially if we consider ritual memory and the rituals of memory; far from being just a clever word play these phrases exemplify the parallel tracks on which this study will run. The place where the protagonists of visions – both laymen and clerics – meet kings and queens is half-way between hell and purgatory, a kind of limbo, which the souls can leave (i.e. save themselves) only through the intervention of the living – with prayers and acts of charity. The diffusion of these visions and these travels in the Otherworld emphasize the possibility of an exchange between the dead and the living. (Le Goff, 1981; Février, 1987; Paxton, 1990).

First, I will consider the functioning of memory in the act of re-telling it: i.e. how the act of remembering itself works, with particular attention to the degree of selectivity (and the degree of consciousness in this selectivity) of memory, and to how the events are subsequently reported (what is remembered and what is forgotten, and why). Second, I will focus on the funerary rituals of the Carolingian Era, and in particular on the fact that the attention of contemporary sources shifted from the moment of ritualised burial to that of remembrance, thus, inserting itself into the rituals linked to family memory. It seems to me that the description of the rituals connected to the preservation and keeping of memory offers some models of remembrance which include legitimacy in the succession to the throne and the role played by queens as keepers of family memory (Geary 1994 a, b; Goetz 2002; Schneidmüller 2002; McKitterick 2004).

Surprisingly, the sources relating to the Carolingian and post-Carolingian periods do not describe specific funerary rituals. The moment of succession to power, I would argue, was always fraught with difficulties; especially when there was no legitimate heir (Goody 1966; Dierkens 1991; Nelson 2000). The moment of the break with the past, then, was particularly symbolic and therefore needed to be ritualised. However, if we except the instances offered by Lothar's funeral in 986, described by Richer,[2] and Otto

III's funeral,[3] and some mentions of the ritual practices enacted when a king died, such as the transmission of his symbols of power to his successor (Charles the Bald to his son Louis, Conrad of Francony to Henry I, and Otto III, passively, to Henry II), it seems to me that contemporaries were not interested in describing the staging of funerary rituals, as was the case later on. What is striking in the analysis of the contemporary sources is not so much the lack of description of funerary rituals as the chroniclers' lack of attention in recording the ritual in detail. The fact that many elements occur with a certain consistency in these descriptions leaves room for the suspicion that some rituals were in fact carried out at the death of a king: e.g. funerary processions, lamentations and complaints, transmission of insignia. Janet Nelson remarks that when funerary rituals are the prerogative of laymen – especially of women – their function is not reported with due attention by the contemporary chroniclers, the opposite of what occurred when the Church gained control of funerary rituals (Nelson, 2000).

In January 814, Charlemagne died and was buried in Aachen. Eginhardt tells us that "the body was solemnly washed and prepared... carried to the church and buried... there were doubts about the place where he had wished to be buried, because when alive he had not given instructions on the subject."[4] It is worth noting some elements: a) first the speed with which the burial was carried out: Eginard lets us understand that the burial took place on the same day as the death; b) second, Eginhardt uses a passive sentence, probably to keep anonymous the identity of those who dealt with the king's funeral;

2. Richerio, *Historia*, III 109-110: "Ingenti itaque luctu tota personat domus; fit sonitus diversus, clamor varius; nemini enim eorum qui aderant inlacrimabilis erat ea calamitas." "Interea magnifice funus regium multo divitiarum regalium ambitu accuratur. Fit ei lectus regalibus insignibus adornatus; corpus bissina veste induitur, ac desuper palla purpurea gemmis ornata auroque intexta operitur. Lectum regnorum primates deferebant. Preibant episcopi et celrus cum evangelis et crucibus; penes quos etiam ejus coronam ferebat multo auro gemmisque pretiosis nitentem cum aliis multis insignibus ejulando incedebant. Funebre melos lacrimis impedientibus vix prosequebantur; reliqua quoque manus cum lamentis succedebat. Sepultus est Remis in coenobio monachorum sancti Remigii, cum patre et matre, sicut ante jusserat suis; quod etiam abest

CCXL stadiis ab eo loco in quo finem vitae accepit; multo obsequio universorum parique affectu per tantum spatiideductus".
3. Tietmaro, Chronicon, IV 49-53:
c. 50: "Exin cum ad Pollingun, curtem Sigifridi presulis Augustane, veniret, ab Heinrico duce suscepti lacrimis eiusdem vehementer iterum commoti sunt. Quos singulatim, ut se in dominum sibi et regem eligere voluissent, multis promissionibus hortatur; et corpus imperatoris cum apparatu imperiali, lancea dumtaxat excepta, quam Heribertus archipresul clam premittens suam sumpsit in potestatem".
c. 51: "Dux vero cum his Augustanam attingens urbem, dilecti senioris intestina duabus lagunculis prius diligenter reposita in oratorio sancti presulis Othelrici, quod in onorem eius Liudulfus, eiusdem ecclesiae episcopus, construxit, in australi parte monasterii sanctae martyris Afrae sepulturae honorabili tradidit et ob animae remedium suae C mansos propriae hereditatis concessit. Deindeque dimissa cum pace magna multitudine ad civitatem suam, quae Nova vocatur, corpus cesaris prosequitur."
c. 53: "Cuius corpus cum ad Coloniam veniret, primo susceptum est ab archiepiscopo eiusdem civitatis Heriberto. Ad monasterium sancti Severini post palmas II. Feria, ad sanctum Pantaleonem III defertur feria, ad sanctum Gereonem III die. In cena Domini ad sanctum Petrum portatur, ubi, penitentibus more aecclesiastico introductis et indulgentia resolutis, animae presentis corporis ab archipresule remissio datur, a consacerdotibus autem memoria exposcitur, lacrimabiliter autem a populo supplici impenditur. VI. Feria illucescente funus elevatum, ad Aquisgrani sancto perducitur in sabbato; die vero dominica in aecclesia sanctae Mariae semper virginis in medio sepelitur choro." More concise Rodolph, Historiarum I, 15: "Cernens quoque exercitus quem secum duxerat suo domino destitutum, coegerunt se pariter in unum agmen, ne ab his quos in Italia presserant trucidarentur, imposito ante se in equo defuncti imperatoris corpore, sicque in patriam tuti pervenientes in monasterio Beate semper virginis Mariae Aquisgrani decenter sepelierunt".
4. Eginardo, *Vita Karoli*, c. 31.

c) at the moment of his death, Louis his son, was in Aquitaine, but he visited Aachen exactly 30 days after his father's death: at the most important moment in the remembrance of the dead. Louis did not take part, and did not organise, his father's funeral; on the other hand, he took pains to control the moment of his commemoration. The Astronomer, in contrast with Eginhardt, asserts in quite a generic way that Louis provided for his father's funeral, silencing remarks, as it were, on the king's absence[5] and 'forgetting' the difficult situation in which the king found himself at that moment, emphasising instead his role as legitimate heir, a role expressed specifically by the care he took over his predecessor's funeral; d) it is worth noting that Charlemagne's body was buried in a Late Antique sarcophagus, carved in marble, brought to France from Italy and prepared especially for this purpose. Janet Nelson emphasises two elements of this practice: the choice – made by Charlemagne and later by Louis the Pious – to be buried in a sarcophagus as gesture of *imitatio imperii* towards Byzantium. After the imperial coronation, as a matter of fact, the Byzantine emperor customarily chose the marble for his own sarcophagus; another element stands out in the choice of ornaments for Charlemagne's sarcophagus: the rape of Proserpine, seen in the *interpretatio Christiana* as a symbol of the soul ascending to heaven. But it is also possible to read this choice of theme in light of a "question of gender," i.e. it is possible to postulate that the choice, and indeed the whole funerary ritual, could have been arranged by Charlemagne's daughters. This, moreover, would explain Eginhardt's conscious silence on the funeral – about the sarcophagus and the identity of the organisers of the funeral, and also the fact that, once he ascended to the throne, Louis took great pains to drive his sisters away from the palace. (Nelson 2000).

In the year 1000, Otto III was in Aachen. He dreamt of the place where Charlemagne was buried; the next day, in a well-known episode related by numerous sources, the king had the sarcophagus opened. In the 1030s, the compiler of the *Chronicle of Novalesa*, and later Ademar of Chabannes, built a legend on this find that took on the significance of a symbolic passage of power from Charlemagne to Otto III, and, more significantly still, from the Carolingians to the Ottonians.[6]

In the premonitory dream, the emperor was found sitting upright as if still on his throne. Otto III's gestures towards his predecessor (he dressed him, cut his nails, etc.) must be interpreted within a funerary context. The times and modes of memory – for Louis the Pious as for Otto III – were then strategic for those who intended to legitimate their power.

Re-use – remembrance – women's roles: these are the issues that I intend to examine here. But the concept of re-use must be considered, in my opinion, in its wider meaning: not only the re-use of objects, such as Charlemagne's sarcophagus, but also of gestures and places – as in Otto III's example – to bolster their position in the present through the power and the memory of the past.

In this same direction we must interpret the choice of ritual places – of anointing and burial – made by the first Capetians to ascend to power. The newly elected kings, or kings that had just managed to obtain power, immediately took care to emphasise the connections linking them with their predecessors, and repeat their rituals and gestures in order to enhance the sense of continuity. In the same way, the newcomers trod upon and re-used their ritual places; Hugh Capet was anointed in 987 at Noyon, the same place where Charlemagne had been crowned in 768; he was then buried in St. Denis, the Carolingian family remembrance monastery par excellence. Hugh's son, Robert the Pious, was anointed at Orleans, where Charles the Bald had been anointed (one of the three times he was anointed) and buried in St. Denis as well.

The analysis of Carolingian and Capetian kings' choice of consecration, coronation and burial places highlights the fact that these choices played an important part in the establishment of a dynastic continuity of power (Werner 1985 and 1995). Hugh Capet, for example, chose Noyon as the place for his coronation and unction – following Charlemagne. His choice was meant to affirm dynastic continuity with the Carolingian family (Bautier 1992).

Rituals of memory

In 1002, Otto III died suddenly while in Italy, without heirs and, more important still, without leaving any suggestion as to who should succeed him. Three candi-

---

5. Eginardo, *Vita Karoli*, c. 20.

6. Annales Altahenses, year 1000: "Aquisgrani, magni imperatoris Caroli ossa a pluribus in scia quaesivit" and Annales di Hildesheim, year 1000: "Pentecostes autem celebritatem digna devozione Aquisgrani feriavit quo tunc admirationis causa magni imperatoris Karoli ossa contra divinae rligionis ecclesiastica effondere praecepit, quae tunc in abdito sepolturae mirificas varietatis inventi". Thietmar Marseburgensis, Chronicon, IV, 47: "Karoli cesaris ossa ubi requiescerent, cum dubitaret, rupto clam pavimento, ubi ea esse putavit, fodere, quousque haec in solio inventa sunt regio, iussit. Crucem auream, quae in collo eius ppendit, cum vestimentorum parte adhuc imputribilium sumens, caetera cum veneratione magna reposuit." Ademaro of Chabannes, Historiarum libri tres, III, 31: "Quibus diebus Otto imperator per somnum monitus est ut levaret corpus Caroli Magni imperatoris, quod Aquis humatus erat, sed vetustate obliterante, ignorabatur locus certus, ubi quiescebat. Et peracto triduano

jejunio, inventus est eo loco, quem per visum cognoverat imperator, sedens in aurea cathedra, intra arcuatam speluncam, infra basilicam Marie, coronatus corona ex auro et gemmis, tenens sceptrum et ensem ex auro purissimo, et ipsum corpus incorruptum inventum est. Quod levatum populis demonstratum est. Quidam vero canonicarum ejusdem loci, Adalbertus, cum enormi et procero corpore esset, coronam Caroli quasi pro mensura capiti suo circumponens, inventus est strictiori vertice, coronam ampitudine sua vincentem circulum capitis.... Corpus vero Caroli conditum in dextro membro basilicae ipsius retro altare sancti Johannis Baptistae, et cripta aurea super illud mirifica est fabbricata, multisque signis et miraculis clarescere cepit". Cronaca di Novalesa, III, c. 32. Folz (1973). The smell at the opening of graves is saints' smell. Oldoni, (1971) and H. Günter, (1954). The monk who writes the chronicle reports Count Otto's account. The analysis of memory's rituals depends also by the analysis of the events' memory.

dates stepped forward: Henry of Bavaria, Ekkehardt of Meissen, and Hermann of Swabia.

J. W. Bernhardt remarks that in the year 1003 (15 January) Henry II sent a charter to Strasbourg, thanking Bishop Werner for his loyalty and for his support. At the same time, he punished Duke Hermann of Swabia, who represented their common political opponent and who had opposed the crowning of Henry II by plundering the seat of Strasbourg. The duke was forced to make important concessions in favour of the bishop. The *narratio* of the charter is interesting: Henry II was actually emphasizing his close friendship with the deceased Otto III and also their kinship, something which persuaded the bishop to support him against other candidates. With God's help, the people's consent, and according to hereditary right, Henry II was elected king (Bernhardt 1993).

Henry of Bavaria, who was the winner in the end, did his best to emphasise the legitimacy of his succession, broadcasting the closeness and kinship connecting him to his predecessor. For these reasons he visited Polling, in southern Bavaria, in order to meet the funerary procession carrying Otto's body to Aachen. Thietmar says that he accompanied the procession to Augsburg and Neuburg and that he then let it proceed towards Aachen.

The Duke Henry meets in tears the procession carrying Otto's body at Polling, a meeting during which he has the chance to obtain the royal ensigns. He accompanies the train until Augsburg, where he buries the intestines in St Ulrich Chapel, and donates 100 landunits for the salvation of Otto III's soul. Then he accompanies the procession to Neuburg, on the Danube. Before leaving, he instructs his brother-in-law, Henry of Luxembourg, to follow the body until Aachen.

Adalbold, who basically relied on Thietmar's account, added some details to this description. Two of these details are of crucial importance in the representation of the legitimate succession of Henry II. First, he affirmed that when Henry met the procession, he worshipped the body of his 'kinsman' together with the whole army accompanying him; moreover, the author specified that Henry would have carried Otto's coffin on his shoulders, a clear gesture of humility and piety towards his predecessor. These two distinct moments, worship and humility, represented the public manifestation of the heir to the throne's legitimacy.[7]

Adalbold, however, differed from Thietmar's account in another respect, this time not in something he added but in something he did not write: he omitted the account of the organisation of the funerals carried out by Archbishop Heribert from Cologne to Aachen during Holy Week. Thietmar, reporting the whole episode, says that Otto's body was brought in procession to some churches in Cologne and then brought to Aachen, where it was buried on Easter Sunday in St. Mary's Basilica under the direction of the archbishop.[8] The following year, in 1003, Henry celebrated the anniversary of Otto's death in Aachen. He was, by then, already king (he was crowned and anointed in Mainz in July 1002). Three and a half years later, on 6 July 1005, Henry made a donation in favour of Otto III's burial place, specifying the reason for the donation as: "the salvation of Charlemagne's, Otto III's, Henry's kinsmen and predecessors, and his own salvation as well," thus, constructing a significant royal genealogy. This represents the final moment of Otto III's funerary celebration.

These continuous references to memory are some of the instruments through which the ruling elite asserted and re-asserted their own position and function, justifying themselves through tradition and therefore through their own predecessors. Henry II's gestures served to affirm his position in relation to the past and represented his desire to remember sections of this past, which thus, became the guarantee of his present power. Adalbold, as a matter of fact, specified the fact that Henry joined the procession behaving like a member of the deceased emperor's family, and as such he took the coffin on his shoulders. It is through the commemorative gestures that Adalbod tells the story of Henry's succession to the throne, emphasising some crucial elements and omitting others in order to construct a representation of remembrance and, therefore, of legitimacy.

Funerary rituals – remembrance rituals

Within the context of remembrance rituals, given the enormous breadth of the subject, I will analyse in particular *pro anima* donations as an instance of exchange between the dead and the living (Wollasch 1990). As a matter of fact, between the eight and ninth centuries, we see offices for the deceased spread across the Western world: usually in the form of a series of prayers regularly intoned by a religious community. Roughly in the same period, the custom of organising cycles of three, seven or thirty day suffrages took hold, together with the practice of holding "private" masses for the salvation of the soul of the dead, to be celebrated on the anniversary of their death. During this period, *confraternitae* or *societae*, societies of bishops and abbots, committing their members to the organisation of liturgical services (chanting of psalms and special masses) when one of the brothers died, developed and spread across Europe. Acts of charity towards the poor and donations to monasteries in order to sustain monks and abbots became increasingly

---

7. Adalbold decides not to write about the part of Otto III's funerals that is managed by the archbishop of Cologne. He prefers to note only the part where Henry II is the protagonist.

8. Thietmar V, 15-18: "Bernhardus igitur dux, accepta in manibus sacra lancea, ex parte omnium regni curam illi fideliter committit" and V, 20: "Quo in nativitate sancte Marie a primatibus Luithariorum in regem collaudatur et in sedem regiam more antecessorum suorum exaltatur et magnificatur".

associated with prayers *pro anima* and "special masses." Odilo, to mention an example regarding the liturgy of death at Cluny, includes in his Constitution the maintenance of a poor man for thirty days by the monastic community in order to commemorate a dead brother; on the anniversary of Henry II's death (30 July), the same community sustained twelve poor men for seven days.

In 796 for example, Charlemagne donated a cell to St. Denis where his father was buried and where he himself wished to be buried, specifying that the rents of the donation should serve to sustain 10 to 15 monks, whose role was to pray for him and Pepin. The monks, in fact, prayed for the king's soul and the well-being of the whole kingdom. Otto Gerhard Oexle observes that the *Notitia de servitio monasteriorum*, ca. 819, presents a list of royal monasteries subdivided into three categories according to the service they offered to the king: 1) *dona et militiam*; 2) *sola dona sine militia*; and 3) *nec dona nec militiam, sed solas orationes pro salute imperatoris vel filiorum eius et stabilitate imperii* (Oexle 1993).

These donations comprised an actual exchange between the living and the dead -- rents and remembrance -- through the mediation of churches and monasteries, the currency of which were represented by lands and prayers, material wealth, and salvation of the soul. The lands were bequeathed to churches and monasteries, in the first instance, to ensure the maintenance of memory. The second reason was to reciprocate with masses and prayers, within the model of gift and counter-gift proposed by Mauss. However, the model according to which a gift is given in exchange for another, earlier, gift is not sufficient to explain this particular kind of barter linking the earthly wealth to the Otherworld. It does not take into account the transformation of the goods that takes place during the transaction; the object donated acquires, in the process of being distributed, an added symbolic value. D. Iogna-Prat (1990), in particular, insists on the relevance in this exchange of lands-for-prayers (or funerary lights vs. lunches, maintenance of the community vs. charity to the poor), of the role played by the poor as objects of the *caritas* of the donor. The former was not only the explicit manifestation of the latter's generosity, but also represented some kind of "transformer," altering the nature of the gift.

In 877, the Empress Engelberga had her will drawn up in the monastery of San Salvatore in Brescia. In it she specified that every year a mass should be held in honour of the deceased Louis II and that on the day of the anniversary of his death, 300 poor should be fed, establishing the same procedure exactly for her anniversary. Interestingly, 24 poor were to be fed and clothed, also *pro anima*, twelve in memory of Louis and twelve in memory of Engelberga herself.

The choice of the twelve poor to be fed seems to me particularly significant; the number of the poor summoned up the image of the Last Supper and thus, their

sustenance represented that sacrifice. The procedure itself is quite linear; a donation was made to a monastery (with particular connections to the king), and it served to sustain the monks or the poor or to buy lights for the monastery. In return, commemorative prayers were offered in honour of one (or more) deceased person(s) connected to the donor. A material gift in return for a spiritual one, a spiritual obligation, lands in return for prayers. The distribution of food and wealth took on liturgical functions. To feed the poor, organise lunches/ banquets for the monastic communities as one was able, represented a way to secure salvation of the soul for oneself and one's own family.

The widow as keeper of family memory

In 936, Henry I of Saxony died at Memleben. His wife Mathilda, was in tears at his deathbed (the topos of tears falling at the moment of the death of the king is a continuously repeating emotional model: the crying people, the crying army, etc.). Wracked by pain, she had the deceased king's body brought to Quedlinburg, where a monastery was founded on lands from her dowry. The female section of the monastery was immediately taken under the queen's direction and Mathilda affirmed her wish to be buried in this newly founded place. The site of Quedlinburg became both a place of remembrance and the burial site of the whole Saxon dynasty, a place where, for example, Easter was celebrated by the family.

On her husband's death, Mathilda became the *rectrix* of Quedlinburg monastery. Before her death she made one of the daughters that Otto I had with Adheleid, also named Mathilda, head of the monastery. The practice of placing one of the royal daughters at the head of a monastery, as abbess or *rectrix*, was common not only in the Saxon dynasty but also in the Italian kingdom. For example, in 878, Hermengard, Louis II's daughter became abbess at San Salvatore, the monastery of Brescia; she was followed by Charles the Fat's daughter and then Berengar's daughter (La Rocca 2002; Le Jan 1995, 2001).

Does Mathilda's description fall into a known model of reference? Like, for example, the one presenting her as a devoted widow? At the moment of Henry's death, the widowed queen donated her golden arm-rings to the priest so that he would sing a mass for the salvation of her husband's soul.[9] This donation recalls slightly what we have already observed about the exchange between the dead and the living: material objects for prayers and salvation. In this case, the donation was constituted

9. Vita Matildis reginae posterior, c. 8: "Postea surgens interrogavit, si adhuc aliquis ieiunaret, qui animae sui domini missam decantaret? Audiens hoc Adeldach presbiter, respondit festinus: Domina, nondum quidquam gustavimus. Venerabilis regina olim induerat duas armillas mira arte celatas, quae tanta firmitate brachiis fuerant circumdatae, ut sine auxilio fabri nullatenus possent divelli. Has tunc minimo tangens digito, citus dicto excussit, ita ad presbiterum dicens: «Accipe tibi hoc aureum, et canta missam animarum»."

by jewels, which represented the social status and the wealth of the queen and were also bequeathed in order to show her generosity – an exclusively royal prerogative – in exchange for a long-term commemoration of Henry I, founder of the Saxon dynasty.

Mathilda ensured that Henry's soul received a three-layered commemorative celebration at Quedlinburg, and her acts/gestures already began at the king's deathbed. An activity of intense memory keeping and preservation, which was complemented by the prayers sung by the nuns of Nordhausen, another Saxon foundation *pro anima Regis et carissimi fili*. The son referred to here was Henry, Otto's brother.

P. Corbet observes that Mathilda's biography was written with clear hagiographic aims. He also remarks that the description of Mathilda's widowhood occupies twenty of the twenty-eight chapters which constitute the text. P. Corbet points out all the main features of queen's widowhood, but here we are interested only in the last one, i.e. the practice of prayer and acts for the salvation of the king's soul: "dès le dernier soupir du roi, elle fait dire une messe des ames à l'intention de son mari, un geste que l'hagiographe souligne avec une particulière insistance" (Corbet 1993).

The intent of the *Vita Mathildis Posterior*, this kind of biography of Mathilda ordered by Henry II and composed by an anonymous author in the monastery, was to emphasise and justify the providential succession of Henry II himself. Unfortunately, there is no space here to examine another extremely interesting and complex issue, that of the use of names, but I wish, nonetheless, to emphasise the fact that at least two mechanisms were used in this *Vita* to support Henry's ascension to the throne in 1002: the emphasis on names and the gestures and actions connected with the commemoration of the dead. The young Henry was named after Henry I, with the devoted Mathilda manifesting her preference towards the younger branch of the family while still performing the remembrance rituals for her beloved husband; Henry thus, seemed almost predestined to obtain the crown. In this manner, the act of commemoration became the ultimate argument supporting Henry II's succession. (Corbet 1986).

There is a precedent to this *Vita*, i.e. the *Vita Mathildis Anterioris*, which does not emphasise the same aspects examined here. Composed at the beginning of Otto II's reign and dedicated to him by an anonymous author at Nordhausen, it is concerned not so much with providing elements of legitimacy in favour of Henry II as in finding illustrious and ancient origins for the Ottonian dynasty, by listing the names of legendary ancestors. The image of the devoted widow is found here as well. At the death of her nephew, Mathilda donated cloth for his funeral originally destined for her own burial. This cloth was substituted by a *pallium auro intextum* sent by Gerberga. The *Vita Mathildis Posterior* adds the fact that

on this occasion the queen ordered the poor to be assembled in order to receive charity and thus intercede in favour of William's soul (Corbet 1986; Geary 1994a).

P. Geary, in his *Phantoms of Remembrance*, compares two distinct accounts of the last moments of two Saxon queens: Adelaide and Mathilda. Here we are confronted with two different ways to understand the relationship between the dead and the living, and the role played by men and women in this relationship, two different ways, in short, of constructing memory and commemoration. (Geary 1994a). Also in this case, there are two different aspects of memory: a) the role played by queens in the act of remembrance; b) the queens as objects of memory, i.e. how they themselves were remembered.

Odilo of Cluny, author of Adelaide's epitaph, tells us that when her son Otto II died, Adelaide made a series of donations to different monasteries, among them Montecassino, Cluny, and St. Martin of Tours, so that their monks would pray to the memory of her son. She turned to one monk in particular from the latter monastery, entrusting him with the task of commemorating her son. Odilo portrayed the queen as a charitable and discreet woman, presenting a picture of the queen as a devoted widow (first passage). The acts of remembrance consisted of making donations to male monasteries, asking the monks to pray for deceased kinsmen on the day of the anniversary of their death (second passage). Let us compare this with the image portrayed in the *Vita Mathildis*: if the first passages, i.e. the portrayal of the dying empress, can be considered analogous, the same cannot be said about the second passage, relating to the enactment of the remembrance of the deceased. As the fatal hour of her death draws nearer, the queen called her granddaughter Mathilda, Otto I's daughter, and gave her a *computarium* on which were listed the names of the dead kinsmen to be remembered. Mathilda, moreover, entrusted her granddaughter with the soul of Henry I, her own soul and the souls of all the family members whose names were included in the list. Mathilda's role was active and direct, i.e. the queen acted in the first person for the commemoration of her husband and her kin.[10]

As in the case of other contemporary texts, women – and here I am referring to queens in particular – not only made donations to monastic communities so that they would pray for their deceased husbands and sons, they also prayed, offered alms, and fasted. That is what was expected of a widow. We could say that the role of a

---

10. Vita Mathildis reginae antiquior, c. 13; Vita Mathildis reginae posterior, c. 26: "Post haec praecepit, ut omnes exirent in pace Christi, nisi qui necessaria sibi essent ministraturi. Tunc ad se vocavit suam neptulam abbatissam Mathildam, filiam Ottonis imperatoris, salutaria illi dans monita, ut esset pia et humilis, prudens et cauta, ac sibi commissum gregem custodiret, et ut monasterium raro egrederetur, ne secularibus dedita a Christi servitio impediretur. Dedit etiam ei in manum computarium, in quo nomina defunctorum davit et suam, et omnium fidelium, quorum memoriam recolebat."

widow was strongly connected to the commemoration of the dead, complemented by the obligation not to marry again. This is the model of the good widow who honours the memory of her husband with her behaviour.

The role of keeper of memory, therefore, includes not only prayers, but also alms and fasting, which the Saxon queens more often than not performed themselves instead of leaving it to monasteries. It is clear that not only queens followed this behaviour, as we have already seen, but in their case, thanks to their visibility and economic possibilities, such behavior became more explicit. The queens became, therefore, responsible for the well-being of their husbands' souls in the next life. As Corbet has rightly observed, the opposite is not true. Otto I never prayed for the salvation of the soul of the deceased Edith. (Corbet 1986).

In a Frankish context, however, the sources do not present the same behavioural pattern. In the West, remembrance was confined to the male sphere, and in particular to reformed monks. The studies carried out by David Herlihy in 1962 on the charters of donations made by laymen, like those carried out by Penny Gold (1985) on charters from the Anjou area, confirm that the economic role of women between East and West was similar: the demographic pattern was similar as was the influence exerted by women over propriety (Herlihy 1962; Gold 1985). Moreover, it can be observed that in the West there were queens who appeared politically active, for example, Gerberga, Henry's daughter and Otto's sister. But even in the case of strong and politically active queens, there was no corresponding active role in the safeguarding of family memory. The importance of nunneries directed by members of the Carolingian family is simply not comparable with those in Saxony.

The images of Adelaide and Mathilda reflect two distinct models of remembrance. The first, connected to Cluny and to the sphere of reformed monasticism, committed the prerogative of memory to the monks, and the second, connected to the Saxon and imperial environment, entrusted this role to queens or women in general. The authors of the two accounts, therefore, use the acts of remembrance available through their own models of reference.

In France it was the men who were concerned with the keeping of memory. In a period slightly later than the one considered here, Peter the Venerable, in his *De Miraculis*, contrasted the infidelity of women in exercising their obligations towards memory with the effectiveness of Cluny's intervention. Peter tells the tale of a woman who kept the money destined for the commemoration of her husband for herself. Peter also tells the story of the spirit of a mercenary who appeared to his lord, asking to obtain from the woman the eight *solidos* which she should have spent for the salvation of his soul, but which she had kept for herself instead. The same spirit revealed that it was only thanks to the prayers of Cluny

that King Alphonse had been saved from the torments he was experiencing.

Conclusions

The memory of the past, then, laid the foundations for: a) the legitimisation of present power (Charlemagne; Otto III); b) the aspiration to a guarantee of future power (Henry II controlled Otto's funeral, but also the models presenting women as mediators between past and present); c) the salvation of the soul (the exchange between the present – the lands – and the Otherworld, through prayers for the dead).

I would just like to make some points about what has been said so far:

It seems to me that it is impossible to deny the importance of the practices of remembrance, given the attention to which they were subjected by medieval contemporaries;

The existence of and the desire for continuity in the relationship connecting the dead to the living is equally undeniable, through the mediation of the church and of the monasteries which stood surety for the continuity of memory, for the possibility of perpetuating the memory. The shared implications that can be attributed to this exchange include the concept of transformation of the objects and the idea of giving in order to receive something back.

It appears, therefore, as if the sphere of remembrance and memory was of utmost importance, since – in a way – those who controlled the memory exerted *de facto* authority over the tradition, the past which justified both the present and the future. In exactly the same way, those who controlled writing exerted a strong influence over the account of the events.

Finally, I think it is possible to identify some remembrance models of reference, i.e. to think about the possibility of commemoration in terms of a search for a legitimisation of the present. Therefore, the weight of tradition can be off-set both by written records, and thus by the management of the memory of given events, and by the very practices of remembrance relating to the events which are themselves presented in those [written] accounts.

Acknowledgments

The author thanks all those gave her suggestions and information on the subject and especially to dott. Andrea Pennacchi for her English translation.

Bibliography

Bautier, R. H. 1992. L'avénement d'Hugues Capet et le sacre de Robert le Pieux. In: M. Parisse, X. Barral I Altat, (eds), *Le roi de France et son royaume autours de l'an mil.* Actes du colloque « Hugues Capet 987-1987. La France de l'an Mil » (Paris-Senlis 22-25 octobre 1987), Les Belles Lettres: Paris, pp. 27-38.

Bernhardt, J. W. (1993). *Itinerant Kingship and Royal Monasteries in Early Medieval Germany, 936-1075*, Cambridge University Press: Cambridge.

Carozzi, C. (1990). Les carolingiens dans l'au-delà. In: M. Sot, (ed.), *Haut Moyen Age, culture, éducation, société: études offerts à Pierre Riché*. La Garenne-Colombes-Eitions Européennes Erasme: Paris, pp. 367-376.

Carozzi, C. 1994. *Le voyage de l'âme dans l'au-delà* d'après la littérature latine Ve-XIIIe siècle, Collection de l'Ecole française de Rome: Roma.

Corbet, P. 1986. *Les saints ottoniens. Sainteté dynastique, saniteté royale et sainteté féminine autour de l'an Mil*, J. Thorbecke ed: Paris.

Corbet, P. 1993. Pro anima seniori sui. La pastorale ottonienne du veuvage. In: M. Parisse, (ed), *Veuves et veuvage dans le haut moyen age*. Picard: Paris.

Dierkens, A. 1991. Autour de la tombe de Charlemagne. *Byzantion* 51, pp. 156-180.

Dutton, P. 1994. *The Politics of Dreaming in the Carolingian Empire*, University of Nebraska Press:Nebraska.

Février, P.-A. 1981. Quelques aspects de la prière pour les morts. In: *La Prière au Moyen-Age*, Colloque du CUERMA: Aix en Provence.

Février, P.-A. 1987. La mort chrétienne. In: *Segni e riti nella chiesa altomedievale occidentale*, Settimane del CISAM 37/ II, Spoleto, pp. 881-952.

Fichtenau, H. 1991. *Living in the Tenth Century*. The University of Chicago Press: Chicago.

Folz, R. 1973. *Le souvenir et la légende de Charlemagne dans l'empire germanique médiéval*, Slatkine reprints: Geneva.

Geary, P. 1994a. *Phantoms of Rememebrance : Memory and Oblivion at the End of the First Millennium*, Princeton University Press: Princeton.

Geary, P. 1994b. *Living with the Dead in the Middle Ages*, Cornell University Press: Ithaca.

Goetz, H. W. 2002. The Concept of Time. In: Althoff, J. Fried, P. Geary, (eds), *Medieval Concepts of the Past. Ritual, Memory, Historiography*. Cambridge University Press: Cambridge. pp. 138-165

Gold, P. S. 1985. The Lady and the Virgin: Image, Attitude and Experience in Twelth-Century France. In: *Women in Culture and Society*, vol. number 7, The University of Chicago Press: Chicago, pp. 13-35.

Goody, J. 1966. *Succession to High Office*, Cambridge University Press:Cambridge.

Herlihy, D. 1962. Land, Family, and Women in Continental Europe 701-1200. *Traditio* 18, pp. 89-120.

Kantorowicz, E. H. 1957. *The King's Two Bodies. A Study in Medieval Political Theology*. Princeton University Press:Princeton.

Iogna-Prat, D. 1990. Les morts dans la comptabilité céleste des clunisiens de l'an Mil. In: D. Iogna-Prat,

J.-C. Picard, (eds.), *Religion et culture autour de l'an Mil. Royaume capétien et Lotharingie*. Picard:Paris, pp. 55-69.

Lawers, M. 1996. Le «sépulcre des péres» et les «ancêtres». *Médiévales* 31, pp. 67-78.

La Rocca, C. 2002. Les cadeaux nuptiaux de la famille royale en Italie. In: F. Bougard, L. Feller, R. Le Jan, (eds.), *Dots et douaires dans le haut Moyen Age*. Collection de l'Ecole française de Rome, No.295, pp.123-142.

Le Goff, J. 1981, *La nascita del purgatorio*. Einaudi:Turin

Le Jan, R. 2001. Aux origines du douaire médiéval (VIe-Xe siècle). In : R. Le Jan, (ed.), *Femmes, pouvoir et société dans le haut Moyen Age*. Picard: Paris, pp. 53-67.

Le Jan, R 1995. *Famille et pouvoir dans le monde franc (VIIe-Xe siècle)*. Essai d'anthropologie sociale, Publications de la Sorbonne: Paris.

MacGuire, B. P. 1989. Purgatory, the Communion of Saints and Medieval Change. *Viator* 20, pp. 61-84.

McKitterick, R. 2004, *History and Memory in the Carolingian world*, Cambridge University Press: Cambridge.

McLaughlin, M. 1994. *Consorting with Saints. Prayer for the Dead in Early Medieval France*. Cornell University Press: Ithaca and London.

Nelson, J. 1996. La mort de Charles le Chauve. *Médiévales* 31, pp. 53-66.

Nelson, J. 2000. Carolingian Royal Funerals. In: J. Nelson, F. Thews, (eds.), *Rituals of Power from Late Antiquity to Early Middle Ages*. Brill: Leiden, Boston, Cologne, pp. 131-184.

Oexle, O. G. 1984. Mahl und Spende im Mittelalterliche Totenkult. *Frühmittelaterliche Studien* 18, pp. 401-420.

Oexle, O. G. 1994, Les moines d'occident et la vie politique et sociale dans le haut Moyen Age, in Le monaschisme à Byzance et en Occident du VIIIe au Xe siècle. Aspects internes et relationes avec la société. *Revue Bénédictine* 1-2, pp. 25-372

Oldoni, M. 1971. Agiografia longobarda tra il secolo IX e il X: la leggenda di Trofimena. *Studi Medievali* 12, pp. 623-26.

Paxton, F. S. 1990. *Christianizing Death. The Creation of a Ritual Process in Early Medieval Europe*. Cornell University Press: Ithaca and London.

Rosenwein, B. 1998. *Negotiating Space*. Cornell University Press: Ithaca.

Schneidmüller, B. 2002. Constructing the Past by Means of the Present. In: G. Althoff, J. Fried, P. Geary (eds), *Medieval Concepts of the Past. Ritual, Memory, Historiography*. Cambridge University Press: Cambridge. pp. 167-192.

Treffort, C.1996. *L'église carolingienne et la mort*. Presses Universitaires de Lyon: Lyon.

Van Gennep, A. 1969. *The Rites of Passage*. Johnson Reprint Corp: New York.

Werner, K. F. 1995. Aix-la-Chapelle. In: J. Morizet, H. Möller (eds.), *Allemagne-France. Lieux et mémoire d'une histoire commune*. Picard: Paris, pp. 43-74.

Werner, K. F. 1985. Les sources de la légitimité royale à l'avénement des Capetiens, (Xe-XIe siècle). In: *Le sacre des rois*, Actes du Colloque international d'histoire sur les sacres et couronnement royaux, (Reims 1975), Les Belles Lettres: Paris.

Wollasch, J. 1989. Totengedenken im Reformmönchtum. In: R. Kottie and H. Maurer, (eds.), *Monastische Reformen im 9. und 10. Jahrundert*. Jan Thorbecke Verlag: Sigmaringen, pp. 147-166.

Wollasch, J. 1990. Les moines et la mémoire des morts. In: D. Iogna-Prat, (ed.), *Religion et culture autour de l'an mil: royaume capétien et Lotharingie*. Picard: Paris, pp. 47-54.

THE POLITICS OF MEMORY OF THE LOMBARD MONARCHY IN PAVIA, THE KINGDOM'S CAPITAL

Piero Majocchi

Abstract

In the 7th and 8th centuries, as Pavia developed from Late Antiquity to the Lombard period, the town became the capital of the kingdom. At that time, the Lombard monarchy initiated commemoration practices such as the building of a royal palace and increasing the establishment of churches and monasteries founded directly by kings and queens, where inscriptions were used to commemorate the presence of royal graves. A few of these churches were located in pagan necropoli that had existed since the time of the Roman Empire. The capital also played a specific role in the Lombard monarchy's cultural production, especially "memory texts" like the *Origo gentis Langobardorum* and the "Prologus" of the *Edictum of Rotari*, both produced in Pavia during the AD 7th century.

Pavia remained the capital of the Italian kingdom from Carolingian times until the period of the Saxonian empire of the Ottonians; in 1024 the royal palace was destroyed by the populace. From the AD 11th to 14th centuries, during the confrontation between Pavia and Milan, both cities used the memory of "royal traditions" as political and ideological propaganda. This "permanent war" of the communes was also affected by the military expeditions of the German emperors, especially Friedrich I Barbarossa. His regency in Italy, during which Pavia was the military capital of the imperial communal league, was characterized by a great use of symbols by the Lombard monarchy as means of legitimizing imperial power. In the AD 14th century, during the regency of Galeazzo II e Gian Galeazzo Visconti (1359-1402), the memory of the capital's role and the Lombard traditions of Pavia were used in the official propaganda of the new masters of Pavia, the Visconti family.

Keywords: Memory, Lombard kingship, Pavia, propaganda

***

The Rise of a New Capital: Pavia in the Early Middle Ages

In the AD 4th century the transfer of the Roman imperial capital from Trier to Milan favoured the development of Milan, the largest city in Northern Italy, which retained its pre-eminence among the urban centres of the region. The increasing military instability at the beginning of the AD 5th century encouraged the Roman Emperor Honorius to move the capital to Ravenna, which could be defended more easily if attacked. Ravenna became the most prestigious bishopric in Italy with the exception of Rome. For similar reasons, Pavia, a smaller urban centre hosting military troops, grew in importance as a better defended town, connected to the Adriatic Sea through the Ticino and Po rivers (Cracco Ruggini 1984).

Pavia increased its important role in the Po Valley in the late AD 5th to early 6th centuries, as a result of the military events that led to the rise of the first post-Roman kingdom in Italy, founded by Odoacer. Furthermore, during the war caused by the arrival of Theoderic and the Ostrogoths in Italy, the new king of Italy chose Pavia, along with Ravenna and Verona, as *sedes regia* (Pohl 2000c: 41-58), while the presence of bishops such as Epifanius and Ennodius lent the city prestige and importance (Hoff 1943: 41-55). However, Pavia took over Milan's position at the time of the Greek-Gothic war, when, due to the loss of Rome and Ravenna, the capital of the Ostrogothic kingdom since AD 540, was moved to Pavia, where kings Ildibad, Totila, and Teia were elected and the royal treasure was kept (Pohl 2000c: 101-148). In AD 553, the capitulation of the last Gothic warriors in Pavia marked the official end of the Greek-Gothic war and showed the primary military role of the city (Cracco Ruggini 1984: 308-312).

Events occurring between the Byzantine conquest in AD 553 and the Lombard arrival in Northern Italy show how the imperial military control of the area was merely formal. On the one hand, rebellions of Gothic and Eruli chiefs seem to have been endemic, and, on the other, the Roman army was not able to stop Frankish raids on the southern side of the Alps. Within this framework, in

AD 569, various confederated peoples entered Italy, led by the Lombard King Alboin. Recent historical interpretations have noted that the Lombards, allied with the Roman empire for almost a century, entered Italy at the invitation of the Byzantine commander, Narsis, to oppose the Frankish expansion, and only a few years later they rebelled against the empire (Gasparri 2003; Pohl 1997; Pohl 2000c: 137-179; Pohl 2002; Barbiera 2005). In fact, there are no traces of fights with the Byzantine army in the sources for the first years after their settlement in Italy except for the three-year siege of Pavia. Even this celebrated event is doubtful, however, because in all the works of Paul the Deacon every siege lasted three years and the narration of this siege is identical to the narration of the siege of Antioch led by the Roman Emperor Aurelianus as narrated in the *Historia Augusta* (Settia 2000; Pohl 2000c: 167-179; the source is Paulus: II 26-27).

Until the beginning of the AD 7th century the Lombard kingdom was characterized by instability of the royal residence. Alboin died in Verona and Agilulf and Theodelind stayed in Milan and Monza, but Pavia remained the most important military centre of the kingdom, where the king often resided and yearly gathered free men for the army. During the regency of Arioald and then Rothari in the first half of the AD 7th century, along with creation of the military and institutional structure of the Lombard kingdom, Pavia became the capital of the kingdom and the regular residence of the monarchy (Pohl 1997: 98-112; Gasparri 2004a). The echo of Ostrogoth royal traditions probably played a significant role in the choice of Pavia as the capital of the Lombard kingdom, as suggested by the long-lasting attribution of the royal palace to the age of Theoderic (Gasparri 1987: 20-44; see also Paulus: II 31, III 35).

The specific role of the capital

The archaeological evidence of the urbanization standards in Northern Italy in the Early Middle Ages shows a general decrease in the town area (Brogiolo, Gelichi 1998), but in the Ostrogothic and Lombard ages the state administration was still based on city districts. The urbanization levels in the Po Valley, compared to other provinces of the Roman Empire, remained at a high level (Gasparri 2004a; Wickham 2005: 644-656). The urban centres, as in Roman times, maintained their commercial role of regional surplus distribution and they were still the main residence place of the aristocratic class, adding the consumption of goods to urban dynamics (Wickham 1998; Wickham 2005: 602-609).

The role of the capital in the seventh and eighth centuries implies the residence of the royal court, the presence of the central administrative structure of the kingdom, and the city's pre-eminence over the other urban centres in the military organization of the seasonal wars

(Gasparri 1987: 51-58). Here the army, composed of all free Lombard men, was yearly convoked together with the legislative assembly. During one of the assemblies in AD 643, the Edict of Rothari was promulgated (Gasparri 2005; Everett 2003: 163-171).

During this period, thanks to the close relationship between the monarchy and the bishopric of Pavia, the capital was exempted from the archbishop of Milan and placed under the direct jurisdiction of the Roman papacy. The cathedral in the centre of town and the bishop's palace beside the cathedral were built in the same period (Bullough 1966: 100-101; Panazza 1969: 479-483). Pavia also hosted the celebration of the ecclesiastical council, a privilege it kept all through the Carolingian period, until the AD 11th to 12th centuries. In AD 699, the synod that ended the "Three Chapters" Schism was solemnly celebrated in the royal palace and cathedral (Hoff 1943: 102-121). The residence of the Lombard monarchy in the city for two centuries had another significant consequence: the donation to the capital of its most important relics, including the body of the Church Father, St. Augustine, donated by King Liutprand to the monastery of St. Peter *Coeli Aurei* in the first half of the AD 8th century (Tomea 2001: 34-46).

The urban development of the city seems to have been greatly affected by the fact of its having been the capital. Archaeological excavations in Pavia in the 1970s have shown how High Middle Ages stratigraphy is characterized by thin layers of "dark earth," generally a reflection of a high level of urbanization (Peroni 1967; Hudson 1981: 23-27; Ward-Perkins 1984: 180-181; Hudson 1987: 258-259; Brogiolo, Gelichi 1998: 78-95; Blake 1995a; see also in general Brogiolo 2000b). The main source describing the urban structure of Pavia during the Lombard kingdom is the *Historia Langobardorum* by Paul the Deacon, in which urban walls with at least two gates, a royal palace, public baths, at least twelve churches, and three monasteries are attested (Paulus: II 27 palace, IV 31 St. Peter, IV 42 St. *Eusebius*, IV 47 St. John *in Burgo* and St. John *Domnarum*, IV 48 St. *Salvatore* and the *Marenca* urban gate, V 3 St. Michael, V 33 St. Ambrose, V 34 St. Agatha *ad Montem* and St. Mary *ad Perticam*, V 36 urban gate near the *palatium*, V 37 baths and St. Mary *Theodotae*, VI 5 St. Peter *in Vincolis*, VI 6 St. Roman, VI 58 royal chapel and St. Peter *Coeli Aurei*). Recent studies and archaeological excavations have confirmed the high level of urbanization of the city in the Lombard period. It was a stage of urbanization that did not fill the empty spaces left by the crisis of the Roman town with pastures and wooden houses, but one that consciously adapted the urban topography to the exigencies of the population and its political, ecclesiastical, and cultural elites (La Rocca 2003; Ward-Perkins 1984: 30 palace, 128 amphitheatre, 134 drains, 147 baths, 179-181 streets, 183-184 main square, 187-189 bridge, 192 urban walls; Hudson 1987: 238-260; Bullogh 1966: 82-

98; Maccabruni 1991: 27-36; Brogiolo 2000a: 144-150; see also Peroni 1972; Nepoti, Corsano 1995; Arslan 1995b; Blake 1995b).

The material and cultural means used in the Lombard kings' perpetuation of memory

The capital seems to have been a privileged place where the monarchy tended to adopt places of memory. The functioning and the maintenance of the royal *palatium*, intended to host the residence of the king and the chancellery, i.e., the kingdom's central administration, was the best way of commemorating royal power in the Lombard period. The royal palace (or probably a part of it) is likely to have been built by the Ostrogothic King Theoderic at the beginning of the AD 6th century, as mentioned by the historian Anonymus Valesianus (324, *Item Ticino palatium thermas anphiteatrum et alios muros civitatis fecit*). Theodoric's foundation of the palace is also mentioned by the AD 7th century Frankish chronicler Fredegar (82, *Theoderich palatia quoque splendidissime Ravennae urbis, Veronae et Papiae, quod Ticinum cognomentum est, fabricare iussit*) and by Paul the Deacon, who lived in the palace around the middle of the AD 8th century (II 27, *in palatium, quod quondam rex Theudericus construxerat*). In the AD 9th century, the Carolingian chronicler Agnellus of Ravenna himself saw a mosaic in the royal palace representing King Theoderic (Agnellus, 337-338), and (probably) the same mosaic is attested in a *placitum* held at the beginning of the AD 10th century – during the regency of Berengar I – *in sacro palacio, hubi domnus Berengarius rex preerat in laubia magiore ubi sub Teuderico dicitur* (*I Placiti del "Regnum Italie":* I 122, 456-459). This shows that the part of the palace built by Theoderic survived beyond the Lombard age; Ward-Perkins (1984: 163) says that "both the Ravenna and the Pavia palace-mosaics were certainly meant to impress in the grandest Roman manner." Unfortunately, no specific archaeological research in the area of the palace which might allow dating the different building phases is available and the area of the palace itself is still undefined because the palace was completely destroyed by the citizens of Pavia in 1024 (Hudson 1987: 260-263, 293).

Thanks to a few written sources from the AD 9th to the AD 11th centuries, we know that the royal palace comprised a complex of different buildings containing the residence of the king and his family, the court, a main hall where the throne was located and justice was administered, the chancellery, and the mint. Furthermore, one or more churches, a prison, a commercial emporium, baths, a large courtyard where the *placita* were held, and a garden – the *Viridarium*, with exotic animals – also lay within the palace; many of these buildings may date back to the Lombard period (Ward-Perkins 1984:159-160, 168; Hudson 1987: 260-263, 293; Settia 1987: 103-108; Brühl 1969: 189-206; Bougard 1996:

181-188; Gasparri 2004b: 57-60; Bougard 2002: 44-48; on the mint see Arslan 1995a). As Ward-Perkins (1984: 168) says, the palace of Pavia was certainly in Lombard times a dominant and admired building in the city, since an early AD 8th century inscription describes the splendor of (St. Mary) Theodota's monastery in these words: 'nor do buildings exist in this world to rival it, except the palace of kings.'

The heart of the kingdom looked to visitors like an impressive work, a kingship manifesto recalling a glorious past, as shown by the mosaic of the palace representing Theoderic, who initiated royal ideology in Italy.

During the Early Middle Ages, Pavia was a centre where the ideology of kingship was elaborated and diffused; an example is offered by the continuity of the royal symbol of the spear. In the Ostrogothic and Lombard kingdoms, in contrast to traditions in the Frankish kingdom where the crown was presented in a sacred ceremony, access to royal dignity was symbolized – as Paul the Deacon notes – by the delivery of a spear to the king once he was elected by the army (*contum, sicut moris est, traderent*, see Paulus, VI 55). Dynastic policy and blood links were important factors in the choice of a new king, although approval of the Lombard warriors was required. Sources do not refer to any specific crowning ceremony, the only royal symbol being the spear (Gasparri 1983: 61-67; Gasparri 2000: 95-101; Tomea 2001: 30-32; Bougard 2002: 34-39; Elze 1976: 571-573).

The royal spear remained a symbol of Italian kingship in the following centuries, becoming from the Ottonian Age (AD 10th to 11th centuries) one of the main symbols of imperial power; the lance of St. Maurice, the Holy Lance, still preserved in Vienna, might have originated in the *palatium* of Pavia (Elze 1976: 583-585). The AD 10th century chronicler Liutprand, bishop of Cremona, but born in Pavia, having lived for many years in the palace, tells in his history of the Italian kingdom, *Antapodosis*, that the lance was a gift from Sansone, the palatine count of Pavia, to the future King Rudolf of Burgundy in 921, and then to Henry I of Saxony and his descendants, the Ottonians (Liudprandus: IV 25, 118-119). In fact, during the regency of the Ottonians, the royal chapel in the palace of Pavia was dedicated to St. Maurice (Hudson 1987: 262-263; the source is *Ottonis III diplomata*: 411, 844-846 *in palacio domni imperatoris in laubia ipsius palaci que extat ante capellam Sancti Mauricii*).

While patronage of public secular buildings almost disappeared in Late Antiquity, the Ostrogoth and Lombard monarchies still promoted the erection of new public buildings in the capital. Theoderic built or repaired the walls, baths, the palace, and the amphitheatre in Pavia (Ward-Perkins 1984: 30, 115). Ostrogoth work on the amphitheatre of Pavia is confirmed by an inscription of Athalaric (Panazza 1953: 10 232-233), and in the second half of the AD 7th century King Perctarit built a new town gate near the royal palace, called the *porta Palacensis* (Paulus: V 36), on which an inscription listing the first ten Roman emperors was probably displayed (Maccabruni 1991: 32 109-110). To quote Ward-Perkins (1984: 169), "the evidence concerning the Pavia palace suggests that the Lombards, though scarcely matching the Ostrogoths, were not wholly insensitive to the role of palace architecture as a backdrop to the display of power." Another urban gate of Pavia, preserved until the AD 16th century, called the "Boetius tower," dated to Late Antiquity; it was richly decorated and was used as a prison during the Commune (Maccabruni 1991: 14-20).

The main and lasting means of preserving the memory of the Lombard monarchs was the increased establishment of churches and monasteries founded directly by kings and queens. Until the middle of the AD 6th century, only two Christian churches – both outside the urban wall – are attested in Pavia, while during the Lombard period almost 21 churches or monasteries were built in the city between AD 569 and 774 (Hudson 1987: 241-245, 247-254, 308-309). In this explosion of religious zeal the role the monarchy played seems to have been decisive; from the first half of the AD 7th century the foundation of an ecclesiastical institution became the main act by which Lombard kings showed and advertised their belonging and adherence to the Christian world (Bullough 1966: 99-100, 119-129; Brogiolo 2000a: 149-150). This phenomenon, common to all the post-Roman kingdoms in the Early Middle Ages (La Rocca 2002: 503-505), originated in Italy at the time Queen Theodolinda founded the St. John church in Monza and King Agilulf founded the Bobbio monastery (Pohl 2000a). Most of the royal foundations are located in Pavia, however; Paul the Deacon gives information about eight royal foundations, six churches (St. John Domnarum by Gundiperga, St. Salvatore by Ariperth I, St. Ambrose by Grimoald, St. Mary *ad Perticas* by Rodelind, St. Adrian by Ansprand, the royal chapel in the palace by Liutprand), and two monasteries (St. Agatha *ad Montem* by Pertarith and St. Peter in *Coeli Aurei* by Liutprand) (Paulus: IV 47, IV 48, V 33, V 34, VI 58). In the Lombard period, circa four more churches are attested under episcopal patronage, and two churches and two monasteries were founded by secular and clerical aristocrats (Ward-Perkins 1984: 244-245).

A few of these churches were located on sites characterized by the continuity of necropoli from the Roman Age to the Early Middle Ages: during this period Pavia had three main cemeteries sited outside the urban wall, still identifiable in the AD 14th century – as reported by the Pavian chronicler *Opicinus de Canistris* – probably because of the occasional finds of burials (Anonymus Ticinensis: XX). While the burial church of the first bishop of the city, Syrus, was constructed in one necropolis, probably at the beginning of the AD 5th century AD, ecclesiastical buildings in other cemeteries are attested only in the Lombard period (Hudson 1981, pp. 23-27). The church of St. John "in Burgo," where King Rothari was buried according to a AD 13th to 15th century tradition, and the church of St. Mary *ad perticas*, which was founded at the end of the AD 7th century by Queen Rodelinda in a Lombard cemetery characterized by – as Paul the Deacon reports – poles with doves on the top marking the empty graves of dead warriors that had been buried far from Pavia (Zironi 2000). In the AD 8th century, the church of St. Mary became a "mausoleum" of Lombard kingship; here were royal and aristocratic burials and in this area the newly elected king received the spear in front of the army (Hudson 1987: 241, 248). The continuity of the "pagan" cult and burial rituals in a new Christian form seems to have been used by the Lombard monarchy to assure the maintenance of the royal memory (Gasparri 1983: 61-67).

The perpetuation of the monarch's memory mainly relied on his burial in a Christian church, often founded by the monarch himself (Ward-Perkins 1984: 79-80; Hudson 1987: 247-254; Brogiolo 2000a: 158-159: La Rocca 1998b: 270-272). While Alboin was buried in Verona and Theodelind probably in Monza, after the foundation of St. John *Domnarum* by Queen Gundiperga, Theodolind's daughter, in the first half of the AD 7th century, the monarchy's practice of founding ecclesiastical institutions in Pavia implied that an explicit choice was made to be buried there. Queen Gundiperga was buried in St. John *Domnarum* (ca. AD 640), Rodelind and Ragintrud in St. Mary *ad Perticas* (ca. AD 680-740), Grimoald in St. Ambrose (AD 667), Ariperth I, Pertarith, Cunincpert and Ariperth II in St. Salvatore (AD 660-712), Ansprand and Liutprand in St. Adrian near St. Mary *ad Perticas* (AD 712-744) (Paulus: IV 47, IV 48, V 33, V 34, V 37, VI 17, VI 35, VI 58).

It is notable that the transformation of burial rites during the AD 7th century in Italy was characterized by the passage from burial with grave goods to burial in or near ecclesiastical buildings, in which the social memory of the dead no longer relied on an articulated ritual but on an inscription in Latin (La Rocca 1997). This phenomenon was gradual and not exclusive; there is archaeological evidence of burials with grave goods in ecclesiastical buildings and the Roman practice of using written inscriptions to commemorate the dead was never completely abandoned in Italy between the AD 5th and the 8th centuries (La Rocca 1998a; Effros 1997; De Rubeis 200b; De Rubeis 2002). There is evidence of barbarian chiefs being buried in Christian churches in Pavia as early as the AD 6th century, when, at the end of the Greek-Gothic war, Asbadus, a Gepid commander in the Roman army, who – according to Procopius – was the man who killed the Ostrogoth King Totila just after the battle of Gualdo Tadino, died in Pavia and was buried in the church of St. Nazarus with an inscription in

Latin. The inscription was reported by the anonymous continuator of the historian Prosperus, who even provided the text (Prosperus: 337 *Asbadus…moritur Ticinio sepultusque in basilica beati Nazarii martyris his super sepulchrum versibus descriptis…* on Asbadus see Prosopography, III 133).

The role played by the Lombard monarchy, using inscriptions to commemorate the presence of royal graves, seems to have been relevant in the diffusion of this practice in Italy during the Early Middle Ages. Although it is known that Alboin and Rothari were buried with grave goods, from the beginning of the AD 7th century the Lombard kings were buried in Christian churches, with gravestones written in Latin almost from the end of the century. The Pavian epitaphs named monarchs, members of the highest aristocracy such as the duke of Liguria, Ansoald, priests, and abbesses related to the royal court (Consolino 1987; Everett 2003: 248-262). Few of the gravestones have survived (Panazza 1953: 244-273); many of them are preserved only in medieval transcriptions, such as those published in the Monumenta Germaniae Historica (*Epytaphia civitatis Papiae*: 101-107). The epigraphic production in the Lombard capital, where the social role of the dead was particularly stressed (De Rubeis 2000a), was so characteristic in script and decoration as to be considered a specific style and was exceptional for quality and quantity in the epigraphy of the kingdom (De Rubeis 2002). It also testifies to royal patronage of epigraphic production in Pavia and its subsequent diffusion among the aristocracy and lower social classes and into the peripheral areas of the kingdom.

The capital also played a specific role in the cultural production of the Lombard monarchy, especially "memory texts" such as the *Origo gentis Langobardorum* and the "Prologus" of the *Edictum of Rotari*, both produced in Pavia during the AD 7th century. In AD 643, King Rothari promulgated the first *corpus* of Lombard laws in a field outside Pavia during the annual military draft. They were valid throughout the kingdom, not discriminating on ethnic descent because the term *Romanus* denoted those who came from Romania, the part of Italy controlled by Byzantium (Pohl 2000b: 12-15; Pohl 2000d: 418-419; Everett 2003: 92-99). The "Prologus" of the written redaction of the Edict contains a list of kings which identifies the origin of royal legitimacy long before its arrival in Italy, and declares the monarchy's right to settle disputes (*Le leggi dei Longobardi*: 14-16). The *Origo gentis Langobardorum* is a brief text that tells the story of the origins of both the Lombard nation and its name, the (mythical) long migration that took the Lombards from Scandinavia to Italy, the catalogue of the kings until the AD 7th century, and a brief narration of the principal events in the Italian kingdom (*Origo gentis Langobardorum*). This work was written in Pavia during the regency of Perctarit, actively promoted

at the royal court, in order to legitimate the Bavarian dynasty which came back to power with Perctarit after Grimoald's *coup d'état*. It perpetuated the royal memory by creating a new ethnogenetic collective text (Pohl 2000b: 15-28; Pohl 2000d: 416-418; Everett 2003: 87-92). Finally, another memory text related to the capital is *Carmen de synodo Ticinensi*, a poem commemorating the ecclesiastical council held in Pavia in AD 698, which brought the Church of the Lombard kingdom under Roman orthodoxy (*Carmen de Synodo Ticinensi*). The *Carmen*, probably written in Bobbio, describes royal efforts to promote Roman Christianity in the kingdom (Everett 2003, pp. 262-265).

The use of the memory of the Lombard capital in the Middle Ages

Pavia was the capital of the Italian kingdom during the Carolingian Age and the *Regnum Italicum* until the Saxon empire of the Ottonians. From AD 774 to 1024 the royal palace was restored and enlarged and at least 24 additional churches and monasteries were founded in the city (Hudson 1987: 260-290). While none of the Carolingian, Italic, and Ottonian kings that resided in the palace were still buried in Pavia, the capital began to host coronations in the Italian kingdom, celebrated in the palatine church of St. Michael (Settia 1987). Furthermore, after the Carolingian Age the royal practice emerged of donating the primary royal nunneries to the widows or daughters of the monarch (La Rocca 1998b: 279-281; La Rocca 2002: 506-508).

In 1024, the royal palace was destroyed by the Pavian population. This dramatic act of political memory-caesura was caused primarily by the need of the Pavian citizens to escape the payment of taxes and royal rights. As in the contemporary destruction of the episcopal palace in Cremona, at the beginning of the AD 11th century the violent reaction of the urban population of Northern Italy against the German emperors and their local administrators – the bishops – signalled the birth of communes. The dynastic union of the Italian and the German kingdom made the Italian capital meaningless because after the regency of Henry II at the beginning of the AD 11th century, the German emperors no longer resided in the southern part of their kingdom, except for short periods while on the road to imperial crownings in Rome (Settia 1992).

From the AD 11th to the 14th centuries, in the confrontation between the communes of Pavia and Milan, both cities used the memory of royal traditions as political propaganda. The privilege of hosting the celebration of a crowning or a royal burial (real or invented) in the city became an ideological weapon in the clash between Pavia and Milan. Milan hosted a royal burial in the church of St. Ambrose in the Carolingian Age and tried to seize the Pavian prerogative of Italian coronation. In this "permanent war" of Italian communes, the military expeditions of the German emperors, especially Friedrich I Barbarossa, played an important role. Barbarossa's regency in Italy, during which Pavia was the military capital of the imperial communal league, was characterized by a broad use of the symbols of Lombard kingship as a means of legitimizing imperial power. Friedrich I celebrated two coronations in Pavia (the first in 1155 celebrating the conquest of Tortona, the second one in 1162 after the victorious siege of Milan), and resided in a new imperial palace near the royal monastery of St. Salvatore. The "revival" of the capital in the second half of the AD 12th century is also shown by the translation of the relics (and of the burial epitaph) of the Lombard King Liutprand and his father Ansprand to the royal monastery of St. Peter *Coeli Aurei* (Majocchi 2005).

In the Communal period the ancient capital retained the memory of its early medieval role. The permanence of the Lombard law code favoured the memory of the capital, where most of the laws had been promulgated. Some chronicle and hagiographic texts related to Pavia tell legends about kings who lived in the capital, mainly about the siege of AD 774 by Charles the Great. In such texts, victory goes to Lombards and the Lombard kingdom never came to an end. Furthermore, the Pavian ecclesiastical institutions retained the memory of their royal founders and benefactors; from the AD 13th century, royal burials were counted in the relics' catalogue of the city. The main evidence for the perpetuation of the Lombard period as collective memory in Pavia is the *Libellus de laudibus civitatis Papie* by the AD 14th century chronicler Opicinus de Canistris. In this work, the Lombard period, to which the city owed all its privileges and the significant role it played in the history of the Italian kingdom, is described as the "golden age" in the history of Pavia (Majocchi 2008: 69-150).

In 1359, at the end of the Middle Ages, Pavia was finally conquered by the Visconti family, which lacked legitimacy. The conquest of 1359 did not mean that the city took on a secondary role in the new regional lordship of the Visconti; during the regency of Galeazzo II and his son Gian Galeazzo Visconti (1359-1402) the memory of the capital's role and the Lombard traditions of Pavia jointly entered the "official propaganda" of the new masters of Pavia. When Galeazzo II conquered Pavia he knew very well that it was not a city like the others, but the ancient capital of the Lombard kingdom, of which the Visconti claimed to be legitimate descendants. A few years after the conquest, Galeazzo promoted a far-reaching urban project recalling the Lombard capital. Between 1361 and 1365 a new palace with a major park was built, which became the official residence of the dynasty in the following years; in 1361 the university was founded and impressive works were added to the main square and the bridge. In the same period, the Visconti founded churches and monasteries

and chose St. Peter *Coeli Aurei* , where St. Augustine and King Liutprand were buried, as a dynastic burial church (Settia 1997; Majocchi 2008: 151-225). A last piece of evidence for the perpetuation of the Lombard memory in Pavia is the Dal Verme codex, a collection made at the Pavian castle in the late AD 14th to early 15th centuries by the cultural entourage of Gian Galeazzo. He controlled the area of the ancient Lombard kingdom and declared himself to be the new *rex Lombardie*. The manuscript contains the famous *Honorantie civitatis Papie* and other texts about the capital from Ostrogoths and Lombards to the Ottonian Age; catalogues of Lombard kings, queens, and bishops; lists of churches founded by monarchs and the royal burials of Pavia. Finally, it included evidence of Gian Galeazzo's royal dream, such as a poem comparing Gian Galeazzo with Liutprand and documenting the ducal coronation celebrated in 1395 (the Dal Verme code is published in Majocchi 2008: 223-307).

Acknowlegments

The author would like to thank Irene Barbiera, who kindly offered me the opportunity to write this article, and Cristina La Rocca, who steered me towards a deeper and deeper comprehension of the Lombard world.

Bibliography

Primary sources:

Agnellus. *Liber pontificalis ecclesiae Ravennatis*. O. Holder Egger (ed.), in Monumenta Germaniae Historica, Scriptores rerum Langobardicarum et Italicarum saec. VI-IX. Impensis Hannover: Bibliopolii Hahniani, 1878, pp. 265-391.

Anonymus Ticinensis. *Liber de laudibus civitatis Ticinensis*. R. Maiocchi and F. Quintavalle (eds.). In Rerum Italicarum Scriptores 11, No. 1. Città di Castello: Lapi, 1903.

Anonymus Valesianus. *Pars posterior*, in *Consularia Italica*. T. Mommsen (ed.). In Monumenta Germaniae Historica, Auctores Antiquissimi, 9. Berolini: Weidmannos, 1892, pp. 306-328.

Carmen de Synodo Ticinensi. L. Bethmann (ed.). in Monumenta Germaniae Historica, Scriptores rerum Langobardicarum et Italicarum saec. 6-9. Hannover: Impensis Bibliopolii Hahniani, 1878, pp. 189-191.

Epytaphia civitatis Papiae. E. Duemmler (ed.). In Monumenta Germaniae Historica, Poetarum latinorum medii aevi, 1. Berolini: Weidmannos, 1881, pp. 101-107.

Fredegar. *Chronicarum libri IV*. B. Krusch (ed.). In *Fredegarii et aliorum chronica*, Monumenta Germaniae Historica, Scriptores rerum Merovingicarum, 2. Hannover: Impensis Bibliopolii Hahniani, 1888, pp. 1-200.

Le leggi dei Longobardi. Storia, memoria e diritto di un popolo germanico. C. Azzara and S. Gasparri (eds.). Rome; Viella, 2005.

Liudprandus. *Antapodosis*, in Liudprandus, *Opera*. J. Becker (ed.). Monumenta Germaniae Historica, Scriptores rerum Germanicarum in usum scholarum separatim editi. Hannover: Impensis Bibliopolii Hahniani, 1915, pp. 1-158.

Origo gentis Langobardorum. F. Bluhme (ed.). Monumenta Germaniae Historica, Scriptores rerum Langobardicarum et Italicarum saec. 6-9. Hannover: Impensis Bibliopolii Hahniani, 1878, pp. 1-7.

Ottonis III diplomata. Monumenta Germaniae Historica, Diplomata regum et imperatorum Germaniae, II, No. 2. Hannover: Impensis Bibliopolii Hahniani, 1893.

The Prosopography of the Later Roman Empire, Vol. 3, *AD 527-641*. J. R. Martindale (ed.). Cambridge: Cambridge University Press, 1992.

Prosperus. *Continuatio Hauniensis*, in *Consularia Italica*. T. Mommsen (ed.). Monumenta Germaniae Historica, Auctores Antiquissimi, 9. Berolini: Weidmannos, 1892, pp. 298-339.

Paulus. *Historia Langobardorum*. L. Bethmann, G. Waitz (eds.), Monumenta Germaniae Historica, Scriptores rerum Langobardicarum et Italicarum saec. 6-9. Hannover: Impensis Bibliopolii Hahniani, 1878, pp. 12-187.

I Placiti del Regnum Italie, vol. 1, *776-945*. C. Manaresi (ed.), Fonti per la storia d'Italia 95. Rome: Tipografia del Senato, 1995.

Secondary sources:

Arslan, E. 1995a. La moneta a Pavia. La monetazione dei Goti e dei Longobardi. *Bollettino della Società Pavese di Storia Patria* 95, pp. 53-70.

Arslan, E. 1995b. Il ripostiglio di S. Giovanni Domnarum. In: *Archeologia urbana a Pavia*. I. H. Blake (ed.). Pavia: Emi, pp. 251-256.

Barbiera, I. 2005. *Changing Lands in Changing Memories. Migration and Identity during the Lombard Invasions*. Florence: All'insegna del Giglio.

Blake, H. 1995a. Archeologia urbana a Pavia. In: *Archeologia urbana a Pavia*. I. H. Blake (ed.). Pavia: Emi, pp. 4-6.

Blake, H. 1995b. S. Maria alle Cacce: lo scavo archeologico del 1979. In: *Archeologia urbana a Pavia*. I. H. Blake (ed.). Pavia: Emi, pp. 163-192.

Bougard, F. 1996. Palais princiers, royaux et imperiaux de l'Italie carolingienne et ottonienne. In: *Palais royaux et princiers en Moyen Age*. Acts du colloque international du Man (octobre 1994). Le Man: Université du Maine, pp. 181-196.

Bougard, F. 2002. Public Power and Authority. In: *Italy in the Early Middle Ages 476-1000*. C. La Rocca (ed.). The Short Oxford History of Italy. Oxford: Oxford University Press, pp. 34-57.

Brogiolo, G. P. 2000a. Capitali e residenze regie nell'Italia longobarda. In: G. Ripoll and J. Gurt (eds.), *Sedes Regiae (ann. 400-800)*. Barcelona: Reial Academia des Bones Lletres, pp. 135-162.

Brogiolo, G. P. 2000b. Towns, Forts and Countryside: Archaeological Models for Northern Italy in the Early Lombard Period (AD 568-650). In: *Towns and their Territories between Late Antiquity and the Early Middle Ages*. G. P. Brogiolo, N. Gauthier, and N. Christie (eds.). The Transformation of the Roman World 9. Leiden: Brill, pp. 299-323.

Brogiolo, G. P., S. Gelichi. 1998. *La città nell'alto medioevo italiano. Archeologia e storia*. Bari: Laterza.

Brühl, C. 1969. Das *Palatium* von Pavia und die *Honorantie civitatis Papiae*. In: *Pavia capitale di regno*. Atti del 4° congresso internazionale di studi sull'alto medioevo. Spoleto: Centro Italiano di Studi sull'Alto Medioevo, pp. 189-220.

Bullough, D. 1966. Urban Change in Early Medieval Italy: The Example of Pavia. *Papers of the British school at Rome* 34, pp. 82-130.

Consolino, F. E. 1987. La poesia epigrafica a Pavia longobarda nell'VIII sec. In: *Storia di Pavia, L'alto medioevo*, vol. 2. Pavia: Banca del Monte di Lombardia, pp. 159-175.

Cracco Ruggini, L. 1984. Ticinum: dal 476 d.C. alla fine del regno gotico. In: *Storia di Pavia*, vol. 1, *L'età antica*. Pavia: Banca del Monte di Lombardia, pp. 271-312.

De Rubeis, F. 2000a. Le iscrizioni dei re longobardi. In: *Poesia dell'alto medioevo europeo: manoscritti, lingua e musica dei ritmi latini. Atti delle conferenze per il corpus dei ritmi latini IV-IX secolo*. F. Stella (ed.). Florence: Edizioni del Galluzzo, pp. 223-240.

De Rubeis, F. 2000b. La scrittura epigrafica in età longobarda. In: *Il futuro dei Longobardi. L'Italia e la costruzione dell'Europa di Carlo Magno. Saggi*. I. C. Bertelli, and G. P. Brogiolo (eds.). Milan: Electa, pp. 71-83.

De Rubeis, F. 2002. Epigraphs. In: C. La Rocca (ed.), *Italy in the Early Middle Ages 476-1000*. The Short Oxford History of Italy. Oxford: Oxford University Press, pp. 220-227.

Effros, B. 1997. Beyond Cemetery Walls: Early Medieval Funerary Topography and Christian Salvation. *Early Medieval Europe* 6, pp. 1-24.

Elze, R. 1976. Insegne del potere sovrano e delegato in Occidente. In: *Simboli e simbologia nell'alto medioevo*. Settimane di studio del Centro italiano di studi sull'alto medioevo XXIII. Spoleto: Centro Italiano di Studi sull'Alto Medioevo, pp. 569-593.

Everett, N. 2003. *Literacy in Lombard Italy, c. 568-774*. Cambridge: Cambridge University Press.

Gasparri, S. 1983. *La cultura tradizionale dei Longobardi. Struttura tribale e resistenze pagane*. Spoleto: Centro Italiano di Studi sull'Alto Medioevo.

Gasparri, S. 1987. Pavia longobarda. In: *Storia di Pavia*, vol. 2, *L'alto medioevo*. Pavia: Banca del Monte di Lombardia, pp. 19-68.

Gasparri, S. 2000. Kingship Rituals and Ideology in Lombard Italy. In: *Rituals of Power from Late Antiquity to the Early Middle Ages*. F. Theuws and J. Nelson (eds.). Leiden: Brill, pp. 95-113.

Gasparri, S. 2003. I germani immaginari e la realtà del regno. Cinquant'anni di studi sui Longobardi. In: *I Lingobardi dei ducati di Spoleto e Benevento*. XVI congresso internazionale di studi sull'alto medioevo. Spoleto: Centro Italiano di Studi sull'Alto Medioevo, pp. 1-28.

Gasparri, S. 2004a. Il regno longobardo in Italia. Struttura e funzionamento di uno stato altomedievale. In: S. Gasparri (ed.), *Il regno dei longobardi in Italia. Archeologia, società e istituzioni*. Spoleto: Centro Italiano di Studi sull'Alto Medioevo, pp. 1-92.

Gasparri, S. 2004b. Il tesoro del re. In: S. Gelichi and C. La Rocca (eds.), *Tesori. Forme di accumulazione della ricchezza nell'alto medioevo (secoli VI-XI)*. Rome: Viella, pp. 47-68.

Gasparri, S. 2005. La memoria storica dei Longobardi. In: *Le leggi dei Longobardi. Storia, memoria e diritto di un popolo germanico*. C. Azzara and S. Gasparri (eds.). Rome: Viella, pp. xvii-xxvii.

Hoff, E. 1943. *Pavia und seine Bischofe im Mittelalter. Beitrage zur geschichte der Bischofe von Pavia unter besonderer berucksichtigung ihrer politischen stellung*. Pavia: Fusi.

Hudson, P. 1981. *Archeologia urbana e programmazione della ricerca: l'esempio di Pavia*. Florence: All'insegna del Giglio.

Hudson, P. 1987. Pavia: l'evoluzione urbanistica di una capitale altomedievale. In: *Storia di Pavia*, vol. 2, *L'alto medioevo*. Pavia: Banca del Monte di Lombardia, pp. 237-315.

La Rocca, C. 1997. Segni di distinzione. Dai corredi funerari alle donazioni *post obitum* nel regno longobardo. In: *L'Italia centro-settentrionale in età longobarda, Atti del convegno*. Florence L. Paroli (ed.). Florence: All'Insegna del Giglio, pp. 31-54.

La Rocca, C. 1998a. Donare, distribuire, spezzare: pratiche di conservazione della memoria e dello status in Italia tra VIII e IX secolo. In: *Sepolture tra IV e VIII secolo*, VII seminario sul tardo antico e l'alto medioevo in Italia centro-settentrionale (Gardone, 24-26 ottobre 1996). G. P. Brogiolo, and G. Cantino Wataghin (eds.). Documenti di Archeologia 13. Mantua: Società Archeologica Padana (S.A.P.), pp. 77-87.

La Rocca, C. 1998b. La reine et ses liens avec les monastères dans le royaume d'Italie. In: *La royauté et les élites dans l'Europe carolingienne (début IX siècle aux environs de 920)*. R. Le Jan (ed.). Lille : Centre d'histoire de l'Europe du Nord Ouest, pp. 269-284.

La Rocca, C. 2002. Les cadeaux nuptiaux de la famille royale en Italie. In: *Dots et douaires dans le Haut Moyen Âge*. F. Bougard, L. Feller, and R. Le Jan (eds.). Collectione de l'École Française de Rome 295. Rome: École Française de Rome, pp. 499-526.

La Rocca, C. 2003. Lo spazio urbano tra VI e VIII secolo. In: *Uomo e spazio nell'alto medioevo*, Settimana di studio del Centro Italiano di Studi sull'alto medioevo. Spoleto, Centro Italiano di Studi sull'Alto Medioevo, pp. 397-436.

Maccabruni, C. 1991. *Pavia: la tradizione dell'antico nella città medievale*. Pavia: Emi.

Majocchi, P. 2005. *Papia civitas imperialis*. Federico I di Svevia e le tradizioni regie pavesi. *Bollettino della Società Pavese di Storia Patria* 105, pp. 19-52.

Majocchi, P. 2008. *Pavia città regia. Storia e memoria di una capitale medievale*. Roma: Viella.

Nipoti, S., Corsano, M. 1995. I reperti dello scavo del Seminario nel 1970. In: *Archeologia urbana a Pavia*. I. H. Blake (ed.). Pavia: Emi, pp. 87-110.

Panazza, G. 1953. Lapidi e sculture paleo-cristiane e pre-romaniche di Pavia. In: *Arte del primo millennio*, Atti del II° convegno per lo studio dell'arte dell'alto medioevo. Turin: Viglongo, pp. 211-302.

Panazza, G. 1969. Le cattedrali pavesi. In: *Pavia capitale di regno*, Atti del 4° congresso internazionale di studi sull'alto medioevo. Spoleto: Centro Italiano di Studi sull'Alto Medioevo, pp. 479-484.

Peroni, A. 1967. *Oreficerie e metalli lavorati tardoantichi e altomedievali del territorio di Pavia. Catalogo*. Spoleto: Centro Italiano di Studi sull'Alto Medioevo.

Peroni, A. 1972. Il monastero altomedievale di S. Maria Teodote a Pavia. *Studi Medievali* 13, s. 3, pp. 1-93.

Pohl, W. 1997. The Empire and the Lombards: Treaties and Negotiation in the sixth century. In: *Kingdoms of the Empire. The Integration of Barbarians in Late Antiquity*. W. Pohl (ed.). The Transformation of the Roman World 1. Leiden: Brill, pp. 75-133.

Pohl, W. 2000a. Deliberate ambiguity: The Lombards and Christianity. In: *Christianizing Peoples and Converting Individuals*. G. Armstrong and I. N. Wood (eds.). Turnhout: Brepols, pp. 47-59.

Pohl, W. 2000b. Memory, Identity and Power in Lombard Italy. In: *The Uses of the Past in the Early Middle Ages*. Y. Hen and M. Innes (eds.). Cambridge: Cambridge University Press, pp. 9-28.

Pohl, W. 2000c. *Le origini etniche dell'Europa. Romani e barbari tra antichità e medioevo*, Rome: Viella.

Pohl, W. 2000d. Paolo Diacono e la costruzione dell'identità longobarda. In: *Paolo Diacono. Uno scrittore fra tradizione longobarda e rinnovamento carolingio*. P. Chiesa (ed.). Atti del convegno internazionale di studi, Cividale del Friuli-Udine, 6-9 maggio 1999. Udine: Forum, pp. 413-426.

Pohl, W. 2002. Invasions and Ethnic Identities. In: *Italy in the Early Middle Ages 476-1000*. C. La Rocca (ed.).

The Short Oxford History of Italy. Oxford: Oxford University Press, pp. 11-32.

Settia, A. 1987. Pavia carolingia e postcarolingia. In: *Storia di Pavia*, vol. 2, *L'alto medioevo*. Pavia: Banca del Monte di Lombardia, pp. 69-158.

Settia, A. 1992. Pavia nell'età precomunale. In: *Storia di Pavia*, Vol. 3, Part 1, *Dal libero comune alla fine del principato indipendente*. Pavia: Banca del Monte di Lombardia, pp. 9-25.

Settia, A. 1997. Il sogno regio dei Visconti, Pavia e la Certosa. *Annali di Storia Pavese* 25, pp. 13-15.

Settia, A. 2000. Aureliano imperatore e il cavallo di re Alboino. Tradizione ed elaborazione nella fonti pavesi di Paolo Diacono. In: *Paolo Diacono. Uno scrittore fra tradizione longobarda e rinnovamento carolingio*. P. Chiesa (ed.). Atti del convegno internazionale di studi, Cividale del Friuli-Udine, 6-9 maggio 1999. Udine: Forum, pp. 487-504.

Tomea, P. 2001. Intorno a Santa Giulia. Le traslazioni e le *rapine* dei corpi santi nel regno longobardo (Austria e Neustria). In: *Culto e storia in Santa Giulia*. G. Antenna (ed.). Brescia: Grafo, pp. 29-102.

Ward-Perkins, B. 1984. *From Classical Antiquity to the Middle Ages. Urban Public Building in Northern and Central Italy AD 300-850*. Oxford: Oxford University Press.

Wickham, C. 1998. Aristocratic Power in Eighth-Century Lombard Italy. In: *After Rome's Fall. Narrators and Sources of Early Medieval History. Essays presented to Walter Goffart*. A. Callander Murray (ed.). Toronto: University of Toronto Press, pp. 153-170.

Wickham, C. 2005. *Framing the Early Middle Ages. Europe and the Mediterranean, 400-800*. Oxford: Oxford University Press.

Zironi, A. 2000. *Historia Langobardorum*, Vol. 5, 34: la *colomba dei morti* fra bibbia gotica e sepolture franche. In: *Paolo Diacono. Uno scrittore fra tradizione longobarda e rinnovamento carolingio*. P. Chiesa (ed.). Atti del convegno internazionale di studi, Cividale del Friuli-Udine, 6-9 maggio 1999. Udine: Forum, pp. 601-625.

MEMORY, POLITICS AND HOLY RELICS: CATHOLIC TACTICS AMIDST THE HUSSITE REFORMATION

Kateřina Horničková

Abstract

Several different approaches to applying Reformation ideas impacted Bohemia in the 15th century, varying in their distance from Roman Catholicism in theology, liturgy, and religious practices. Emotionally charged medieval objects (relics) were used in the politically motivated manipulation of a particular medieval memory to return the people to Catholicism. Bishop Phillibert, a Catholic prelate, called on memories of the past and began to re-stage earlier Catholic ceremonies and celebrate relics collected by Emperor Charles IV before the Reformation. His selection of relics was made judiciously so as not to offend those who followed Reformation doctrines, but he seems to have intended to lead people back to Catholicism by evoking memories of the past.

Keywords: Memory, relics, Bohemia, Hussites, Charles IV, Phillibert of Montjeu, bishop of Coutances

***

Introduction

Le Goff defines medieval memory as privatised and internalised public memory embodied in a liturgy and commemoration of the saints that is not a memory of the past, but rather a *re-enactment of the actual*; Wallis calls it an "unhistorical quality" of medieval memory (Wallis 1995: 79). Together with the "presence of the present," medieval memory is defined by attachment to places, and objects (Nora 1989:23) – this conjunction strengthens its already multiple meaning, which is open to future re-interpretations. This article takes the form of a narrative of the politically motivated manipulation of a particular medieval memory using emotionally charged objects within a specific context decades after the original events, although still in a medieval context.

Setting the scene

Aware of the dangers of reducing public manipulation of memory to simple political aims, the case offered here is that of reiterated, guided memory imbued with political and religious meaning, which can be traced only because it occurred in the politically evident context (see Confino 1997: 1401-2) of the early Bohemian Reformation (Šmahel 1993: 9, 44). After the Hussite religious conflict of the 1420s and early 1430s, the citizens of Prague began to follow Utraquism, a moderate direction of the Hussite movement. The city had been Protestant for almost two decades when the Catholic Phillibert of Montjeu, bishop of Coutances, arrived and became active in Hussite Prague (1436-1439). He was an envoy of the Council of Basel, a body working – among other issues – to establish an accord between the Roman Catholic Church and the Hussites. The context of the presence of a Catholic bishop in Utraquist-oriented Prague, the capital of Protestant Bohemia, encouraged a search for a means of persuasion, the development of a political and religious agenda to bring the faithful back to Catholicism. Phillibert's public manipulation of traditional Catholic piety in the churches of Utraquist Prague involved the peaceful but pragmatic use of objects – relics – in the conflict. Phillibert's deliberate manipulation of public memory, I would argue, was based on history, but essentially modern in its conception. Not by chance, it occurred in the period bridging the Middle Ages and the Modern era.

In the Middle Ages, holy relics were important vehicles of public memory. Their religious significance and miraculous effects stemmed from their specific spiritual and material substance, present on earth but with links to heaven (Legner 1995:7). There is a long history of both preserving and manipulating them. Holy relics are both transferable and attached to places, capable of creating a topographic network of places and rituals resulting in sacralisation of time and geography.

Emperor Charles IV of Luxembourg (died 1378) was among the most important collectors of relics in the Late Middle Ages. He fostered the public manifestation of the cult of relics and anchored it in his concept of government. Through a range of iconographic subjects, he promoted his relics in various art media (Otavský 2003: 396), housing them in a variety of religious structures

(Birnbaum 1947). By establishing the Feast of the Holy Lance and two major Prague relic displays, he brought the saintly intercessors close to the faithful and helped build a common memory of these value-laden material objects that was shared by the citizens of Prague. His passion for relics provided important relics for the metropolitan treasury of St. Vitus and other Prague church treasuries. Along with a number of monasteries, Charles' policy also encompassed the parish churches of Prague, some of which received important relics from their patrons, as well as elaborate and valuable reliquaries for them, documented, for instance, in the 1390 "Inventory of St. Gallus (Havel) in Prague" (Borový 1883: 345). These sites became part of the city's religious topography, woven around major churches. As late as in 1471, Pavel Žídek, mentor of the "Hussite" King George of Poděbrady, urged the king to return to the Prague tradition of showing relics, enumerating their benefits: for the economy, protection and sanctification of the land, the greater glory of the royal dynasty, safe-guarding the morals of the people, and keeping kings on a righteous path (Žídek, 1908: 21-22).

Many monuments of Charles' grand building programme survived in Prague; his policy of making Prague a pilgrimage centre became a model, a remembered golden age. Charles IV's son, Sigismund of Luxembourg, and his ally, Bishop Phillibert, first made use of the memory of Charles' policy in 1436-1439 with the aim of returning Utraquist Prague to Catholicism. After 1420, Prague inclined to the Protestant "Bohemian church," following the teachings of John Hus. Although these moderate Hussites (Utraquists) accepted the authority of the Roman Church, the movement was considered to be a deviation from Catholic unity, posing a serious challenge. The purpose of this paper is to examine one aspect of Phillibert's confessional policy of promoting a return to Catholic religious practices in Hussite Prague, particularly his manipulation of historical memory through material relics.

Phillibert's strategy

After the unsuccessful war years, long negotiations, and a peace treaty, the Emperor Sigismund and council representatives were reluctant to continue their oppressive measures, but did not give up the idea of Catholic restoration in Prague. Once their return was accepted by the Utraquists in the city, they resorted to "soft propaganda," pressure translated into the public language of Catholic piety and ritual, which became a means of restoring Catholic pastoral care within the limits of the treaty (Kavka, 1998: 229). The expressions of Catholic piety appealed to the collective memory of Prague citizens, as the older pre-revolution generation was still able to recall their personal memories. The use of such means of conversion was eased by the fact that – although their

theologians decisively rejected more excessive forms of Catholic piety – more conservative Utraquists were far from the radicalism of the Taborites (Hussites with a rather fundamentalist utopianism) in the sphere of religious practice and more open in their acceptance of traditional forms of Christian piety.

The central figure in this story, French Bishop Phillibert of Montjeu, bishop of Coutances, was an interesting personality, an important political figure who became a legate for the Council of Basel (Kleinert 2004). In 1433, he was charged with the uneasy task of reconciling the "heretic" Czechs with the Roman Church. After studying the situation and in agreement with Emperor Sigismund's aims, Phillibert chose moderate pressure as a means to his end and promoted peaceful reconciliation among the Czechs. His actions were documented in the diary of his secretary, Master Jean de Tornis, who recorded his moves around Prague, important meetings, and political decisions (Zilynská 1992:56, 60; Birk 1857: 787-867). In the first phase of his mission, between 1433 and 1436, he led several delegations that were sent to negotiate with the Czechs. As a result of his mission, the Hussite party made concessions to the Council of Basel, which in effect resulted in the Czech Hussites returning to Catholic rituals (Palacký 1844: 453-455).

The second period of Philbert's mission, from the summer of 1436 until his death in 1439, led him directly to Hussite Prague. From his arrival on August 21, 1436, his stay was marked by great efforts to isolate the radical opposition and return the city to the Catholic faith. He participated in the staging of the arrival of the Emperor Sigismund of Luxemburg in Prague (Bartlová, 2008: 4-5), crowned the Empress Barbara of Celje on February 11, 1437, and probably helped organise the last *ostensio reliquiarum* (display of relics) in its original place in the Corpus Christi chapel in the New Town's Ox Market in 1437. These relics had last been shown on the Feast of the Holy Lance in 1417, before the Hussites came to prominence. What gave this event a specific political flavor was the fact that the showing presented not only the imperial and royal relics housed in royal castle of Karlštejn, southwest of Prague, but included the official announcement of the content of the *Compactate* Accord of 1433 (confirmed in 1436 in Jihlava) claiming Czech Utraquism to be a part of the universal Church. This was a key treaty between the Czechs and the Roman Church that created a mode for the existence of the first officially recognised non-Catholic enclave in Catholic Europe (although in the end the papacy never accepted it officially).

To promote his cause, Phillibert turned to conventional Catholic ceremonies and public appearances in his role as a bishop during his time in Prague. Between September 1436 and April 1438, he reintroduced monastic orders back into Prague (Zilynská [1992: 91], fifteen of them before his death), a move not welcomed by the

Hussites, ordained priests (Zilynská 1991: 361-71), and held pontifical services in the cathedral. In addition, he also held pontifical masses in at least five other important Prague churches. De Tornis, Phillibert's secretary, recorded the churches that acted as stages for Phillibert's activity: he held four masses on September 9, 1436, at St. Michael's; on September 30, 1436, at the Emmaus Monastery; on November 8, 1436, in the church of Our Lady at the Týn (Tyne) church; on March 14, 1437, at St. Jacob's church; and on May 5, 1437, at St. Henry and Cunigunde's church.

It appears that Phillibert concentrated on strategically important Prague churches, specifically those connected with the recent Hussite revolt or otherwise important parishes; to some extent these two criteria overlapped. The Our Lady at the Týn church was one of the most important parish churches in Prague (Eckert 1884:293), where Utraquist-elected Archbishop Jan Rokycana had preached and which was also dedicated to the Corpus Christi. St. Michal's was the first church where the chalice was offered to laymen during the celebration of the Eucharist (Holeton 1996: 24-27; Holeton 1998: 94-126). The name Utraquism comes from this practice – *communio sub utraque*, i.e., under both kinds, both bread and wine; in Catholic ritual only priests received the wine (Graham 2006). The use of the lay chalice was a key issue in the Bohemian Reformation controversy. Phillibert also consecrated several altars in St. Michael's, possibly at the invitation of a conservative Hussite priest, Master Křišťan of Prachatice. St. Henry and Cunigunde's church, founded by Charles IV, was an important parish church with an imperial and dynastic tradition. Phillibert also consecrated the chapel of the Corpus Christi, where a display of relics took place, and a chapel at the university (Zilynská 1992:90). Finally, he consecrated St. Jacob's church, originally a monastic church of the Franciscans, for those who communicated *sub una* (only the Body of Christ).

In mid-June 1437, Jan Rokycana left Prague with the priest of St. Stephen's church; the priest`s absence might have played a role in Phillibert's calculations. On April 19, 1438, Phillibert consecrated an altar or altars in the important parish church of St. Stephen, located in the eastern part of the New Town of Prague, although this consecration was not recorded in de Tornis' diary. This church was considered among the most important of the New Town parish churches and was known as a place of Hussite radical excesses in the early stages of the Hussite movement. The patronage rights to this ancient church belonged to the Czech hospital order of the Knights of the Cross with a Red Star. During the reign of Charles IV, 90 years earlier, the parish had been enlarged to such an extent that it was considered a new foundation in some sources (Eckert 1884:105). Following its enlargement, a new church was built at the same location and endowed; a silver gilded bust, in the pos-

session of the church in 1379-1380, might have come from the imperial endowment (Hlaváček and Hledíková 1973: 62). Charles IV, who held St. Stephen in special esteem, brought his relics from Rome to Prague in 1355 and donated them to St. Vitus' cathedral (Podlaha and Šittler 1903: IV, XII, XXVII, XXXI). It might have been Charles who initiated an annual procession from the cathedral treasury of St. Vitus to St. Stephen's church carrying the bust reliquary of St. Stephen the Protomartyr and a stone from the stoning of St. Stephen (Eckert 1884:105-106), which were then shown in that church on the feast day of the saint. The church had been the site of two violent episodes during an early phase of the Hussite revolt. First, a priest was attacked in 1410 when announcing an interdict against the leader of the Hussite party, Jan [John] Hus, and the radical priest Jan Želivský [John of Želiv] led an attack on the church in 1419 which ended in the pillaging of the church and parsonage (Eckert 1884:107).

The relics selected

Phillibert's consecration of altars in St. Stephen's in 1438 clearly reveals the strategy behind his activities in Prague. It aimed at the collective public memory of important relics as testimonies to Prague's glorious past as a pilgrimage centre, and reminded the Utraquists of their Catholic origin. A written record of Phillibert's relics offered to the church is preserved (Inventory of Relics…1438) in the archive of the Karlov Augustinian monastery. The consecration took place on the second Sunday after Easter and the parish church was given truly important relics for the consecration.

A° Dni 1438 die 19 Ap(ri)lis ^{hore(?) Domi(ni)ca Secunda post Pas-} ^{cha} *Templu(m) hoc Consecrata e(st) per venerabilem in χo patrem et Dominum Philibertum gratia Dei Episcopum Coutancien(sem?) p(ro)vincia(m) Bo(Bohemiam?) a S. Concilio Basiliensi Legatto sc(?) (sacras?) eade(m) reconduntur hac reliquia(s)*

De ligno S. Crucis
De Columna in qua fuit Chrs(Christus) flagellatus
De Lapido in quo stetit Crux Sita(m)
Reliq Stephani Prothomarty(ris)
De Beato Petro ^{in primo}
De Sanguino Beati Pauli
SS. Simonis et Juda(m) Ap(osto)lor(um)

S. Venceslai M.
S. Laurentii M.
S. Mauritii Martyris in 2do
S. Clement(is) Papa(m) Confesoris
St(?) (…Ilybros, Hybros?, Ilarie?) Martyri(s?) (sc?)

Ossa ss. 11 Milliu(m) Virginu(m) Mart.
S. Catharine V. et M. in 3^{tio}

S. Margaritha(e) V. et M.
S. Ursula(e) V. et. M. in 4to
S. Sabrina(e) V. et M. (sc?) 18 Elisabeth Vidua(e)
Titulus Vero annotatur S. Stephano Prothomartyrii

[On April 19, 1438, (…on the second Sunday after the Easter) this church was consecrated by Philibert, Bishop of Coutance, Legate of the Holy Council of Basel to the province of Bohemia, and the following relics were brought there: from the Wood of the Holy Cross, from the Column where Christ flagellated, from the Stone in which the cross was positioned, a relic of Stephen the Protomartyr, of St. Peter, the Blood of St. Paul, St. Simon and St. Jude the Apostles… for the first (altar). Relics of St. Wenceslaus the Martyr, St. Lawrence the Martyr, St. Mauritius the Martyr, St. Clemens the Pope and Confessor, St. Hilarie? the Martyr…for the second (altar). The bones of the holy Eleven Thousand Virgins, the Martyrs, St. Catherine the Virgin and Martyr…for the third. St. Margaret the Virgin and Martyr, St. Ursula the Virgin and Martyr, St. Sabrina the Virgin and Martyr and, (St.?) Elisabeth the Widow. The titular dedication is to St. Stephen the Protomartyr.]

The inventory is written in this order in four parts, possibly denoting caskets in which the relics were enclosed, or even more likely, the altars where they were to be kept. They included pieces of: the True Cross, the column where Christ was flagellated, and the stone which held the Cross in Golgotha. Relics of the most important saints of Christianity followed, starting with the titular saint, St. Stephen the Protomartyr, followed by St. Peter, the blood of St. Paul, and the apostles St. Simon and St. Jude. All of these relics were placed in the first altar. In the second group, the main patron saint of Bohemia, St. Wenceslaus, was placed together with the early martyrs Laurentius, Mauritius, and the confessor pope, St. Clement. In the third altar, bones from the Eleven Thousand Virgins and St. Catherine were deposited. In the last group were the virgin female saints Margaret, Ursula, Sabrina, and Elisabeth.

Such a composition of consecration relics is surprising for an important, but still only a parish, church in Prague. In agreement with the Christian hierarchy of saints and the tradition of Charles IV, the accent was placed on relics of the Passion and the apostles. The choice is impressive and – in this ambivalent confessional environment – avoided being too controversial. The Passion relics echoed the centrality of Christ's figure and the Corpus Christi in the Hussite rite (Holeton 1996, 23-47, Holeton 1998, 94-126). There were no Virgin Mary relics, which can be explained as Phillibert's concession to Hussite theology, which disputed the role of the Virgin in Salvation History. The composition also aimed at careful promotion of Roman saints (Sts. Lawrence, Stephen, Peter, and Paul) and papal authority; two uncontroversial sainted popes – St. Peter and St. Clement – were included. Churches had

been dedicated to St. Clement since Christianity arrived in Bohemia and his cult resonated with Czech-Slavonic feelings. His were the first relics that consecrated churches in Bohemia, as Sts. Cyril and Methodius had brought him to Magna Moravia in the 9th century and from there to Prague; later, this saint's relics were included in the annual Prague showing of relics begun by Charles IV (Kubínová 2006:291-4). Finally, the reason for the use of St. Wenceslaus' relics is clear. The main patron saint of Bohemia was there to remind the Protestants of the martyrs of their past and their own saintly tradition.

Phillibert's activity aimed at re-Catholisation was not limited to solemn pontifical masses, processions with relics, and episcopal ritual acts. Another opportunity for public promotion of traditional forms of Catholic piety was provided by the practice of inserting relics into images or sculptures, known from Charles IV's Karlštejn decoration designed by Master Theodorich. In Karlštejn, the images had relics inserted in their frames – this verified the visual representation in the painting through the physical touch of the saint's relic. This practice then became popular with the Virgin Mary's images during Wenceslaus IV's reign (Šroněk 2007: 84-5). On 11 March 1439, important Passion relics were inserted into the head of the sculpture of Christ in the famous Týn church Calvary, which stood in the triumphal arch between the choir and the nave in the church of the Our Lady at Týn, carved by the anonymous master who was named after this Calvary (Bartlová 2004: 23-5). Either the parish priest, Master Jan Papoušek (Parrot), Phillibert's adherent who had been confirmed as priest of the church by Phillibert earlier (on 24 April 1437) (Zilynská 1992: 90) or Phillibert himself initiated this consecration of the sculpture in clear reference to a fourteenth-century practice.

The relics inserted in the Týn Christ's head read as follows:

Infrascriptae reliquiae sacrae continentur in vertice huius crucifixi amarissime: Passionis Christi, primo de ligno domini, de petra in qua stetit crux, de statua circa quam flagellatus est, de panno domini, de lapide ubi Christus predicavit, de operibus misericordiae aliae reliquie his recondite a.d. MCCCCXXXIX m. Xima.

Below are sacred relics that are placed in the head of this crucifix: of the Passion of Christ, first of the wood of the Holy Cross, of the stone, in which stood the Cross of the column at which he was flagellated, of the veil of Christ, with which his nakedness was covered, of the stone, where Christ preached, and other relics of the deeds of mercy are here inserted in 1439.

This time, relics of Christ's Passion were used exclusively, and, again, they ranked among the most venerated tokens of Christianity. Interestingly, the first three relics are identical with those used in the consecration of

St. Stephen's. The *pannum*, the Virgin Mary's veil, with which Mary covered Christ's nakedness on the Cross, was a clever choice – it was a venerated relic in the St. Vitus Cathedral, and simultaneously a relic referring to Christ's Passion and the Virgin.

When considering Phillibert's fostering of traditional Catholic piety it is notable that two images of the Virgin dating from the second third of the fifteenth century originated from two of the churches Phillibert was associated with (the Our Lady at Týn and St. Stephen). In the Týn church, the panel painting of the Virgin was of the *Beata* type (Bartlová, 2005: 389-90) that closely followed the St. Vitus prototype; Bartlová dates the painting to before the mid-15th century. Another panel painting of the Virgin, this time of the Vyšší Brod type, was created for St. Stephen's church. Both are late, conservative examples of the Beautiful Style, copying famous Bohemian prototypes (Bartlová 2005:389-390, pl. 148; Matějček 1940: 154, pl. 254-5). The Týn church had its own Catholic-oriented decoration programme in sculpture by the Master of the Týn Calvary, designed in the late 1430s to 1440s, whose iconography promoted the most important relics in Prague church treasuries (Horníčková 2007: 223-225).

Another church where Phillibert is known to have been active is St. Henry and Cunigunde's, consecrated by Phillibert the day before St. Stephen's day, that is, on April 18, 1438 (Eckert 1884, vol. 2: 7). The act was commemorated by a Baroque inscription based on an older text naming Phillibert as consecrator and ennumerating the consecration relics used: St. Luke, St. Mark, St. Mathias, St. Bartholomew, St. Jacob the Minor, St. Andrew, St. John the Baptist, St. Paul and other Apostels, as well as the Wood of the Holy Cross and Christ's Sepulchre. Master Prokop of Plzeň, a conservative Utraquist and ally of Phillibert in the reconciliation between the Czechs and the Roman Catholic church, was established in this parish by Phillibert on May 5, 1437 (Zilynská 1992:90). Probably soon after that date, but before 1448 (Prokeš 1927: 144), he authored a tractate: *De Adoratione reliquiarum et de processionibus* [*On the veneration of relics and processions*], where he defended traditional Catholic forms of piety, especially public veneration of relics and the processions related to it. He used the argument of the ancient Bohemian origin of their tradition in the translation of the body of St. Ludmilla, reminded readers of Charles IV's annual showings of Karlštejn relics, and defended the Virgin Mary relics (Prokeš 1927: 153, 183, 259, ft. 845). In his sermons delivered in St. Henry's in 1437 or 1438, that is, before Phillibert's death and possibly under his aegis, he preached the traditional Catholic forms of cult to the Prague public; in the outlines for his sermons he promoted the veneration of saints and their images, ceremonies, feasts, and pilgrimages, sacraments, prayers to the saints, and argued against iconoclasm, destruction of sacred places and vessels (attempts to destroy material memory), and serving mass outside of churches (Prokeš 1927: 237-8, ft. 628-638).

A carved Crucifix by the workshop of the Master of the Týn Calvary comes from another Prague church, the church of St. Jiljí (Eligius). Here, in April 1437, Phillibert confirmed and established Master Jan of Příbram, another of his conservative Utraquist allies. All four Utraquist Masters, Prokop of Plzeň, Jan Papoušek, Křišťan of Prachatice, and Příbram were apparently regarded as reliable supporters of Phillibert's cause, as all of them consequently backed those few petitioners to clerical grade that were ordained by Phillibert in 1437-8 (Zilynská 1991: 366-7). Next to religious images, the sculptures of Crucified Christ by the Master of the Týn Calvary were ordered for two of their four churches. This suggests an interesting link between the sculptures produced by this workshop and the bishop's activity in Prague and lends support to the claim by Aeneas Silvio Piccolomini that Phillibert "returned images of saints back" to the churches (Hadravová, Martínková, and Motl 1998: 169).

At least four of the churches consecrated by Phillibert or where Phillibert served pontifical masses (the Týn church, St. Henry and Cunigunde's, St. Stephen's, and the Emmaus monastery) already had their own historical memories of Charles IV and his successful effort to make Prague a pilgrimage centre. The forms Phillibert used to foster Catholic piety influenced the common memory of the people of Prague in support of the contemporary revival of Charles IV-style veneration of relics, especially of Passion relics. Prague's forgotten treasures – the most important relics of Western Christianity – were called on to help in a time of need, when the Catholic cause was under threat. Phillibert calculated on the unifying potential and possibly patrimonial value of Christ's relics, which, on the one hand, had strong persuasive capacity as the most venerated of relics, and on the other hand, seem to have been less controversial for the Hussites than those of the Virgin would have been.

Where did the Phillibert's relics come from? Although there is no direct source of information, judging by the composition of relics it is probable that they originated from St. Vitus cathedral, which – thanks to Charles IV – held one of the most impressive collections of relics in Central Europe. It was a handy resource for several reasons. First, it was an excellent collection, containing the most important Passion relics, relics from all over Europe and many from Rome itself. Second, Phillibert was able to exercise a certain influence over the Prague chapter as he paid its expenses with his own money after Sigismund appropriated most of its own resources and stopped paying after he left Prague (Zilynská, 1992:67). Third, the relics were already present in Prague. In the spring of 1437, they had been brought to Prague from Karlštejn by imperial order for display on the feast of the Holy Lance to make a respectable framework for the Emperor Sigismund's claim to the Bohemian throne.

Conclusions

More than half a century after Charles IV's reign, under different confessional conditions, Bishop Phillibert, by imperial order or consent, embraced the memory of Charles IV's era and put it to the service of the Catholic cause. Making direct reference to Prague (Catholic) history, Phillibert employed methods of persuasion including relic manipulation, ceremonies and processions, and engaged the public by showing relics on special feast days. Phillibert counted on a twofold effect. First, the public ceremony with a procession was a sort of public ritual imbued with memory of the past. At the same time, these public appearances expressed a point in contemporary polemics on the format of church ritual – one of the key conflicting issues the radical Hussites had had with the Catholics and conservative Utraquists since the 1420s. Phillibert counted on the emotional effect of these relics on Prague citizens, who were more likely to tolerate donations and solemn ceremonies than less conservative groups. He might also have played on public resentment over the loss of the prime position of Prague among imperial cities as the seat of the Holy Roman emperor following the war years of the Hussite revolt. One cannot be sure of the direct reaction of Prague's public to Phillibert's effort, but the harking back to a glorious tradition and the fame of the relics themselves would have worked well together.

In any case, Phillibert seems to have followed a deliberate plan, influenced not only by the adherence of certain parish priests, but by a well-thought-out program. Behind Phillibert's activities when he toured the city was his concept of "soft" Catholic propaganda. His activities around Prague – thanks to their historical context – took on specific meanings in the minds of his contemporaries; these meanings corresponded to local memory.

The outcome

Whose idea it was originally to employ this cunning strategy to reverse the confessional balance in Prague in favour of Catholicism one can only guess. Phillibert was well acquainted with the Prague political and religious situation and was able to exploit this knowledge. He read the psychology of the people, which balanced between sympathy to the Reformation and inclinations to traditional piety at a time when nothing had yet been decided upon and there was a threat of new conflict. He opted for persuasion, a "peaceful" strategy, rather than more extreme action, but his calculations proved only partially successful. The rituals must have caused – and did cause – indignation among more radically oriented individuals, although no large-scale revolt occurred; in

fact, his adversary, Jan Rokycana, fled Prague as a result of Phillibert's clever policy. The burghers did not fail Phillibert's hopes, and partially embraced – or tolerated – the return to what was clearly Catholic practice. This might have been meant as a concession; more likely, however, the conservative Utraquist party, then predominant in Prague, had no problem with traditional religious practices. Memory worked for the moment – albeit not for long. Sigismund died in December 1437, followed by Phillibert two years later. Although Phillibert's policy spawned followers who continued his work till 1457, Phillibert's death from plague on June 19, 1439 closed the first phase of "peaceful" efforts to return the Catholics to power in Prague. George of Poděbrady's siege of Prague and the return of Jan Rokycana in 1448, and the sudden death of young King Ladislaus Posthumus in 1457 and papal rejection of the Compactate Accord in 1462 finally put an end to this late medieval confessional propaganda strategy until the Jagellonians took the throne in 1471.

Bibliography

Hadravová, Alena, Dana Martínková, and Jiří Motl, (eds.). 1998. *Aeneae Silvii Historia Bohemica/Enea Silvio Historie česká* [History of the Czechs by Aeneas Silvio], Preface František Šmahel. Prague: Koniasch Latin Press.

Bartlová, Milena. 2004. *Mistr Týnské kalvárie. Český sochař doby husitské* [The Master of the Tyn Calvary. Czech skulptor of the Hussite Era]. Prague: Academia.

Bartlová, Milena. 2005. *Poctivé obrazy* [Truthful images]. Prague: Argo.

Bartlová, Milena. 2008. "Sigismundus Rex Bohemiae: Royal Representation after the Revolution." In: *Kunst als Herschaftsinstrument unter den Luxemburgen*, Jiří Fajt and Andrea Langer, (eds.). Berlin, (forthcoming).

Birnbaum, Vojtěch. 1947. *Karel IV jako sběratel a Praha. Listy z dějin umění* [Charles IV as a Collector in Prague. Papers from art history]. Alžběta Birnbaumová, (ed.). Prague.

Borový, Klement. 1875-1889. *Libri erectionum archidieocesis Pragensis saeculo XIV. et XV.* Vol. 4, No. 1. Prague: Pragensis doctorum theologiae collegii, 1883. cat. oo: 458, 345.

Confino, Alon, 1997. "Collective Memory and Cultural History: problems of Method," *The American Historical Review* 102, No. 5, pp.1386-1403.

Eckert, František. 1884. *Posvátná místa král. hl. města Prahy. Dějiny a popsání* [Sacred Places in the Royal Capital City of Prague]. 2 vols. Prague: Dědictví sv. Jana Nepomuckého.

Graham, Barry F.H. 2006. The Evolution of the Utraquist Mass, 1420-1620. *The Catholic Historical Review* 92, No. 4, pp. 553-573.

Hlaváček, Ivan Hlaváček, and Zdeňka Hledíková, (eds.). 1973. *Protocolum visitationis archidiaconatus Pragensis annis 1379 - 1382 per Paulum de Janowicz archidiaconum pragensem factae* [The Visitation Protocol of the Archdiaconates of Prague of 1379-1382]. Prague: Academia.

Holeton, David R. 1996. The Bohemian Eucharistic movement in its European context. *The Bohemian Reformation and the Religious Practice* 1, pp. 23-47.

Holeton, David R. 1998. Evolution of Utraquist Eucharistic Liturgy: A Textual Study. *Bohemian Reformation and Religious Practice* 2, pp. 94-126.

Horníčková, Kateřina. 2007. Eucharistický Kristus mezi anděly z Týna [The eucharistic Christ between angels from the Týn church]. In: *Žena ve člunu*. Kateřina Horníčková and Michal Šroněk, (eds.). Prague: Artefactum, pp. 211-238.

Inventory of relics in the church of St. Stephen in Rybníček (1438). National Archive, section of Dissolved Monasteries, AZK ŘA Karlov, Spisy (unsorted administrative material), inv. no. 2535 fasc. 11. (Holinka no. 1111).Year 1438, appended to Sermon Dominica + Post Pascha *Ira enim viri justitiam Dei non operatur*, 17th century copy.

Kavka, František. 1998. *Poslední Lucemburk na českém trůně* (The Last Luxembourg on the Bohemian Throne). Prague: Mladá fronta.

Kleinert, Christian. 2004. *Phillibert de Montjeu (ca. 1374–1439): Ein Bischof im Zeitalter der Reformkonzilien und des Hundertjährigen Krieges*. Ostfildern: Jan Thorbecke.

Kubínová, Kateřina. 2006. *Imitatio Romae* [Imitation of Rome]. Prague: Artefactum.

Legner, Anton. 1995. *Reliquien in Kunst und Kult. Zwischen Antike und Aufklärung* [Relics in Art and Cult between Antiquity and the Enlightenment]. Darmstadt: Wissenschaftliche Buchgesellschaft.

Matějček, Antonín. 1940. *Česká malba gotická. Deskové malířství 1350-1450* [Czech Gothic painting. Panel painting 1350-1450]. Prague: Melantrich.

Birk Ernst. Ed. 1857. *Monumenta Conciliorum Generalium Saeculi decimi quinti, Concilium Basileense* [Writings of the General Council of the 15th century, Basel Council], Scriptorum tomus I. Vienna, 1857, pp. 787-867.

Nora, Pierre. 1989. "Between Memory and History: Les Lieux de Mémoire," *Representations* 26, pp. 7- 24.

Otavský, Karel. 2003. K relikviím vlastněným císařem Karlem IV, k jejich uctívání a jejich schránkám [On the Relics Owned by the Emperor Charles IV, their Veneration and Reliquaries]. In: *Court Chapels of the High and Late Middle Ages and their Artistic Decoration*. Jiří Fajt (ed.). Prague: Národní galerie v Praze, pp. 392-398.

Palacký, František, (ed.). 1844. Artikulové smluvení na držení kompaktát w Čechách 10.3. 1437 [Articles on keeping the Compactate Accord in Bohemia on March 10, 1437]. In: *Archiv český čili staré písemné památky české i moravské*. Vol. 3, Prague: F. Palacký, pp. 453-455.

Tobolka, Zdeněk (ed.). 1908. *M. Pavla Žídka Správovna* [The Corrector by Master Pavel Žídek]. Prague: Česká akademie císaře Františka Josefa pro vědy, slovesnost a umění.

Podlaha, Antonín, and Eduard Šittler, (eds.). 1903. *Chrámový poklad u sv. Víta, jeho dějiny a popis* [The Church Treasury of St. Vitus, its History and Description]. Prague: Nákladem dědictví sv. Prokopa.

Prokeš, Jaroslav. 1927. *M. Prokop z Plzně. Příspěvek k vývoji konzervativní strany husitské* [Master Prokop of Plzeň. Contribution to the Evolution of the Conservative Hussite Party]. Prague: Nákladem společnosti Husova musea.

Šmahel, František. 1993. *Husitská revoluce* [The Hussite Revolution], vol. 1. Prague: Univerzita Karlova Praha 1993.

Šroněk, Michal. 2007. Karel IV, Jan Rokycana a šlojíř nejistý [Charles IV, Jan Rokycana and the "Uncertain Veil"]. In: *Zbožnost středověku* [Piety in the Middle Ages], Martin Nodl, (ed.), Colloquia Medievala Pragensia 6, pp. 79-110.

Wallis, Faith. 1995. "The Ambiguities of Medieval "Memoria" *Canadian Journal of History /Anales canadiennes d'histoire* 30, pp. 77-83.

Zilynská, Blanka. 1991. "Svěcení kněžstva biskupem Filibertem v Praze v letech 1437-39" [Ordinations of clergy by bishop Phillibert in 1437-39]. *Documenta Pragensia* 9, No. 2, pp. 361-386.

Zilynská, Blanka. 1992. "Biskup Filibert a české země" [Bishop Phillibert and the Bohemian Lands]. In: *Jihlava a Basilejská kompaktáta*. Dana Nováková, Karel Křesadlo, and Eva Nedbalová, (eds.) Jihlava: Muzeum Vysočiny, pp. 57-94.

THE ROLE OF THE PEACOCK "SANJAK" IN YEZIDI RELIGIOUS MEMORY; MAINTAINING YEZIDI ORAL TRADITION

Eszter Spät

Abstract

This paper aims to discuss the role of the holiest object of the Yezidis, the peacock "*sanjak*" or standard in preserving communal religious memory. The *sanjak* is a physical representation of the Peacock Angel, and the rituals connected with it are an important occasion for the recitation of orally transmitted religious texts. As Yezidis formerly lacked books or formal religious education, such occasions were paramount for the survival of a Yezidi religious identity. As oral traditions change, the role of oral recitation is being taken over by books, so the role of the peacock image is evolving from a symbol of divinity at the core of oral religious lore to a more fixed symbol meant to remind Yezidi of their communal identity in general.

Keywords: memory, oral tradition, peacock *sanjak*, sacred objects, Yezidis

***

Introduction

Sacred objects do not merely have the power to evoke religious feelings, but through their symbolism and physical presence they are closely connected to perpetuating religious traditions and lore through memory and connections to a constructed past. This is doubly so in the case of societies relying on oral traditions, where the place of sacred books and voluminous learned writings has to be taken by a few key material images capable of triggering memories of an enduring set of associations. Besides serving as a link to their past, and to the world of religious oral lore inherited from their forefathers, these material images may simultaneously also be used to reinforce traditional religious authority. Although Yezidis have but a few sacred objects, such a multiple role is served by their most sacred object, the peacock *sanjak*, a representation of the Peacock Angel. The *sanjak* is a metal statue showing a peacock-like figure, surmounted on a candlestick (Fig. 1).

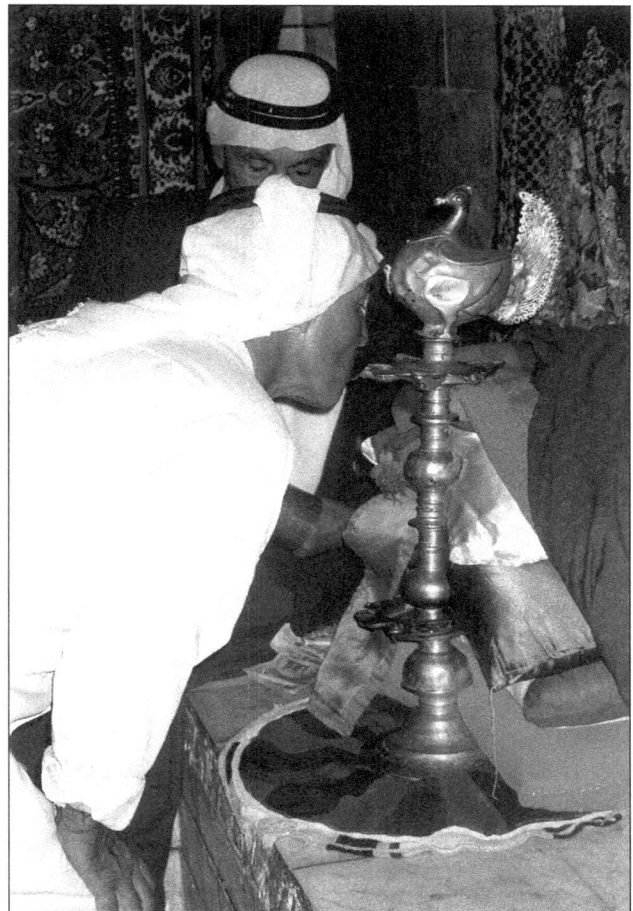

Fig. 1. Yezıdi Pilgrim kissing the Sheikhani Sanjak.

The Historical and Religious Context

Yezidis are a Kurdish speaking religious minority living throughout the Middle East, mainly in Iraq,[1] but also in Syria, Turkey, Iran, and the Caucasian states. They follow a highly syncretistic religious system based on oral tradition. Their faith bears the marks of the influence of numerous religions once flourishing in the region and displays an amazing ability to adapt and

1. My field research was carried out in Iraq between 2002 and 2004 in two Yezidi regions: the Sheikhan, the religious center for all Yezidis, lying between Mosul and Duhok, and in the Sinjar region, an isolated mountain area along the Iraqi-Syrian border.

reshape any "foreign" elements, building up from them a totally new and original system. Historically, Yezidis can be traced back to a 12th c. Sufi brotherhood, the "al-Adawiya", founded by *Sheikh* Adi bin Misafir in the valley of Lalish in the Kurdish mountains near Mosul (ancient Niniveh). With time this Sufi order incorporated so many pre-Islamic elements from its environment that it ceased to be a part of Islam and became an independent religious entity. Though some Yezidis today like to call themselves "Sufis", Muslims see them either as heretics, or, even worse, as infidels who worship the Devil. This Devil, according to Muslims, is none other than the Peacock Angel, whose *sanjak* or image in the form of a brass statuette plays a central role in the perpetuation of Yezidi oral tradition. Although called an angel, the Peacock Angel, or Tawusi Melek, is not an angel, at least not in the sense Christianity or Islam utilizes this word. Yezidi angels are not creations or creatures of God, but are emanations or hypostases of the Godhead, who came into being, as the Yezidis say, as candles lit from another candle. The most important of all these angels is the Peacock Angel. He is simultaneously the head of the Seven Angels, the viceroy of God on earth, and the special protector angel of the Yezidis.

The *sanjak*, known in Western literature as the peacock standard, is the material image or symbol of the Peacock Angel and the most sacred object that the Yezidis possess. It is worshipped only as a sacred object made by and symbolizing a deity, and not as a deity itself. Layard (1854) noted in the mid 19th c. that *Sheikh* Nasr, the religious head of the community "was careful to explain it was only looked upon as a symbol, and not as an idol."

Objects of sanctity and memory: *Sanjaks, nishans, holy clothing and the Black Snake*

In order to appreciate the significance of the *sanjak*, one must be aware that though Yezidis have a rich religious oral tradition, they possess few objects connected with it. These few sacred objects, however, are inextricably bound up with the details of a Yezidi mythical past characterized by the intervention of divine or angelic figures. Among the Yezidis of Iraq such objects include the so-called *nishans*, literally "signs," which are small metal objects belonging to *sheikh* and *pir* families. (Fig. 2). *Sheikh*s and *pir*s are the hereditary castes of religious leaders. Both words mean "elder," in Arabic and Kurdish respectively. Each Yezidi must have a *sheikh* and a *pir*, which probably reflects the influence of Sufism on Yezidism and its master-teacher relationship. According to Yezidi belief, the ancestors of *Sheikh*s and *pir*s were holy beings possessing the divine mystery or *sir* (secret.) Besides their leading position and some miraculous powers, they have inherited the so-called "signs," small metal objects of great sanctity, from these ancestors. These *nishans* denote the special descent of the family, and are

Fig. 2. Nishans, attached to a bag containing sacred berat, small balls of dust from the holy valley of Lalish.

simultaneously believed to possess supernatural powers themselves. The followers of a *sheikh* or *pir* regularly pay visits (and money) to see these signs, which are affixed to a special bag. The bag itself contains small sacred balls of dust or earth from the holy valley of Lalish, called *berat*, which are believed to bring blessings and good luck. All Yezidi households possess such *berats*, kept in a bag especially made for this purpose and often conspicuously displayed hanging on the wall.

Interestingly, items of clothing must also be counted among the sacred objects connected with communal memory. Thus, for example, traditionally Yezidis should wear an (under)shirt with a round opening (*gerivan*) around the neck – as opposed to the usual open shirt neck worn by people in surrounding communities. The undershirt with a *gerivan* is considered sacred and a Yezidi must kiss the round opening of his shirt before praying. The religious necessity to wear such a round-necked shirt, was emphasized by the 1872 Petition addressed to the Ottoman Government that listed the reasons why the Yezidi community should be made exempt from military service. The obligation to wear such a round-necked shirt is explained by the events in the Yezidi mythical past. The myths recounted vary, but all agree that originally all people had round shirt necks.

106

However, then the neck-line of the Muslims was torn open, signifying that it was the Muslims who had left the path or true religion, whereas the Yezidi community had carefully preserved it. Yet another consideration lending a great relevance to this piece of clothing is the fact that this opening must be made by the Brother or Sister of Hereafter (*Birayê or Xwişka Axreti*) of the owner of the shirt. The Brother (or Sister, as the case be) of Hereafter is one of the five religious obligations a Yezidi must observe. Each Yezidi must have a Brother or Sister of Hereafter coming from the higher castes of *sheikhs* or *pîrs*, who will intercede on his or her behalf after death when the soul is judged. (Others say it is the eponymous ancestor of the lineage of the Sister or Bother who will plead the case of the deceased.) Thus, wearing the *gerîvan* is connected with memory of the Yezidi constructed past not only through the myths explaining its origin, but also through the myths that deal with the origins of Yezidi caste system. The role of the Brother of Hereafter in making the *gerivan* reinforces respect for a religious institution perceived as vital for maintaining Yezidi religious traditions. Furthermore, the *gerîvan* underlines Yezidi identity by highlighting the difference between Yezidis and Muslims even in their apparel mediated through the story of a divine ancestral past.

Another sacred item of clothing whose significance can only be appreciated in light of Yezidi sacral history is the *khirqe*, the coarse, black, woolen shirt of the *feqirs*, or Yezidi ascetics. *Feqirs* are expected to lead a life of piety and abstinence, by fasting, refraining from drinking and smoking as well as avoiding any violent behavior. Their special shirt, the *khirqe* is dyed black with a substance made from the sacred *zerguz* tree. This shirt is held in such awe that no one can strike someone wearing a *khirqe*, however great the provocation and its owner may demand anything he wishes (though abusing his prerogatives may eventually lead to the loss of his *khirqe*). According to Yezidi religious tradition the *khirqe* is remembered as originally being the clothing of God, as well as of his Angels. As a symbol of the divine mystery and gnosis it was also worn by Yezidi *khas*, that is, the angelic beings who became incarnated as humans in order to lead the Yezidis on the path of true religion. It was the attire of *Sheikh* Adi, the incarnation of the Peacock Angel and the central figure of Yezidi mythology, from whose *khirqe* light is said to have emanated. An ancient *khirqe*, claimed to have been that of *Sheikh* Adi, is still preserved at the Central Sanctuary in the holy valley of Lalish. It is worn by the leader of the *feqirs* during the sacred Evening Dance, where he is said to represent *Sheikh* Adi, and the other dancers to represent the Seven Great Angels circling around God. (Fig. 3). The *khirqe* then is a sacred item of clothing which represents the whole chain of Yezidi religious history, from the moment of creation to the moment when the *khirqe* was left on earth by the holy beings so that it could be worn by those who follow the true religion, that is,

Fig. 3. The Evening Dance. The leading feqir at the front is wearing the "khirqe of Sheikh Adi."

the Yezidi *feqirs*. It serves as a visual reminder of Yezidi religion and the special place it is believed to occupy as compared to other religions.

Though not strictly speaking an object, the Black Snake standing on its tail, carved or painted next to the door post of many Yezidi shrines must be mentioned in connection with objects associated with the collective religious memory of Yezidis. Whenever asked about the meaning of the Black Snake, Yezidis expound myths, which connect present-day Yezidis with their constructed past. According to one myth it was a black snake that saved the pious Noah, a Yezidi himself, and his precious cargo from drowning in the waters of the Flood, when his ark foundered on the peak of Mount Judi and started to leak. A black snake coiled itself over the hole thus securing the survival of human and animal kind. Another legend tells of how Sheikh Mend, a companion of Sheikh Adi, and himself an earthly manifestation of one of the divine Angels, turned himself into a black snake and drove the tribe of Haweris back home on their way to becoming Muslims. The *sheikh* family of Sheikh Mend, that is his descendants, are believed to be blessed with power over snakes. Not only do snakes not bite them, but they can cure the snakebites of others.

Among these few sacred objects central to Yezidi collective memory the *sanjak* of the Peacock Angel is by far the most important. It is actually considered the most important by the Yezidis themselves, as the representation of the Peacock Angel, the protecting angel of the community. Unlike other objects, it does not belong to one caste, or to one family line, but is equally held in awe by all the Yezidis. It can also be considered the most significant object from the point of view of researchers, as it plays (or played) a vital role in helping perpetuate Yezidi oral traditions, and through this communal religious memory.

The *sanjak*, or rather *sanjak*s, as there used to be seven of them, are considered very ancient objects, harking back to divine events from the very beginnings of Yezidi history. Just like the *nishans*, the *sanjaks* were handed down from one generation to the next, forming a continuous chain in Yezidi history. According to some traditions, the *sanjaks* were fashioned by the Peacock Angel himself in his own image (Lescot 1938: 73). Other sources simply mention one of the Seven Angels (Empson 1928: 29-30; Joseph 1909: 226) while a portion of a Syriac manuscript relating to the Yezidis, translated and edited by Chabot (1896: 121) says that each of the Seven Gods created one *sanjak*. The *sanjaks* were given to Solomon the Wise, who bequeathed them to the next king. Finally, when Yezid, that is, Yezid bin Muawiya, the sixth caliph, who is identified by the Yezidis as an incarnated divinity and seen as one of their ancestors, was born, the *sanjaks* came into his possession and he left them for his people, the Yezidis. Originally, there were seven bronze peacocks, corresponding to the seven Yezidi districts, also known as *sanjaks* (a word probably adopted from Ottoman administrative terminology). There seems to be some disagreement as to the original identity of these seven geographical *sanjaks*, but they covered all the territories where Yezidis lived, from Aleppo to Iran and from Iraq to the Moscovy *sanjak* (that is, the Caucasus mountains). The *sanjaks* were traditionally kept in Lalish, the sacred valley of the Yezidis near Mosul, or at other times in the house of the Yezidi Prince at Baadra, also near Mosul, investing him with a kind of authority through their ancient links to tradition and divine power.

At regular intervals, however, the *sanjaks* were taken on a tour to visit the Yezidi villages, each one in its own district, accompanied by the *qewwals*, or singers of sacred hymns.[2] This was called the Parading of the Peacock. The *sanjaks* belonging to districts near the center were paraded two or three times a year. Those for districts further away were taken only once, or, when there were political troubles even less often.[3] Most of the money collected by the *sanjaks* during their circuit accrues to the Yezidi *Mir*, or prince, in whose possession they reside officially. Possession of the *sanjaks* helped maintain the spiritual legitimacy of the Yezidi *Mirs* as representatives on earth of the Peacock Angel. The peacock standard is therefore a symbol and reminder of the princely power on which Yezidi political structure is based. The Parading of the Peacock in the Yezidi villages "emphasized the prince's links with the supernatural power of Tawus [Peacock Angel] thus, strengthening his authority vis-à-vis the believers" (Fuccaro 1999: 21), especially among Yezidi communities settled on the periphery, far from the center where religious leaders reside. Furthermore, these tours have always provided the prince and princely family with an opportunity to intervene in the life of Yezidi communities far from the center, through the intermediary of the *qewwals* chosen by the prince, and occasionally other dignitaries accompanying the Peacock. (Fuccaro 1999: 22)

Peacock as an ancient symbol and the possible origin of the Peacock *Sanjak*

Due to the lack of sources, very little is actually known about either the origin of the worship of the Peacock Angel or of the *sanjak* itself. The peacock is certainly an old religious symbol and can be found in the symbolic imagery of most of the major religions that may have exerted their influence in the region (Amirbekian 1997). The peacock was frequently depicted in Christian art. Christians adopted the symbol of the peacock to represent immortality in Christian catacombs and on sarcophagi, possibly connected with an ancient legend that the flesh of the peacock did not decay. It is also associated with the resurrection of Christ, for the same reason, and also because it sheds its old feathers every year and grows newer, brighter ones.

In India, the peacock, probably of Dravidian origin, is associated with several divinities in the Hindu pantheon. It also holds a prominent place in Indian folk tales and tribal beliefs (Nair 1974). In the Christian art of India, the peacock is a symbol of immortality, as well as of St. Thomas, the Apostle of Indian Christians. Peacocks can be seen above the gates of the churches, and on old crosses (information provided by István Perczel, Professor, Central European University, Budapest).

The position of the peacock in Islam seems to be more ambiguous. On the one hand, it can be a cosmic symbol. A Sufi legend, probably of Persian origin, tells that God created the Spirit in the form of a peacock and showed it its own image in the mirror of the Divine Essence. The peacock was seized with reverential awe and let fall drops of sweat and from these all other beings were created. The peacock's outspread tail imitates the cosmic deployment of the Spirit (*Christ Story Bestiary*, http://ww2.netnitco.net/users/legend01/peacock.htm, last accessed 08.11.07). In Islamic folklore, however, the peacock is associated with the Devil. It was the peacock, who – in one way or another – helped Iblis gain entrance to paradise and then seduce Adam and Eve to eat from the forbidden fruit. As a punishment God took away its

---

2. The word *qewwal*, literally "the one who chants or recites" originally referred to Sufi singers who sang ecstatic Sufi poems during *semas*, that is, spiritual sessions. They performed the "qawwali," the devotional music of the Chishti Sufis of the Indian Subcontinent, and they were hereditary specialists.

3. The *sanjaks* have had a troubled history. They were the favorite spoils of the hostile Ottoman armies and even of warring Yezidi fractions. Five of the *sanjaks* kept in Lalish were or example taken as war spoils to Baghdad in 1892, though they are said to have been returned later (Guest, 1993: 166, 171.) Today, some of the original *sanjaks* seem to have been lost for good, though it is impossible to know how many are actually left. Fuccaro (1999: 139) writes that in the 1920s only 3 images toured the Yezidi districts. My Yezidi friends in Iraq claimed that today only two are left, those of the Sheikhan and Sinjar district in Iraq, while Dr Jasim Murad (1993: 129) claims that the Aleppo and Diyarbakir *sanjaks* still remain and occasionally visit their district.

Fig. 4. The Sinjari Sanjak.

voice (Knappert 1985: 37). This may, at least partially, explain why Muslims identify the Peacock Angel with the Devil, especially since Yezidis also attribute the Peacock Angel with tricking Adam into tasting the forbidden fruit (or rather wheat), although they see it as a positive act in accordance with the wishes of God. However, trying to tie the worship of the peacock, as a symbol of divinity, to either of these religions or to any worship of birds in earlier religions of Mesopotamia or Iran, as some early researchers attempted to do (Ainsworth 1861; Badger 1852) is futile given the present state of our knowledge about the origin of Yezidi tenets.

This painful lack of written sources also creates obstacles in tracing the origin of the *sanjak* itself. According to Ainsworth (1861:26), a Father Garzoni, whose tract was published in 1807, was the first European to call attention to the Yezidis, "paying adoration, or at least a sort of worship, to the figure of a bird placed on a kind of candlestick, and called Melek Taus. Mr Rich and Mr Fraser corroborated the fact. 'Once a year' says the latter 'they worship the figure of a cock, which is called Melek Taus, placed before the assembly on a sort of candlestick."

Their information was corroborated by the traveler Frederick Forbes in the 1830s, who said that "at the village of *Sheikh* Adi is the figure of a peacock in brass, called Malik Taus (King Peacock), which is venerated as the emblem or representative of David and Solomon" (cited in Ainsworth 1861:27).

For a long time it was strictly forbidden for any non-Yezidi to set eyes on the *sanjak* and some Western travelers even doubted its existence (Ainsworth 1861: 27). The first European to actually see a *sanjak* was the archeologist Layard, the discoverer of Niniveh, in the first half of the 19th c. Even though he was much respected by the Yezidis, seen as their friend and protector, he was refused permission to see the Peacock by his friend, *Sheikh* Nasr, then the head of the sheikhdom, for fear that many Yezidis would take such an indiscretion amiss. However, having later helped to secure an Imperial *firman* from the Porte granting religious tolerance to the Yezidis and exempting them from the much-hated military conscription (Layard 1853:3-4), his esteem among the Yezidis rose so high that he was granted a viewing of the holy *sanjak* when he met a group of *qewwal*s doing their circuit near Redwan, on the upper Tigris. He made a drawing of the *sanjak*, which he described "as a fanciful image of a bird supported by a stand resembling a candlestick, the whole being of bronze," (Layard 1854:Ch. 8, Note 3). In another passage (1854:40) he writes:

"a stand of bright copper or brass, in shape like the candlestick generally used in Mosul and Baghdad, was surmounted by the rude image of a bird in the same metal, and more like an Indian or Mexican idol than a cock or peacock. Its peculiar workmanship indicated some antiquity, but I could see no traces of inscription upon it."

He also noted (1854: Ch. 8) that:
"There are several of these figures – one always remains with the great *sheikh*, and is carried with him wherever he may journey. When deputies are sent to any distance to collect money for the support of the tomb (of Sheik Adi) and the priests, they are furnished with one of these images, which is shown to those among whom they go, as an authority for their mission."

This is the Parading of the Peacock of which I shall speak later.

The next European to see the Peacock, after much pleading, was Mrs. Badger (1852:124), the wife of a British missionary, who happened to be present at a Yezidi festival.

"The figure is that of a bird, more resembling a peacock than any other fowl, with a swelling breast, diminutive head, and wide spreading tail. The body is full, but the tail flat and fluted, and under the throat is a small protuberance intended perhaps to represent a wattle. This is fixed on top of a candlestick... the whole is of brass, and so constructed, that it may be taken to pieces and put together with the greatest ease. Close by stand was a copper jug filled with water, which we understood

Fig. 5. Peacock censers of Indian Hindus, photos courtesy of István Perczel.

was dealt out to be drunk as a charm by the sick and afflicted."

Her drawing and description of the peacock calls to mind the Sheikhani *sanjak* (see photo above in Fig. 1). It seems that the seven standards were not exact replicas of each other. Each district may have had it own peculiar image of a peacock – at least the two *sanjak*s I was lucky enough to see, those of Sheikhan and Sinjar (both in present-day Iraq) were quite different, although both were mounted on candlesticks. The latter *sanjak* resembled a duck rather more than a peacock. (Fig. 4). Roger Lescot was of the same opinion "L'animal reproduit est censè être un paon, cependant, il ressemble plutôt à une colombe ou à un canard." (Lescot 1938:73).

The most important of the *Sanjak*s is from the Sheikhan region or "home of the *Sheikh*s" north of Mosul, the spiritual center of Yezidism. It is here that the Yezidi prince, most other religious leaders, and all the *qewwal*s reside. The valley of Lalish, the "Yezidi Mecca" also lies in this region. The so-called Sheikhani *Sanjak* is clearly fashioned after the Peacock censers of Indian Hindus (Fig. 5) – or perhaps it *is* a Hindu censer. Strange as it may sound at first, using a sacred object of another religion as the most important Yezidi holy symbol does not contradict the independent spirit and ethos of Yezidi faith. Rather, it reflects the amazing ability Yezidis have displayed in adopting and adapting motifs taken from other religions into their own system. Yezidi mythology is a living monument to this creative ability of incorporating external elements into their own oral tradition, but eloquent traces of it exist in the material side of religious culture as well.

A good example of such creative adoption is the sacred *nishan*, or "sign" I was shown in a *sheikh* family of

Sinjari origin. This particular *nishan* bore the words *dieu et mon droit*, and was in all probability a belt clip from a British uniform from the time of the British Mandate (1920-32). The most revealing part of the story of this beltclip-cum-*nishan* was the fact that though its owners knew Latin writing (in fact, the daughter of the house was a physics undergraduate), they never doubted the authenticity and ancient nature of the object as an "heirloom" from their distant ancestors and perhaps never even recognized that it was inscribed with a text written in Latin letters. Thus, if even such mundane objects can morph into sacred ones one can imagine with what great ease the already ritual censer, hailing from a place generally thought of as a mysterious land of true believers, might have been adopted as an ancient Yezidi religious object at one point. (Of course, the question of whether the Indian censer was the model for the Yezidi *sanjak* or whether there was some sort of a peacock standard already in existence cannot be answered.)

The connection with India comes up again and again in Yezidi mythology and their constructed past. Many are convinced today that there are Yezidis living in India, and evidently this idea is not a new one. Lady Drower (1941:99-100) also reported that *qewwals* told her how they used to travel far and wide before the time of borders, wars, and passports, including the lands of India. When she said she did not know there were Yezidis in India, they answered in the affirmative. Others see India as their ancient homeland. According to one of my informants, Feqir Haci of Baadra, one of the best known experts in Yezidi oral lore, the Yezidis used to live in India at the time of the Flood, from whence they later spread westward. The Yezidi website *Yezidi Truth Organisation* (http: yeziditruth.org/yezidi_religious_tradition, last accessed 08.11.07) recounts how:

110

"Following the last flood the Yezidis settled in the Indian sub-continent. Then, about 4,000 years ago many of them began to migrate west, moving into ancient Persia and the Middle East, where they participated in the Sumerian, Babylonian and Assyrian civilizations."[4]

Interestingly, the site also adds: "The *Sanjak*s, which came from the Yezidi homeland of India, are the most precious sacred objects among the Yezidi." Upon enquiry, the site webmaster, Mark Amaru Pinkham, confirmed that both pieces of information were "*oral testimony passed down through the Faqir family of Kaawal Hassan.*"

Although an Indian origin for the Yezidis does not sound too likely from a historical point of view, connection between Kurdistan and India, especially on a religious plane, must have been continuous and many-sided. The Nestorians of Mesopotamia (and Kurdistan) kept intensive connection with the Indian Christians throughout the Middle Ages. There is also Islamic Sufism, popular in Kurdistan, to be reckoned with. Yezidis themselves may have once started as a Sufi order, and even the name of their qewwal order may reflect Indian Sufic origins. The two Sufi orders followed in Kurdistan, Naqshibandi and Qadri, both have branches in, and therefore a connection with, India. What is more, Mewlana Salid, a Kurd of the powerful Jaf tribe, who brought the Naqshibendi order to Kurdistan at the beginning of the 19th c., received his initiation into the order in Delhi. According to the Kurdish Naqshibendi tradition a dream inspired him to go on a quest to India for mystical knowledge (Bruinessen 1978: 282). This would explain the possible adoption of an object of a religious nature from India as a Yezidi sacred object connected with the central symbol of their religious traditions, that is, the Peacock Angel.

Parading of the Peacock and maintaining Yezidi oral traditions

The *sanjak*, through the rituals associated with it, played an important role in maintaining and preserving Yezidi oral tradition, and thus, Yezidi religion itself. Yezidi faith was until recently a strictly oral religion. In fact it was forbidden to write down any of the sacred texts, the hymns and myths, and religious lore was transmitted orally from father to son. This transmission, however, was restricted in its nature. Traditionally, memorizing and reciting the religious texts, hymns, and myths was primarily the task of a special class, the so-called *qewwal*s or singers of the sacred hymns.

Qewwals acted as the living memory of the Yezidi community. These singers, to whom European travelers somewhat erroneously alluded to as "teachers of the doctrines of the sect" (as did Layard 1854:Ch. 8) traditionally resided in the twin villages of Beshiqe-Behzani near Mosul, from whence they traveled to other villages. *Qewwal*s officiated at ceremonies like the Autumn Festival at Lalish, at burials, and at the ceremonial mourning in graveyards on the morning of New Year; however, these activities were (and are) usually confined to their immediate district. It was only during the Parading of the Peacock, when the *sanjak*s were accompanied by a group of *qewwal*s, that these singers really ventured far from home, going as far as Aleppo or the Muscovy *sanjak*.[5]

One must bear in mind that Yezidi faith, like all oral religions, never developed a formal, unified theology. According to Kreyenbroek (1995:19-20) there is no "'official' form of the faith, – a monolithic, coherent system of dogma... different people have been taught different things... The lack of written tradition... has prevented the development of a formal theology, or a single, monolithic system of beliefs". There is not even universal agreement on the name of the seven holy angels of the Yezidi Pantheon (Allison 2001: 34; Drower 1941: 24; Lescot 1938: 46-47). Even "the form of prayer (word or gesture) or even the time of the day when prayer is made, often seems a matter of great variation" (Allison 2001: 34), a fact that missionaries of the past found "shocking to a Christian mind" (Badger 1852:117-118). Travelers have never failed to be amazed by the lack of common knowledge Yezidis display in matters of their religion, for "Yezidism" does not involve familiarity with a well-defined theological system or even with basic religious teachings, rather, as a sort of orthopraxy, it is based on the observations of certain religious taboos, and participation in rituals (Kreyenbroek 1995: 18-19; Murad 1993: 385, 388, 391). Conversely, these rituals are the main channels of acquiring some knowledge of Yezidi mythology. Under such circumstances the importance of the institution called the Parading of the Peacock, including the recital not only of *qewl*s (hymns), but also of the so-called *meshabet*s (sermons, preaching) cannot be overstated. The sermons preached by the *qewwal*s on these occasions are (or rather were) all the religious education and spiritual food most lay Yezidis are (or were) ever likely to receive.

If times are calm, the standards are taken around their region twice a year, in the spring and in the fall. Old people in the Sheikhan claim that the *sanjak* used to 'walk' three times a year in the past, but due to the poverty of the people this was reduced to twice a year. It seems likely that the *sanjak* may have been taken to more outlying regions only once a year or even less often. Some of the minor details of the Parading may have varied from region to region (or rather from *sanjak* to *sanjak*) but the

---

4. Mention of the Yezidi contribution to ancient Mesopotamian civilizations, however, is a recent development, connected with the spread of literacy and the wish of "modernizing" Yezidis. On this topic see Spät "Religious Oral Tradition" 2008.

5. Beside the *qewwal*s, religious leaders, basically an inherited family position, may also have had a more profound knowledge of the religion, but they were few, and just like the *qewwal*s, they mostly lived in the Sheikhan region, the center of "Yezidiland."

Fig. 6. Qewwals performing hymns during the Parading of the Peacock.

Fig. 7. Ceremonial meal during the parading of the Peacock.

most important features of the Parading are the same everywhere, however.[6]

The *sanjak*, carefully covered, is carried into the village by the delegation of *qewwal*s playing on their sacred instruments, the flute and the tambour. While the appropriate prayer is recited, the small bronze statuette of the Peacock is ceremoniously set up in the guest room of the host, next to a jug containing sacred water from the White Spring, a bag of sacred dust formed into balls (*berat*) from the holy valley of Lalish, and a sacred candle stick. Believers then begin arriving in long queues to pay their respects, that is, to kiss the standard and the hand of the leading *qewwal* and leave some money.

Later, the *qewwals* perform religious hymns accompanied by the sacred instruments (Fig. 6). The highlight of the event is the sermon preached by the leading *qewwal*. The topic is chosen after consulting the wishes of the audience, and the recitation of the sacred hymns is mixed with the retelling of myths and learned expositions on the subject. Yezidi laymen listen avidly in awed silence. A ceremonial meal consumed together with the guests is usually a part of the proceedings as well (Fig. 7). In the Sheikhan following the meal there is another session of hymn singing, when the elderly men present can request which hymns they would like to hear. These usually center around *Sheikh* Adi, the Peacock Angel, and Yezidi ancestors, and a special hymn is recited in honor of the ancestor *sheikh* to whose lineage the host belongs (Murad 1993:134-135). Once the allotted time is over and the trickle of visitors dries up, the Peacock is carefully wrapped in its protective sacred clothes and taken to a new house or a new village, where the proceedings are repeated again.

In earlier times the peacock was not only visited by Yezidis, but Muslims and Christians as well. According

to Mrs. Badger (1852: 124), when she saw the *sanjak* "a *Fakir* was in the room relating all the benefits that had been conferred on Christians and Mohammedans, as well as on Yezeedees, by the contribution to the Senjak." I was also told by a Kurd politician, a native of the Sinjar that decades ago in his childhood, all the Muslims used visit the peacock standard during its circuit. Thus, the Parading of the Peacock was also an important social occasion for strengthening the often tenuous alliance or strained relations with neighboring non-Yezidi tribes and communities

The Parading of the Peacock provided one of the rare opportunities when common Yezidis could get some form of religious instruction. Thus, the rituals surrounding the holy object of the *sanjak*, when the village community assembled to see the peacock and the *qewwal*s sang hymns and recited sermons explaining Yezidi myths and concepts, were of a great importance in preserving Yezidi religion as they secured the continuance of the oral tradition by providing an opportunity for the recitation of oral texts.

The relevance of the ritual of the Parading of the Peacock in disseminating and keeping alive religious knowledge in the Yezidi community is highlighted by the fieldwork carried out by the anthropologist Jasim Murad, himself a Yezidi of Sheikhan, among the German diaspora. Speaking of the "unawareness of these Yezidis [living in Germany] of the basic doctrines of their religion," (Murad 1993: 381), he claims that this can be attributed to the fact that:

"unlike the Yazidis who grew up in their native villages and hamlets, these younger generations grew up in an alien cultural environment that impedes the acquisition of a rich ritual life as a Yazidi. For example, the Standard of the Peacock Angel does not circulate among them, a ritual containing a major source for hearing the sacred

---

6. Earlier descriptions of the Parading of the Peacock seem to be in accordance with what I saw in the Sinjar region in the spring of 2004.

poems as well as being instructed in the basic doctrines of the religion."

This is corroborated by the interviews made with older Yezidis now living in Germany. Most of them mentioned the Parading of the Peacock as among the most important aspects of their earlier life "living as Yezidis" in their homeland, though the same informants made it clear that otherwise they had little knowledge of Yezidi tenets and religious texts. As a Yezidi woman from a mixed village in Syria said, "It was during the ritual of the Peacock Angel that my feelings as a Yazidi would become strengthened" (Murad 1993: 390). It must finally be mentioned that the Parading of the Peacock was an important tool for religious standardization, as far as this is possible in an oral tradition, for it ensured continuous contact between the religious center and periphery, preventing independent religious development in the latter. The Yezidi tribes of Armenia, shut off from the center after the creation of the Soviet Union, went through an independent development that is most intriguing for researchers.

Emergence of literacy, the twilight of oral tradition and transformation of the *Sanjak*

For centuries Yezidi faith was strictly based on oral tradition. This traditon, however, has changed over the last few decades. Elementary education has become widespread, illiteracy is gradually becoming a thing of the past and there is a slowly emerging Yezidi professional class with middle and higher education. Access to Western-style schooling and a growing familiarity with book-based religions and philosophy, coupled with the awareness that modernization and changing life-style may lead to the eventual loss of oral tradition, has led to Yezidi intellectuals writing down their sacred texts. The trend started in the 1970s, and the first publication was soon followed by several others published by Yezidi institutions like the state-backed Lalish Cultural Center in Iraq or its European counterparts. Many of these publications are easily available to most Yezidis. For example, *Lalish* and *Roj* magazines, which publish sacred hymns, religious tales, folktales and essays on Yezidi religion, can be found in many Yezidi homes.

This "bookish trend" was further accelerated by the sizeable Yezidi community now settled in the West, especially in Germany. These Yezidis are cut off from all the old forms of Yezidi religious life constituted by holiday rituals, visits to holy places or being visited by religious leaders. At the same time, living in close proximity with other religions for the first time, they are increasingly discomfited by the fact that, unlike other religions, they lack a holy book to which they can refer or a clear history of their own religion. Their children, confronted by the embarrassing lack of knowledge of their own religion when compared to their Western schoolmates or friends, are increasingly turning to books to make up for this perceived deficiency (Jasim 1993: 318-19, 382-398).

The diaspora, in its turn, further influences Yezidis back in the home country. (Kreyenbroek 2005: 45) This has led to a changing attitude toward books and oral tradition in general opinion, at least in the Iraqi Sheikhan and in the European diaspora, where the place accorded to oral tradition is fast becoming usurped by books written on, and mainly by, Yezidis. The isolated and impoverished Sinjar Mountain on the Iraqi-Syrian border, a refuge of Yezidis for centuries and under Saddam Hussein's rule until recently, seems to present a more traditional picture at present, although this may change in the near future.

During my fieldwork it was not unusual to have my informants, who were referred to by others as "knowledgeable on religion", refer to books and periodicals on Yezidis. Once I was even offered the book of John Guest, *Survival among the Kurds*, a thorough analysis of Yezidi history, to read by my host, who was avidly reading it with the aid of a dictionary. I was repeatedly referred to the two Yezidi periodicals, *Lalish* and *Roj*, as the "best sources of information." In one case, a university undergraduate even painstakingly translated a folktale, sentence by sentence, for my sake from *Roj* magazine. On more than one occasion I was glad to "collect" new information, which subsequently turned out to be not oral tradition, but merely gleaned from writings by Yezidi authors, who have tried to look for the roots of Yezidi faith and give a philosophical explanation to religious and mythical ideas (Spät 2008). Simultaneously with the emergence of books, the standing and respect of the *qewwal* class is also presently undergoing a rapid decline. In the past *qewwal*s were seen as the ultimate source of religious knowledge, and Europeans avid for information on Yezidi faith were almost automatically directed to them (Drower 1941: 14-15.). *Qewwal*s were much respected in the Yezidi community not only as the keepers, and consequently sources, of religious knowledge, but also as "men of the world," who travel far and wide (Drower 1941:16, 99-100). All this has come to an end with the advent of books, which seem to be slowly usurping the authority previously accorded to *qewwal*s. Since *qewwal*s are no longer as free to travel around the region as they used to during Ottoman times, their reputation as men of experience is also gone (while common Yezidis are often far more well-traveled thanks to modern technology and the economic and political necessity of emigration). Respect for the *qewwal*s seems to have diminished greatly even among the more traditionally minded. During my trip in 2003 and 2004 to Beshiqe-Behzani, the village of the *qewwal*s, for example, local people generally preferred to introduce me to "laymen," whom for some reason they saw as knowledgeable on the topic of religion, and accompanied me to meet *qew-*

Fig. 8. Drawing of a peacock with its fan tail fully open used on internet websites.

Fig 9. Stylized image of the Peacock sanjak based on Layard's drawing.

*wal*s only at my own request. One of my informants from Behzani, a man very interested in Yezidi religion who had been collecting Yezidi hymns for years, even expressed an opinion to the effect that *qewwal*s (and religious leaders for that matter) were no longer what they used to be and their knowledge can in no way be compared to the *qewwal*s of the past.

The change wrought by the emergence of "bookish religion" can perhaps best be exemplified by the foundation of the Yezidi "Sunday school" in Beshiqe, a school set up in the 1990s to teach the children of the twin villages their religion. The need was felt for such a school, with secular teachers and where all children, regardless of their class and caste, and book-based access to religious knowledge previously reserved for the privileged caste of *qewwal*s, the "memory keepers" of the very same village. The existence of such schools shows the change in mentality rather eloquently.

Under such circumstances, where oral tradition is being replaced by books, and *qewwal*s by teachers and writers or Yezidi intellectuals, rituals are slowly beginning to lose their ancient importance, as they are no longer seen as the sole or the most important means of gaining information on the Yezidi faith. Furthermore, for many Yezidi intellectuals intent on reforming and modernizing religion, rituals are worthy of attention only if they prove the ties of Yezidi religion to ancient cults, especially of an Iranian (that is, proto-Kurdish) origin. Rituals, like the Parading of the Peacock, which do not fit this new, up-to-date constructed past, may be tolerated for the sake of tradition, but they do not arouse much interest among the new "keepers of memory." Consequently, the Parading is fast losing its earlier importance. Due to the restrictions imposed by new political borders after World War I, the Peacock is, in any case, unable

to visit communities in the Caucasus and Turkey nor can a visit to the German diaspora be realistically envisaged. It is still a central event in the isolated region of the Jebel Sinjar, where illiteracy is high and contact with the outside world limited. It is of much less importance, however, in the Sheikhan region, especially in the settlements that lie within the borders of the Autonomous Kurdish Region established in 1991. Thus, for example, in the fall of 2002, my Yezidi acquaintances in the Yezidi Center of Duhok failed to inform me that the Parading of the Peacock was taking place in a nearby village. I assume this was simply due to the fact that they did not attribute special importance to this event anymore. Since the war, due to the dangers of terrorism, the Sheikhan Peacock no longer tours the Sheikhan, while the Sinjar Peacock still makes its rounds regularly, though the Sinjar is certainly no safer than the Sheikhan.

One might expect that the *sanjak*, as a physical representation of the Peacock Angel, would lose "prestige" and become a mere object of antiquarian interest. This is not exactly what is happening, however; the peacock standard seems to be continuing its career of adapting to new circumstances. While the importance of the Parading of the Peacock, and the accompanying rituals is slowly diminishing in some Yezidi communities, the same communities seem to be embracing the image of the peacock as a symbol of Yezidi identity, religion and culture, in a word of "Yezidiness". Many Yezidi publications in the diaspora and most Yezidi websites now carry the image of the peacock. Presently, there seems to be no agreement about what form to use. Beside the photo of real peacocks, the two most popular images are the drawing of a peacock with its fan tail fully open (Fig. 8), and a stylized image of the Peacock *sanjak* based on the drawing of Layard (Fig. 9), the first European to have seen the Peacock.[7] (http://www.yezidi.org/, http://yeziditruth.org/the_peacock_angel, h ttp://www.nadir.org/nadir/initiativ/kurdi-almani-kassel/kultur/yeziden/yezidism.htm, http://www.andrewcollins.com/page/articles/thecygnusmystery_heaven.htm to mention a few, last accessed June 20, 2008)

A third image, showing a young Indian woman dressed in a sari and facing a peacock *sanjak*, is just becoming popular. This image has recently even been painted on a wall near the White Spring where Yezidi children are baptized in the center of the holy valley of Lalish. (http://dailyhawler.blogspot.com/2008_05_01_archive.html, see entry "Tawsi Melek *Sanjak*," last accessed June 20, 2008) [8]

As the globalization of Yezidism and its break into cyberspace is still relatively new, it would be safe to assume that with time a generally accepted image will emerge, and while the peacock *sanjak* was a sacred object in the past destined to help preserve Yezidi oral tradition, the new peacock image will be the symbol of a conscious effort to keep alive the memory of Yezidism in modern times.[9]

Conclusions

The Yezidis, without books or written history, have traditionally employed a limited number of objects as material manifestations of ancient religious traditions and authority. Some of these objects, like the *nishans*

and the *sanjaks* are real heirlooms, handed down from generation to generation. In the case of other objects, like the sacred items of clothing, it is not the actual item, but the idea of what a Yezidi should wear and the connotations such objects bring to mind which is inherited. All these objects, however, are similar in their main function: they connect Yezidis with their past and their ancestors, both mythical and real, thereby becoming objects evoking communal memory. The peacock *sanjak*, a bronze image symbolizing the Peacock Angel, the angel protecting Yezidis and serving as an instrument for keeping alive the religious memory of Yezidis is by far the most important object. Its importance must be understood in relation to the absence of written religious texts and formal religious education among the Yezidis, which could have led to a rapid fragmentation or even the complete disappearance of Yezidi religion, had these factors not been counterbalanced by a number of institutions, including the Parading of the Peacock. The rituals, connected with the parading of the *sanjak* provided a venue for the recital of sacred texts and myths. The *sanjaks*, together with the ritual telling of these stories, helped keep alive constructed religious memory and contributed to the continuance of a religious tradition, which otherwise relied on oral tradition, that is, active memory, instead of written texts. The Parading of the Peacock also ensured, through the presence of religious experts accompanying the peacock, that a relative religious unity was maintained within the far-flung and sometimes isolated Yezidi communities, checking independent developments to a certain degree, despite the distances separating the settlements.

With the arrival of literacy, modern life and increasing contact with the non-Yezidi world, these traditional ways of preserving religious memory have changed. Oral tradition relying on memory is slowly being replaced by book learning. These changes have profoundly affected the role of material culture in religion, including such objects as the peacock *sanjak* as a "trigger" of religious memory.[10] As the position previously filled by *qewwals* and rituals is being taken over by written materials, the role of the peacock *sanjak* in helping sustain religious memory, or oral tradition is fast diminishing in importance. Instead of becoming an obsolete object however, it is gaining a new role as the symbol of Yezidi identity

---

7. One may wonder why it is not one of the *sanjaks*, preferably the Sheikhan one, that is reproduced. The explanation is probably not unconnected with the secrecy that used to shroud the *sanjaks* from foreign eyes. It must be noted that – as far as I know – no photos were available of the Sinjari *sanjak* prior to the publication of my book (Spät 2005), and only one rather blurry photo of the Sheikhan *sanjak* in the book of John Guest (1993: fig 31.)

8. When I last visited Lalish in 2006, September, this painting was not yet there. As has been said above, the idea that they have come from India can be found among Yezidis today, though its popularity is limited. However, it seems fairly certain that with this image in such a prestigious place, Indian origins will in a few years' time become a common motif among Iraqi Yezidis, and thus, we shall witness the birth of a new oral tradition, and a new kind of constructed past arising out of an object (or a painting this time).

9. After having finished this article, I received a draft article from Khanna Omerkhali, a researcher of Yezidis in Armenia, about the recent reappearance of one of the *sanjaks* in Armenia. In her draft article she gives an account of how according to her Yezidi informants, the *sanjak* was just touring the region of Kars (then Russia, now Turkey) when WW I began and could not return to the Sheikhan. At the time of the Armenian genocide, when the persecution of Yezidis was also renewed, its temporary owner managed to carry it away to the territory that is today Armenia. There it stayed hidden for over seven decades, first for the fear of the atheist regime, then – after the fall of the Soviet Union – for the fear it would be stolen and sold by criminal elements. Since 2000, however, this alleged *sanjak* is no longer in hiding. On holidays and Wednesday, the Yezidi holy day, it is publicly and ritually exhibited to followers, many of whom have made a pilgrimage to see it. Such pilgrimages are said not to be inferior to the traditional pilgrimage to Lalish, and confer great grace on the pilgrims. (Her article complete with photos can be found on the websites: http://www.bahzani.net/services/forum/showthread.php?t=18194 and http://www.rojava.net/03.11.2007_X_Omerxali.htm (Sites last accessed on June 20, 2008).

10. As regards the changes in the role of other sacred objects, such as *nishans* or items of clothing, it is hard to make comparisons between their role in the past and at present, as earlier publications on Yezidis make no (*nishans*) or very little (items of clothing) mention of them. It may be assumed that as religious feelings in general decline among modernized Yezidis and the traditional casts lose their high social standing, these objects are slowly becoming less significant. Fewer and fewer Yezidis, for example, wear the special undershirt, and paying to see the *nishans* may be less and less popular with time. Whether these objects will be assigned a new role in emerging "modern Yezidism" like the Peacock *Sanjak* is yet to be seen, though one must keep in mind that among the sacred objects it was doubtlessly the *sanjak* which carried the most profound and universal associations for the community as a whole.

per se, detached from rituals, sacred texts. Thus, the peacock *sanjak* is evolving from an ancient instrument of religious memory into a symbol that recalls the memory of a common Yezidi past in Yezidis living in different parts of the world.

Bibliography

Aisnworth, W. F. 1861. The Assyrian Origin of the Izedis or Yezidis – the so-called 'Devil Worshippers.' *Transaction of the Ethnological Society of London* Vo 1. London: Ethnological Society, pp. 11-44.

Allison, C. 2001. *The Yezidi Oral Tradition in Iraqi Kurdistan*. Richmond: Curson Press.

Amirbekian, R. 1997. Contribution a la Qestion des Symboles Zoomorphes dans l'Art de l'Orient (Le Serpent et le Paon). In *Iran and Caucasus I: Research Papers from the Caucasian Centre for Iranian Studies, Yerevan*. Garnik Asatrian, (ed.) Tehran: International Publications of Iranian Studies, pp. 147-158

Badger, R. G. P. 1852. *The Nestorians and Their Rituals: With the Narrative of a Mission to Mesopotamia and Coordistan in 1842-1844*. Vol 1. London: Joseph Masters.

Bruinessen, van M. 1978. *Agha, Shaikh, and State: On the Social and Political Organization of Kurdistan*. Utrecht: Rijswijk.

Chabot, Abbé, J.-B. 1896. Notice sur les Yézidis: Publiée d'après deux manuscrits syriaques de la Biblothèque Nationale. *Journal Asiatique series* 9. vol.7, pp. 100-132.

ChristStory Bestiary, http://ww2.netnitco.net/users/legend01/peacock.htm

Drower, E. S. 1941. *Peacock Angel*. London: John Murray.

Empson, R. H. W. 1928. *The Cult of the Peacock Angel* 29-30. London, Witherby.

Fuccaro, Nelida. 1999. *The Other Kurds: Yazidis in Colonial Iraq*. London – New York: Tauris.

Guest, J. S. 1993. *Survival among the Kurds: A History of Yezidis*. London: Kegan Paul International.

Joseph, I. 1909. Yezidi Texts. *The American Journal of Semitic Languages and Literatures* 25.2, pp. 111-56.

Kreyenbroek, P. G. 1995. *Yezidism, its Background, Observances and Textual Tradition*. Lewiston (New York): The Edwin Mellen Press.

_____ 2005. *God and Sheikh Adi are Perfect: Sacred Poems and Religious Narratives from the Yezidi Tradition*. Wiesbaden: Harrasowitz.

Knappert, J. 1985. *Islamic Legends: Histories of Heroes, Saints and Prophets of Islam* vol. 1. Leiden: Brill.

Layard, A. H. 1854. *A Popular Account of Discoveries at Nineveh*. New York: Derby. http://mcadams.posc.mu.edu/txt/ah/Layard/DiscNineveh08.html

_____ 1853. *Discoveries Among the Ruins of Niniveh and Babylon*. London: John Murray.

Lescot, R. 1938. *Enquète sur Les Yezidis de Syrie et du Sjebel Sindjār*. Beyrouth: Institut Français de Damas.

Murad, Jasim Elias. 1993. The Sacred Poems of the Yezidis: An Anthropological Approach. (PhD Thesis, University of California at Los Angles.)

Nair, T. 1974. The Peacock Cult in Asia. *Asian Folklore Studies* 33. 2, pp. 93-170.

Polo, Marco and Rustichello of Pisa. *The Travels of Marco Polo*, Volume 2, Eds. Henry Yule and Henri Cordier. Release Date: May 22, 2004 [eBook #12410] http://www.gutenberg.org/catalog/world/readfile?fk_files=58430

Spät, E. 2005. *The Yezidis*. London: Saqi Books.

_____ 2008. Religious Oral Tradition and Literacy Among the Yezidis of Iraq. *Anthropos* 103.2, pp. 393-404.

Yezidi Truth Organisation, http: yeziditruth.org/yezidi_religious_tradition

CREATING A PLACE OF MEMORY: OLVERA STREET, LOS ANGELES

Judith A. Rasson

Abstract

Places of memory (*lieux de memoir*) are adapted from many different kinds of places (structures, ruins, sites of significant events, sacred locales, and so on). They are culturally defined and created and each one has its own history nested into a larger historical picture. This paper examines the elements needed to create (and modify) a place of memory in a case study of Olvera Street, in Los Angeles, California. A place of memory needs: a foundation myth or mythology; an event, person, thing, or place to accommodate memories; input from society, both upper and lower strata; reception of the memory; associated items of material culture, and time for development. The Olvera Street development was started in the 1920s mainly by European-Americans as a nostalgic place for an imagined 18th century Mexican past; changes over time have led to it to be increasingly integrated into regional Hispanic culture.

Keywords: Place of memory, California history, Olvera Street, Los Angeles

***

Olvera Street, a short street in downtown Los Angeles devoted to the memory of Mexican heritage, can serve as a case study of the formation and perpetuation of collective memory over a period of about 80 years (Fig. 1). The street, now known formally as the El Pueblo de Los Angeles Historic Monument, was developed as a commercial enterprise to celebrate nostalgia for California's Hispanic past. The project began in 1926 as a tourist-oriented "Mexican marketplace;" the street was opened in 1930, and still attracts residents and visitors (Fig. 2). This theme has been maintained, but practice over time has changed and added layers of meaning. What began as a commercial venture based on nostalgia has been transformed by many different forces into a place of memory (*lieu de memoire*).

Memory is a topic intimately linked to culture. The general concept of Culture includes the idea that people, in particular regional and national cultures, try to make sense of the surrounding natural, social, and supernatural worlds. This "making sense" includes classifying people into Us and Them (the Other) and using the past to help explain the present. Memory, personal and collective, is one way of managing the past. Every society constructs and uses memories for the maintenance of its own culture. Furthermore, since all cultures change over time, so do group and individual memories and the understanding of the meaning of these memories.

Many scholars have contributed to understanding how memory works and how it is used (Nora 1989; Connerton 1989; Middleton and Edwards 1990; Kammen 1991; Olick and Robbins 1998). A short definition that sums up a great deal of literature is that the study of memory "focuses creatively on how people construct the past through appropriation and contestation" (Confino 1997: 1403). Appropriation and contestation are part of the dynamics of collective memory formation because group memories are compounded of personal memories seen through a cultural filter that suggests to individuals what is important to remember and why. Memory is often aided by items of material culture and often associated with particular locales of varying sizes (Nora 1989; Schwartz 1982).

Memories can be created by the powerful in society, often the political or social elite, those associated with institutions. Formal or informal, this is rather a top-down creation, like the fixing of Veteran's Day or Thanksgiving Day by an act of Congress or the establishment of the Colonial Williamsburg historic site museum by John D. Rockefeller, Jr. Memories are also created from the bottom up in society, by the aggregation of individual acts (spontaneously putting flowers and candles at the site of an accident; putting flowers and cards outside Buckingham Palace after Princess Diana's death). Often a complex interweaving of public and private acts and ideas goes into developing memory (Kammen 1991:10). Once a collective memory, whatever its origin, is internalized by individuals and groups, additional processes of cultural adaptation and change can take effect. Thus, memory creation and maintenance are the result of com-

Fig. 1. Aerial view of the Plaza and Olvera Street in the 1920s (Reproduced courtesy of Los Angeles Public Library).

plex cultural and social behaviors (potentially) across a wide spectrum of a society.

The elements of memory construction are: A foundation myth or mythology; an event, person, thing, or place (or a combination thereof) to accommodate the memories; input from society, both upper and lower strata; reception of the memory and its attributes among different people; associated items of material culture, and time for development.

A foundation myth may originate in the sacred or secular sphere. All societies have a creation mythology that explains the origins of humanity and the natural and supernatural worlds. Ancillary mythology supports the central myth. The mythology provides the theme(s) for commemoration of the memory in culturally appropriate ways, in material items, agency (actions), texts, and oral traditions. A trigger helps to focus the memory. It can be a real or supernatural event, person, place, or thing. Usually several elements combine to provide the focus; these elements may have their own myths attached. Appropriation comes in with mythology and triggers by borrowing ideas and forms from other areas of culture or even other cultures.

To be established, a collective memory requires reception and input from the members of society. These contributions may be planned or unplanned, from the upper or lower echelons. This is where contestation comes into the picture; not everyone necessarily agrees on the content and associated attributes of the memory. This is part of the construction of memory, when different interests vie for inclusion and/or primacy in the formation and celebration of the memory. It is also part of the reception, how different people and groups accept or react to all or parts of the memory.

Time is needed for collective memories to take shape and be more or less standardized culturally. All elements of culture change through time, and memory (both individual and collective) is no exception.

Nostalgia (Lowenthal 1975; Stewart 1988) is a facet of memory. Both memory and nostalgia can be personal and/or collective and both can act powerfully on human thoughts and behaviors, but nostalgia is more superficial and of shorter duration. Neither requires personal memories of the places, events or people that played parts in the phenomenon memorialized. Both can be learned from the cultural milieu, but the depth of feeling may depend on a perceived personal connection between a person and the person, place or event commemorated. Memory is more deep-seated; it prompts more associations with material and non-material culture and it may also prompt (secular or spiritual) ritual(s). Nostalgia prompts action (re-decorating the kitchen in 1950s style for instance), but not necessarily ritual. Activities arising from nostalgia can become memory when they "stabilize," that is, when they take on chronological depth and deeper meaning. Memory is relatively focused on a cultural item (a person, place, thing, and/or event) and nostalgia is relatively unfocused. Memory acts over longer time frames and encompasses folk memory and acts of remembrance. Nostalgia operates over shorter time frames, although it may come in waves, such as repeated waves of interest in the ancient Egyptians or the flapper era. Nostalgia can become memory when it is operative for the long term, acted upon, and organized selectively, which is more likely to happen when this development is tied to a place or places. The development and longevity of Olvera Street seem to be an example of nostalgia becoming memory. In order to understand the elements that have gone into the construction of this place of memory it is necessary to review an outline of historical events.

Background history

The region now known as the State of California was first settled by Europeans when Spanish colonists arrived from Mexico (including Baja California) in the late eighteenth century (1769). The first settlements were a string of outposts along the coast; later occupation extended inland. The settlers comprised three groups of immigrants: first, Spanish and Mexican soldiers and Franciscan friars, and later Mexican settlers. Although the Jesuits were established earlier in Baja California (today Mexico), Alta California (today the State of California) was the domain of the Franciscans. The soldiers established forts (*presidios*) and the Franciscans began missionary work using the same methods that they had used in Mexico and Europe. The Franciscans converted many Native Americans to Catholicism and established settlements of neophytes where they replicated building techniques used in contemporary Spain. The Mediterranean climates in both areas made

118

Fig. 2. Postcard view of El Paseo de Los Angeles, Olvera Street, ca. 1930; the tall building visible in the background is city hall (Reproduced courtesy of Los Angeles Public Library).

this technology transfer relatively easy as the same raw materials were available in both places: wood and soil. The soil was made into sun-baked adobe brick for construction and into roof tiles fired in wood fires. Wood served for roof beams, door and window frames, furniture, and so on. The style of the buildings was rather plain; peaked roofs were tiled, other roofs were flat, waterproofed with tar (bitumen) from local seeps or collected on the beaches. The mission churches were two stories high with pitched, tiled roofs, often with a square tower (later with bells). The Franciscans duplicated their customary monastic architecture with covered cloister walkways surrounding a small garden adjacent to the church. Dwelling structures for settlers and resident Native Americans were also of adobe, usually single-storied flat-roofed buildings with rooms arranged in a square with doors opening onto a central patio. There was virtually no exterior decoration except plaster. Interiors were plastered and perhaps whitewashed.

The Franciscans left a lasting imprint on California in their choices of place names. Virtually all the early settlements and missions had names that reflected Franciscan devotion: San Franciso (for St. Francis himself), Santa Clara (for St. Clare), San Buenaventura (today Ventura, for St. Bonaventura), San Juan Capistrano (for St. John of Capistran), and Nuestra Señora la Reina de los Angeles (now Los Angeles, for the Virgin Mary). Often the names were selected from the saint's day when a settlement was established.

Along with religion and the Spanish language, the Franciscans introduced European material culture to the Indian converts, including agriculture, viticulture, stock raising, and textile and ceramic production (although some native populations already made pottery and all of them had sophisticated basketry traditions). Mission populations lost many of their native cultural prac-

tices, including language. Some descendents of these neophytes are today known by the name of their missions (Luiseños for Mission San Luis Rey, Gabrielinos for Mission San Gabriel Archangel) rather than by their original tribal names. Many missions incorporated members of different tribal groups, which had their own names and languages but close cultural similarities with neighboring groups. A large literature on the process of missionization details the vicissitudes of the local population, which included epidemics of European diseases like measles as well as loss of their own cultural heritage (Coombs and Plog 1977; Milliken 1995; Green 2002).

The traditional lifeways of California Indians were based on hunting and gathering. At the time the Spanish arrived there was a rather dense population by hunter-gatherer standards with associated social organization such as chiefdoms (in some areas). Social groups moved in a seasonal round to harvest wild resources; they stored food and in chiefdoms the chiefs redistributed it; they also traded with neighboring groups as the opportunity arose. The principal plant food staple was acorns, which had to be processed by leaching the ground acorn meal with water before cooking and eating. Many wild seeds, roots, and greens were also eaten. The principal sources of meat were hunted animals like deer and rabbits, and (along the coast) seafood like fish, shellfish, and sea mammals (Heizer 1978; Kroeber 1925). Of course, individual groups' diets varied depending on regional features such as how far they were from the coast. Relying on wild resources, however, meant that there could be times of hunger during the year when stored foods had run out and wild foods were difficult to find. At such times Native Americans came to the missions in larger numbers. Some stayed on and became residents; some left again, although there was pressure from the Franciscans and converts to remain.

119

Settlers who were neither soldiers nor missionaries began to arrive several years after the first footholds were established. Unlike the Franciscans, many of whom originally came from Spain, and the soldiers, a few of whom were Spanish natives, the settlers were all natives of Mexico. According to contemporary documentary evidence many of them were classed as *mulatto* or *mestizo*, signifying that they were of mixed race; there were a number of Indians and one man classified as *negro* (Mason 1998:45-54). They were assigned land in areas separate from the missions—they received a house plot, a plot with access to water (for vegetables), and land for non-irrigated crops and stock raising. The first settlers were of modest means and the first settlements were mere hamlets of adobe houses centered around a plaza with a church.

In 1821, Mexico became independent of Spain, which changed the government and had the impact in California of increasing the number of large land grants for private ranches. Between 1824 and 1836 the missions were secularized and their lands distributed to local Hispanic residents. In only a few cases was land granted to the converted Native Americans resident on former mission landholdings. Life was based on an extensive economy of raising cattle, with plant foods (grain, legumes, vegetables, fruit, wine) supplied by local production. Landowners with large tracts of land lived part of the year on their estates (haciendas) and part of the year in houses they maintained in town. Cattle were less valued for meat than for hides and tallow, which were exported, mainly through American trading ships.

Starting in the 1820s Euro-Americans began to arrive in California overland from the United States, areas such as New Mexico and Texas, and east by ship around the Horn of Africa. Almost all these immigrants were men; at first their numbers were small and they adapted by using such strategies as Hispanicizing their names and marrying into local families. Many of them were land-hungry and happy to inherit or otherwise acquire land. They seem to have been relatively well integrated into local Mexican society. In the mid-1840s there were several attempts to seize California and claim it for the United States, which was finally achieved in 1847. Life was somewhat "Americanized", but otherwise went on as before economically and socially. California became a state in the United States in 1848.

In 1849, however, things changed—gold was discovered in the Sierra Nevada foothills 25 miles (roughly 40 km) east of the port of San Francisco. This news brought a flood of gold-seekers from the U.S. and Europe that quickly swamped the local population in San Francisco, Sacramento, and the Sierra Nevada foothill areas. The impact on Los Angeles was much less dramatic, mainly seen in the development of trade in cattle and other foodstuffs to supply the mining region.

The goldrush gave an impetus to economic development, often foreshadowed by land speculation. After statehood, Mexican landholdings were required to be documented in U.S. courts, a long and costly process that left many Mexican landowners with mountains of debt that forced them to sell the land after it was finally confirmed to them legally. American and European entrepreneurs introduced large-scale grain agriculture, fruit growing, and stock raising in the agricultural sector (as well as land development and speculation) and services such as banking and shipping.

After the American Civil War (1861-1865), Los Angeles became a modern city with a central downtown with fired brick multi-storey buildings, industrial areas for manufacturing, and business precincts of small shops. The original town center of adobe structures was surrounded by suburbs of wooden dwellings in the American Victorian style, linked with the downtown by street railways. Railroads linked the city itself with other business centers in California and the U.S.

While development spread on previously uninhabited land around the city, older areas of the city center were marginalized by changing transportation routes, shifts in residential areas, and the decay of earlier standing structures. If not maintained, adobe buildings were susceptible to water and earthquake damage. Their floor plans did not suit Anglo-American residential patterns, making them not particularly desirable unless they could be altered.

Euro-American culture swamped the Hispanic nature of California to a large extent. Contemporary Californians of Mexican descent were largely considered marginal, a race apart; they had their own part of Los Angeles called Sonora Town. They were not alone in this; the Chinese population was relegated to a Chinatown area. Native Americans were mostly confined to reservations (*rancherias*) or grouped with the Spanish-speakers. The small group of descendents of the last Mexican inhabitants who had intermarried with the social elite was an exception—they were accepted as white.

Transformations of history

In twentieth-century memory, California Indians did not have the cachet of the Plains Indians, with their horses and feathered headdresses. They had been rather modest and did not have the flamboyant reputation of those like the Apache, Geronimo. Helen Hunt Jackson, a writer and activist for Indian rights, traveled to California as a special commissioner of Indian Affairs in 1882. She had had considerable influence through *Century of Dishonor* (1881), a report on the depredations of Euro-Americans on Native Americans. After her visit to Southern California, based on a true incident, she dramatized the plight of California Native Americans, and incidentally Mexican-Americans, in *Ramona; a Story* (1884), a love story about a Mexican girl who falls in love with and marries an Indian (Ales-

Fig. 3. Memorial statue of Felipe de Neve on the Plaza, with performer (Photograph by Alexander Kules, 2008).

sandro). Portraying the Native Americans as victims, this liaison ended tragically in Alessandro's death, which Jackson well knew was required by the social prohibition on inter-racial marriages. The novel has been in print ever since the first edition and spawned the place name Ramona (in San Diego County) and the Ramona Pageant (staged in Hemet, Riverside County, annually since 1923), a community-based annual re-enactment of the story in an open-air amphitheater (Fish 1995). The novel *Ramona*, despite the intention of dramatizing a social problem, was one of the first pieces of literature to romanticize the Californian past. It began to establish mythological roots for a suitable image of the past that Euro-Americans could relate to.

After the 1900s, Mission-style architecture became wildly popular as a revival trend, adopted by the Arts and Crafts movement. It incorporated Hispanic cultural traditions such as small windows (to conserve coolness or warmth) and rooms connected by opening onto an inner courtyard. Churches were similarly built, inspired by Mexican colonial examples. The revival style was characterized by sometimes a-typical features: stucco finishes over a wood-frame structure, flat tarred roofs with red tile trim, arches in windows and interior doorways, patios (often incongruously attached to the front of the house), and towers. It was used for public buildings such as the Mission Inn in Riverside and for many private homes, modest and grand, throughout Southern California.

Foundation myth

The foundation myth of Olvera Street was created by sentimentalizing and romanticizing the Californian Hispanic past of the 18th and 19th centuries. Strong associations of esteemed people, events, or the place itself, such as George Washington's association with Mount Vernon, were absent, which allowed more scope for malleability of the past. The place was selected by almost coincidence. Olvera Street is short, only (160.47 m long by 19.05 m wide); it does not really lead anywhere except to the Plaza since it parallels Main Street, a larger thoroughfare, and ends at Cesar Chavez Avenue (formerly Macy Street). It was still unpaved in the 1920s. The street name had been changed from Calle Vino (Wine Street) to Olvera Street for Augustin Olvera, the first elected judge in Los Angeles County, who had lived at the Plaza end of the street. His home was torn down before the street was selected as a monument. The only standing structure from the pre-statehood period is the Avila Adobe, an adobe house originally built in traditional materials and style, but later modified by the addition of a pitched roof and other non-traditional features. The remaining structures on the street are brick, mostly 19th century architecture; many structures on the north side of the street back onto the shop fronts facing Main Street but a few face Olvera Street. The only event connected to California history was the surrender of the Mexican army to Commodore Stockton at the Avila Adobe in 1847.

The Plaza (Fig. 1), at the western end of Olvera Street, was originally the center of town during the Spanish-Mexican periods. Subsequently the business center of town moved up-slope to the north and a large brick water tank was erected in Plaza as part of the city's water system (an upgrade of the existing *zanja* Hispanic water delivery and irrigation system). In the 1880s and 1890s the Plaza was treated as a park, planted with decorative trees and shrubs. In the 1910s Chinese vegetable vendors used the Plaza as a market area and in the 1920s it became a venue for radical street orators (Estrada 1999). This feature may have made it unsuitable as an anchor for the original conception of the Mexican marketplace as a wholesome and sentimental location; further, until 1929 the Plaza was cut off from Olvera Street by traffic on the cross-street, Sunset. At the same time as Olvera Street was beginning to promulgate the romantic Anglo-American view of history, immigration officials were rounding up Mexicans from the Plaza for deportation to Mexico (Kropp 2001), even Mexican-Americans with American citizenship.

The negative associations of the 1920s were more or less erased by World War II; with traffic no longer flowing on Sunset the resulting open space served to connect the Plaza with Olvera Street. The Plaza was incorporated into the myth of the Hispanic past by erecting a bandstand, decorative plantings, benches for pedestrians, and a number of statues to commemorate assorted historic events and personalities such as Father Junipero Serra, the Franciscan credited with founding the California missions, and Felipe de Neve, the governor of both Californias from 1777 to 1782 (Fig. 3).

Other than lying near the city center, Olvera Street had little special connection with Los Angeles history. It might equally well have been an Italian street, since a winery (in use from the 1880s to about 1940) and the Italian Hall (built in 1908, used by the Italian immigrant community) and Pelanconi House were located there. The façades of several of these buildings faced Main Street. The link between the relatively recent immigrants from Italy and the deeper historical past was not felt to have the same connection to cultural roots. Anchored in the Avila Adobe, Olvera Street gave a spatial fix to history that could otherwise be embellished freely.

Input from society

Responding to an interest in cultural heritage that was "in the air" in the post-World War I era, Mrs. Christine Sterling, a relative newcomer, took on a project for Los Angeles (Dentzel 1963). She was a middle-class woman from the San Francisco area who found a strong resonance in the idea of a romantic Hispanic past. She was not from local society, which meant she was not embedded in any particular interest group and she was not wealthy. She was supported by the editor of the *Los Angeles Times*, Harry Chandler, and other prominent businessmen. They had their own agenda, which was far from romantic; the city center was seen to need development, which meant moving out resident populations, who were mainly minorities: Mexicans, African-Americans, and Indians. Thus, Sterling's vision, which she implemented with a great deal of hard work, played into the hands of Chandler and others with a more directly gentrifying (even eugenic) program.

There was not much competition for this space, so Sterling did not face barriers put up by developers with other plans. Their interest lay just beyond the street near the Southern Pacific train depot in the area known as Chinatown, where they hoped to (and ultimately did) erect the central train station (in grand Mission style).

Sterling masterminded publicity efforts to save the Avila Adobe from demolition and get the street cleared of trash. She received help from the city, which provided prisoners for free labor. Famously, she noted in her diary: "One of the prisoners is a good carpenter, another an

Fig. 4. The cross at the Plaza entrance to Olvera Street, erected in 1930 (Photograph by Alexander Kules, 2008).

electrician. Each night I pray they will arrest a bricklayer and a plumber" (Elkins 1981). The first developments were quite modest, involving cleaning the street, paving or bricking it over, and adding a central drain paved with cobblestones, which evoked a *zanja*, one of the ditches that supplied the settlement with water in the Hispanic period. At first vendors laid out their wares on the pavement, later street furniture was moveable stands; later still small stalls (*puestos*) were added permanently down the center of the street, which increased the density of shopping opportunities. Some businesses opened in the standing structures, including at least one restaurant.

Local interest in Olvera Street was not unique in the United States. Kammen (1991:13) identifies the period from 1915 to 1945 as a time "when tradition became a by-word yet remained contested." The 1920s saw a burgeoning interest in historical heritage across the country. This was the period when Rockefeller began the development of Colonial Williamsburg (Gable, Handler, and Lawson 1992). Such projects were anchored in places and personalities important in American history. They were initiated by the social elite and often paid for by wealthy benefactors (Chandler 1934, for example).

Associated material culture

Material objects, moveable and immobile, add color and texture to memory. The modern cross on a cobblestone pedestal at the entrance to Olvera Street (Fig. 4) was an early part of the constructed romance, meant to evoke the simple piety of the early settlers. Likewise a small shrine in a courtyard off the street, neither of which was in any way original. Both served as props for photo oportunities, with young girls kneeling before them. Ironically, the original Plaza Church, just across Main Street to the north, a true Catholic locus, was not incorporated in the Olvera Street development. Perhaps it exuded a strong persona of its own that was not as romantic as imagined religion safely in the past.

A picturesque modern fountain, installed near the Avila Adobe, was not connected to the original pueblo water supply system. It served as a backdrop for photgraphs romanticizing what in reality was the hard daily-life task of carrying water for the household (see, for example, "Female Group...", 1936). Ironically, the *zanja* (water delivery system) originally led past Olvera Street, adapted for city use in the early years of American rule; the city pumping station was located in the center of the Plaza.

The Avila Adobe housed one of the few early installations that was truly interpretive instead of commercial. When Sterling started the Olvera Street project the house had long been converted from a family home to a rooming house. She gathered antiques to recreate a period life-style, aided by donations from descendents of Mexican settlers. The furniture and other objects offered visitors a chance to develop a personal sense of past lifeways.

A personal remembrance of a visit could be garnered from a tourist feature in the Plaza: the opportunity to be photographed in a Mexican sombrero or on a donkey. The donkey, originally live, was later preserved through taxidermy and became a popular fixture (see Fig. 7, below). Providing a venue for photographs was a significant way to give visitors a way to take away a small souvenir that could be re-visited for the memory, especially in times when many people did not own cameras.

Commemorating the first settlers at first required a bit of indirection, since all of them were from the lower social strata and at least one of them was described as *negro* in the records (which may have meant of dark complexion rather than of African descent). In a segregated Los Angeles this feature of the earliest settlers' group was originally omitted. The romantic picture of the past relied on the image of handsome white Spanish (not Mexican) men and beautiful white Spanish women. Since the 1960s there has been an acknowledgement of the real identities of the first settlers (the *pobladores*), who are now commemorated individually on bronze plaques. Over time the settlers have become more Mexican, as has the street itself; the romantic Spanish elements are

now down-played (although fancy ladies' fans are still available as souvenirs).

As part of the original Mexican marketplace theme, craft demonstrations were presented and the products were available for sale. At first these demonstrations included candle making, glass-blowing, tortilla making, pottery making, and blacksmithing. A glass blower making and selling small souvenir items is still a fixture. Mexican-Americans now visit the Olvera Street candle store to buy the votive candles in glass containers that are used to commemorate the dead in cemeteries.

The production of items for sale is now overshadowed by the sale of finished items. Fewer demonstrations are presented and modern merchandise like t-shirts predominates, although some items such as Mexican candy continue to be offered. Barthel (1996: 135) notes that when people buy souvenirs they want the liminal state of being a tourist (separated from everyday concerns, taking a trip back in time, having fun) "to continue, but know it can not. This special state can only be recalled through memory. The souvenir provides the visual hook for remembrance of times past, both historically and experientially."

In the vein of craft demonstrators, Leo Politi, an Italian-American trained in art, drew portraits of visitors to Olvera Street beginning in the 1930s. He went on to help create a mythology for the street in a children's book, *Pedro the Angel of Olvera Street* (1946). His distinctive style, not unlike that of the Mexican muralists Diego Rivera, Jose Clemente Orozco, and David Alfaro Siquieros, came to be associated with the history of downtown Los Angeles and it's ethnic communities. He avoided controversial subjects and extended the romantic vision of the Hispanic past textually and visually to children in books like *The Mission Bell*, in which "Father Serra and the Indian boy who accompanies him on his journeys watch their dream come true as the missions are built in California" (Catalog description, www.lapl.org: Los Angeles Public Library, 2007) and *Song of the Swallows*, summarized as: "Sad when the swallows leave for the winter, young Juan prepares to welcome them back to the old California Mission at Capistrano on St. Joseph's Day the next spring" (Catalog description, www.lapl.org: Los Angeles Public Library, 2007), which won the prestigious Caldecott Medal for children's literature in 1950. His mural, The Blessing of the Animals, in a building near Olvera Street, is pictured on the Italian-American website (http://www.italianlosangeles.org/).

Siquieros did not subscribe to romanticism; his brief in 1932 was a mural on Olvera Street on the second story of the former Italian Hall. The expectation behind the title "Tropical America" seems to have been that it would show "a continent of happy men, surrounded by palms and parrots" (Goldman 1974:325 cited in Pinon 1977:7). Siquieros, however, a dedicated revolutionary, portrayed a much more provocative and political image

Fig. 5. Disputed watering trough. Security Pacific National Bank— Ernest Marquez Collection, N.d. (Reproduced courtesy of Los Angeles Public Library).

depicting a crucified Mexican peon surmounted by an American eagle, for which he was deported. Sterling arranged for the mural to be whitewashed over (Goldman 1974: 325, cited in Pinon 1977:9), but beginning in the 1990s it was restored and made visible again (described at: http://www.getty.edu/conservation/field_ projects/siqueiros/ [last accessed May 12, 2008]).

A more enduring if less intrisically complex item of material culture on Olvera Street is a stone trough (Fig. 5) about a meter and a half long, which has, however, proved rather difficult to romanticize and integrate into the Olvera Street story. The Los Angeles Department of Water and Power moved to its present location on Olvera Street from the San Fernando Valley seemingly some time in the 1930s. Local folklore held variously that it had been carved by mission Indians or used by the horses of the mission padres or that it was a stone canoe or that *la canoa* meant "water" in the local Indian language. It had a brief flash of notoriety as a contended artifact because it had supposedly inspired the name of the town of Canoga Park in the San Fernando Valley; in 1962 the town tried to recover it for the fiftieth anniversary of the settlement's founding, but the Olvera Street management would not release it ("Canoga Park Watering Trough Dispute" 1962). Recent research has revealed that the trough was carved by ranch hands from local sandstone in the area of the Chatsworth Reservoir in the San Fernando Valley ("Myth Evaporates", n.d.) and thus post-dates the Mission period. It still stands on the end of Olvera Street as far as is practicable from the Plaza.

Food

Food is a special kind of material culture that can be consumed literally. Food was integrated into the early displays of craft production on Olvera Street

in the form of a booth where women could be seen making tortillas, perhaps photographed in the 1950s (Schultheis, n.d.). A Mexican restaurant was one of the original commercial anchors on Olvera Street, adjoining the Plaza. It was called Casa La Golondrina, managed for many years by Consuelo Castillo de Bonza, "a dynamic and strong willed business and community leader." She had established La Misión Café on N. Spring in 1923, which "catered to all sectors of the Mexican community, as well as to many downtown political leaders" (Estrada 1999:111). When the city planned to demolish the café, her contacts among local politicians resulted in an offer to move into the Pelanconi House, the first brick building in the city (built in the 1850s). "Businesses such as *Casa la Golondrina* [italics in original] contributed to the cultural renaissance of the Plaza area, providing Mexicans in the city with a renewed sense of themselves in spaces where they could be Mexican in public once again" (Estrada 1999:112). De Bonza continued to be active in Olvera Street activities for many years, frequently pictured in comb and mantilla at fiestas and other events (Los Angeles Chamber of Commerce, n.d.). In 1995 the restaurant was still in business, managed by her granddaughter, Vivien Consuelo de Bonza ("La Golondrina" [1995]; http://www.lagolondrina.com/olvera.html [last accessed May 2008]).

Reception of the past

The managers of Olvera Street have encouraged the reception of their version of the past in a series of public events. In the early years, the surrender of California from Mexico to the United States, in the person of Commodore Robert W. Stockton, was re-enacted ("City's Capture..." n.d.), but it may have been difficult

Fig. 6. In 1961 dancing girls (Rosario del Rio [left] and Graciela Flores) in Mexican costumes performed for civic leaders: Judge McIntyre Faries, Supervisor Ernest Debs, Acting Mayor Ed Roybal and Walter Braunschweiger (Reproduced courtesy of Los Angeles Public Library).

to put a romantic spin on this negative Mexican experience. This event was only held in the earliest phase of the street's development.

Fiestas have been more durable and successful ways to commemorate the past. These events were attended by society notables in re-created Hispanic dress (originally owing a great deal to the flounced dress styles of the 1920s and 1930s) complete with mantillas on tall combs and were reported in the newspapers. In the 1940s and 1950s the dress became more of an authentic reproduction—a version of the so-called Poblano or China Girl style romanticized in Mexican folklore (seen in photographs of the period, for example, "Las Posadas Christmas Fete" [1953]).

The Blessing of the Animals has been an annual event almost since the beginning. Not mentioned in the *Catholic Encyclopedia*, this event seems to have been mainly based on a romantic idea of religiosity among Hispanic Californians (see a romantic description at http://www.blessingoftheanimals.com/ [last accessed May 2008]). It fitted in nicely with the image of St. Francis (the namesake of the founders of the California missions) and continues to be of popular interest, providing a chance for people to show off their pets, and photo opportunities.

Olvera Street managers have developed an annual cycle of events more or less loosely tied to Hispanic California history, serving to attract local and foreign tourists to the venue. These events have gradually shifted closer to Mexican history and social practice than strictly California's past. Las Posadas, a re-enactment of a genuine

Mexican and Mexican-American Christmas celebration, is held in December. Cinco de Mayo (May 5th—commemorating the Battle of Puebla, Mexico, in 1862) was celebrated in the 1950s as simply a fiesta, without political overtones. Recently it has become a city-wide celebration and the political tone is more marked. The Day of the Dead (*Día de los Muertos*, November 31), another holiday more Mexican than Californian, also draws crowds.

Olvera Street has been successful as a created place of memory through a foundation myth with input from both upper and lower strata of society, reception of the memory idea by the general public, associated material cultural items, and time for the place to be established and accepted. Visitors go there because they want the experience, the souvenir stalls have stayed in business over time, and Mexican food is on offer. Political dignitaries regularly participate in events (Fig. 6). The street is included in official celebrations such as the Democratic National Convention of 2000 and regularly incorporated in tourist bus tours. Personal memories can be perpetuated in a photograph taken in a decorated sombrero, on the (stuffed) donkey (Fig. 7), or at the cross.

Details have changed with the times: styles of dress (from flapper flounces to the La Poblana/China Girl costume in the 1940s), but the mantilla and comb motif is still strong. Souvenir fans continue to be available in at least one shop. Men wear re-constructed costumes, but less often than earlier and they have always worn them more rarely than women. In the 1930s the Mexican Hat Dance seems to have been integrated, judging

125

Fig. 7. Mexican-American women (among them Déleon Melendez and Ofélia Columba) pose for a souvenir snapshot with the burro, Olvera Street (Shades of LA project. Reproduced courtesy of Los Angeles Public Library).

from photographs taken at the time (photos on file, Los Angeles Public Library Photo Collection). In the beginning, roles in the commemorative events were mostly played by Anglo-Americans acting out history; at the present time many Hispanics take part and Mexican holidays such as Cinco de Mayo and *Día de los Muertos* make logical additions. The reality of the Mexican experience in California, especially in the twentieth century, has been accepted by both the street management and the public. The Siqueiros mural has been restored and is protected by a roof. Plaques commemorating each of the original settlers are on view, acknowledging that people of color were among the first inhabitants of the pueblo.

Olvera Street has been received or accepted by many people. This is evidenced in at least one personal website called Olvera Street (http://www.olvera-street.com [last accessed May 2008]), not under official aegis of the monument. Information on the website notes that it is presented by a descendent of a food-stall owner; the logo selected by author is a Mexican prehistoric figurine that has no connection to California. A number of merchants sponsor a website advertising their businesses at http://www.calleolvera.com/; a number of business have individual websites, such as La Golondrina (noted above), Cielito Lindo (http://www.lasanitas.com/) and others. The official website is part of the larger City of Los Angeles website (http://www.cityofla.org/ELP/el-pau.htm [last accessed May 2008]); it soberly describes the history of Olvera Street in politically correct, inclusive language with limited romantic allusions:

"forty-four settlers of Native American, African and European heritage journeyed more than one-thousand miles across the desert ... Today,... El Pueblo is a liv-

ing museum that continues to fulfill its unique role as the historic and symbolic heart of the city, reflecting the Native American, African American, Spanish, Anglo, Mexican, Chinese, Italian and French cultures that contributed to its early history."

This tone echoes in the website of Las Angelitas del Pueblo (www.lasangelitas.org/), "a wonderful group of volunteer docents who give free tours of El Pueblo de Los Angeles to the public. The group consists of people who have a deep knowledge and love of the history of Los Angeles, a commitment to the city and who want to share this knowledge and commitment with others".

Various ethnic groups connected to California history have linked their presence to Olvera Street, in plaques on the street or the Plaza and on their websites. Among them are Italian-Americans, who were prominent in the area at the time Olvera Street was organized (http://www.italianlosangeles.org/), the "ancestral heritage association, Los Pobladores, descendents of the founders," (www.lospobladores.org) and the Native Americans who are descendents of the pre-Hispanic population. Formerly called Gabrieleños from Mission San Gabriel, they have re-claimed an original name: the Tongva (http://www.tongva.com/), "who have lived on this land for generations and descend from the ancestors buried here."

There is material evidence that Olvera Street is seen by at least some city residents as connected to the present life of the city as well as to the past. A memorial to Eugene A. Obregon, a Mexican-American soldier from East Los Angeles, who was posthumously awarded the Congressional Medal of Honor (Korean War, 1950-1953) has been proposed (http://www.volunteermatch.org/ [last accessed May 2008]). His personal connection to Olvera

Street seems tenuous, but those wishing to honor him feel that this is the appropriate place.

"The monument will stand 20 feet high. Bronze figures of Obregon and Johnson [the man whose life he saved] will sit atop a pyramid made of the same volcanic stone once used by pre-Columbian Aztec artists. The pyramid's base will bear a description of Obregon's heroism and the names of all 40 Hispanic CMH recipients, with the wars they fought in. …The monument will be a touchstone for young Latinos, some of whom are at-risk of falling into gangs, and will be connected to an education/scholarship fund."

Time

Olvera Street was started in a period (the 1920s) with a perceived need for a historic past. It provided a physical place with minimal actual connection to the past that served to ground events associated with constructed and real memories. The venue took root over time; it now has its own history. The stall (*puesto*) owners have earned economic and political clout with the city (Estrada 1999) and their personal memories contribute to the perpetuation of the place.

Reasons for the success of Olvera Street

The Olvera Street development, based on the memory of an imagination-embellished past, has endured for over 70 years despite periodic fluctuations in popularity and profitability. A number of factors have contributed to this longevity.

Olvera Street met a perceived need for a spatial locus in the city linked to Los Angeles' history. The Plaza did not have a physical anchor like the Avila Adobe and may have had too much historical baggage; perhaps the radicalism expressed by street orators in the 1920s was too threatening. The San Gabriel mission, an authentic site of colonization about eight miles away, was too far from the city center for easy access by political dignitaries and casual tourists. Olvera Street is convenient to City Hall, which can be seen behind the street in certain views (Fig. 2). Olvera Street became a place to share in events like the Democratic Party's national convention in 2000—it was good for adding a local flavor to photo opportunities.

In the beginning, Olvera Street was rather innocent and simple. It played on (and played up) nostalgia, a romantic vision of the past. It offered souvenirs, mainly hand-crafted items that were compatible with this view—consumer items like pottery and baskets and nostalgic items like decorative hair combs, mantillas, and fans. It also played on a contemporaneous interest in Mexico and Mexican lifeways.

The interpretation (or backstory) behind the Olvera Street development, especially at the beginning, used a rather selective history. The Franciscan missionary, Junipero Serra, was accepted as a nurturer who brought civilization to the native Indians. The alternate view that he was an exploiter or destroyer of the native inhabitants' ways of life (part of the memory of Native Americans) was never expressed. The mixed racial composition of the first group of settlers (*pobledores*) was ignored at first in favor of a more romantic picture of flirtatious white Spanish señors and señoritas. Olvera Street provided a physical venue linking amateur historians and local genealogical societies with the past. Los Pobladores is a group of people who celebrate their descent from the original settlers; the Native Daughters of California is similar, open to descendents of Euro-American settlers. Part of the process of social and institutional change at Olvera Street has been the acknowledgement of the mixed races of the first settlers.

Furthermore, Olvera Street has been adopted by some segments of the Hispanic community as part of their heritage. This has shaped the practice of public events at Olvera Street. Several holidays originating in Mexico are celebrated, among them *Cinco de Mayo* and *Día de los Muertos*. The potentially humiliating commemoration of the surrender of Mexican California to the United States has long been discontinued. Visits to the venue have been perpetuated in family memories such as photos with the donkey (Fig. 7). This is attested in the Shades of L.A. project the Los Angeles Public Library conducted in 1990s to collect photographs linked to family memories especially of minority groups (www. LAPL.org/catalog/Photo_collection_overview).

Olvera Street had some authentic Hispanic elements, most notably the Avila adobe, which anchored the concept without being too restrictive on the imaginations of the managers (different groups at different times). Sterling's initial idea, although largely based on romantic imagination, has been perpetuated over time in various ways. One way is in the type of souvenirs sold; another way is in the association of aromas and tastes. The street has always had at least one restaurant serving Mexican food, which creates a sense of authenticity.

Olvera Street has been officially integrated into the City of Los Angeles, although it first belonged to the State of California. Proximity to the center of city government downtown helped it "earn its keep." It is used as an adjunct location to official commemorative events and celebrations (such as the Democratic National Convention) and is regularly integrated into tourist activities such as bus tours. It is now managed as a tourist attraction with an annual activity cycle of various events (the Blessing of the Animals, Cinco de Mayo, and so on) designed to keep tourists coming on a regular basis. New features have been added over time: the Plaza itself and adjacent buildings that are less connected to the theme of the street (the Firehouse and the Masonic Hall), but nonetheless historic. In the mid-2000s, a Euro-American Los Angeles resident expressed it thus:

"Of course Olvera St. means different things to different people. But when you talk about collective memory, I wonder which collective memory? Los Angeles is now so much a collection of different ethnic communities who share cultural and historic places but interpret them in different ways. I have been going there since I was three and so has my son. We have individual memories and responses. My son and I are Anglos, and native Angelenos. But my son has been going there regularly for a couple of years now with his girlfriend, whose family is from Mexico. He showed me the shops she goes to, and what she buys, introduced me to the leather worker she patronizes. I wonder what Olvera St. means to her family members who were born in Mexico but have lived in L.A. variously, 20, 40, 50, 60 years? Her parents and especially her grandparents have a strong sense of their heritage; *Posadas* and *Día de los Muertos* are living traditions for them. I wonder if the meaning of Olvera Street has changed for them over time, as the larger society has revised its memories and manipulated the image of this site."

Olvera Street was established and is still managed as a tourist locale. The founder did not set out to create a place of memory, but through time and a series of management decisions that has been the result. Shifting historical interpretations among various social groups have impacted which events are commemorated and which are ignored. It seems as though this monument has been incorporated in collective memories of city residents (judging from publicity photographs of political dignitaries in different periods) and also in the personal memories of many inhabitants (judging from family photographs). Although it is recognizably a place with constructed, or at least tended, features of memory, its survival for close on a century has given it a patina of age that can be and has been modeled to suit changing times.

Acknowledgements

I wish to thank the following for careful reading and suggestions: John Chapman, Alice Choyke, Roberta Greenwood, and Helen Wells.

Bibliography

*Available on-line at www.LAPL.org

Barthel, Diane. 1996. *Historic Preservation. Collective Memory and Historical Identity*. New Brunswick: Rutgers University Press, 1996.

*Canoga Park Watering Trough Dispute. 1962. Photograph on file in the Los Angeles Public Library Photo Database File HCN 3764.

Chandler, Julian Alvin Caroll 1934. The Preservation of Our Shrines. *William and Mary College Quarterly Historical Magazine*, ser. 2, 14, no. 4, pp. 300-303.

*City's Capture by U.S. Observed. n.d. [Los Angeles *Examiner*]. Newspaper clipping on file, California History file, Los Angeles Public Library.

Confino, Alon.1997. Collective Memory and Cultural History: Problems of Method. *The American History Review* 102, No. 5, pp. 1386-1403.

Connerton, Paul. 1989. *How Societies Remember*. Cambridge: Cambridge University Press.

Coombs, Gary, and Fred Plog. 1977.The Conversion of the Chumash Indians. An Ecological Interpretation. *Human Ecology* 5, No. 4, pp. 309-328.

*Dentzel, Carl. 1963. [Christine Sterling obituary.] Reprinted: A Tribute to Christine Sterling. Pamphlet, on file, Los Angeles Public Library, California Vertical File, "Streets—Los Angeles—Olvera Street" and at http://dbase1.lapl.org/ webpics/calindex/ documents/ 09/519212.pdf

*Elkins, Anne. 1981. Olvera Street. A Woman and a Dream. *Civic Center News/ Downtown News*, March 3, 1981, p. 8. Newspaper clipping on file, California History file, Los Angeles Public Library.

Estrada, William D. 1999. Los Angeles Old Plaza and Olvera Street: Imagined and Contested Space. *Western Folklore* 58, No. 2: 107-129.

*Female Group in Ethnic Dress [photograph]. 1936. On file: Los Angeles Public Library, Security Pacific National Bank Collection.

Fish, Peter. 1995. Romance Meets Reality in Hemet. *Sunset* 194, No. 4, p. 18.

Goldman, Shifra M. 1974. Siqueiros and Three Early Murals in Los Angeles. *Art Journal* 33/4, pp. 322-325.

Gable, Eric, Richard Handler, and Anna Lawson. 1992. On the Uses of Relativism: Fact, Conjecture and Black and White Histories at Colonial Williamsburg. *American Ethnologist* 19/4, pp. 791-805.

Green, Terisa. 2002. *Spanish Missions and Native Religion: Contact, Conflict, and Convergence*. Ph.D. dissertation, University of California Los Angeles. Facsimile reprint: Salinas, CA: Coyote Press, 2002.

Heizer, Robert F., ed. 1978. *Handbook of North American Indians*. Vol. 8. *California*. Washington, DC: Smithsonian Institution.

Jackson, Helen Hunt.1881. *A Century of Dishonor. A Sketch of the United States Government's Dealings with Some of the Indian Tribes*. New York: Harper.

Jackson, Helen Hunt.1884. *Ramona; a Story*. Numerous reprints.

Kammen, Michael. 1991. *Mystic Chords of Memory. The Transformation of Tradition in American Culture*. New York: Vintage Books.

Kroeber, Alfred L. 1925. *Handbook of the Indians of California*. Washington, D.C.: Bureau of American Ethnography (reprint: New York: Dover Books, 1976).

Kropp, Phoebe S. 2001. Citizens of the Past? Olvera Street and the Construction of Race and Memory in 1930s Los Angeles. *Radical History Review* 81, pp. 34-60.

*"La Golondrina."[1995]. *Downtown News*, Vol. 13:55. On file: Los Angeles Public Library, California Vertical File: Restaurants, Mexican—Los Angeles—La Golondrina.

*Herald-Examiner. 1953. Las Posadas Christmas Fete. On file: Los Angeles Public Library, Herald-Examiner Collection, file no. HE box 8775.

*Herald-Examiner. 1961. Dancing Girls on Olvera Street. On file: Los Angeles Public Library, Herald-Examiner Collection, file no. HE box 11985.

*Los Angeles Chamber of Commerce. n.d. Mrs. Twyman and Mrs. Debonzo in Ethnic Dress. On file: Los Angeles Public Library, Security Pacific National Bank Collection, file no. S-004-008.1.

Lowenthal, David. 1975. Past Time, Present Place: Landscape and Memory. *Geographical Review* 65, No. 1, pp. 1-36.

Lowenthal, David. 1985. *The Past is a Foreign Country*. Cambridge: Cambridge University Press.

Mason, William Marvin. 1998. *The Census of 1790. A Demographic History of Colonial California*. Ballena Press Anthropological Papers No. 45. Menlo Park, CA: Ballena Press, CA.

Middleton, David and Derek Edwards eds. 1990. *Collective Memory*. Newbury Park, CA: Sage.

Milliken, Randall. 1995. *A Time of Little Choice. The Disintegration of Tribal Culture in the San Francisco Bay Area, 1769-1810*. Ballena Press Anthropological Papers No. 47. Menlo Park, CA: Ballena Press.

Mission Revival Style. n.d. http://www.answers.com/topic/mission-revival-style-architecture.

*Myth Evaporates; Canoga Park's Trough Legend Won't Hold Water, Prof. Says. n.d. Newspaper clipping on file, California History file, Los Angeles Public Library.

Nora, Pierre. 1989. Between Memory and History: Les Lieux de Mémoire. *Representations* 26, pp. 7-24.

Olick, Jeffrey K. and Joyce Robbins, 1998. Social Memory Studies: From 'Collective Memory' to the Historical Sociology of Mnemonic Practices. *Annual Review of Sociology* 24, pp. 105-140.

*Pinon, Jeanette. 1977. A Ghostly Mural Haunts Olvera Street. Unpublished ms on file, Los Angeles Public Library, California Biography File A.

Politi, Leo. 1946. *Pedro, the Angel of Olvera Street*. New York: Scribner.

Politi, Leo. 1948. *Song of the Swallows*. New York: Atheneum Books for Young Readers.

Politi, Leo. 1953. *The Mission Bell*. New York: Scribner.

*Schultheis, Herman. n.d. [Two women making tortillas, Olvera Street]. On file, Los Angeles Public Library, Security Pacific National Bank Collection, File No. N-005-124.2 8x10.

Schwartz, Barry. 1982. The Social Context of Commemoration: A Study in Collective Memory. *Social Forces* 61/2, pp. 374-402.

*Security Pacific National Bank—Ernest Marquez Collection. n.d. "Woman Sitting on Rock, Olvera Street." On file, Los Angeles Public Library, File heading: L.A.-Plazas-The Plaza-Olvera Street.

Stewart, Kathleen. 1988. Nostalgia—A Polemic. *Cultural Anthropology*, 3/3, pp. 227-241.

INDEX OF AUTHORS

Irene Barbiera
Research Assistant
University of Padova
Department of History
Padova, Italy
irene.barbriera@gmail.com

John C. Chapman
Reader
Durham University
Department of Archaeology
DURHAM DH1 3LE, United Kingdom
j.c.chapman@dur.ac.uk

Alice Choyke
Associate Professor
Medieval Studies Department
Central European University
Nádor u. 9.
H-1051 Budapest, Hungary
choyke@ceu.hu

Senior Researcher
Aquincum Museum
Záhony u. 4.
H-1031 Budapest, Hungary
h13017cho@iif.hu

Maria Fiano
Italy
maria_fiano@yahoo.it

Kateřina Horníčková, PhD
Centre for Medieval Studies
Institute of Philosophy, Academy of Sciences of the
Jilská 1
110 00 Prague 1, Czech Republic
katerina.hornickova@hrad.cz

Liam Kilmurray
Visiting Professor
Department of Sociology and Anthropology
University of Ottawa
Ottawa, Canada
liam.kilmurray@uottawa.ca

Piero Majocchi
Research Assistant
University of Padova
Department of History
Padova, Italy
pieromajocchi@libero.it

Judith A. Rasson
Assistant Professor
Medieval Studies Department
Central European University
Nádor u. 9.
H-1051 Budapest, Hungary
rassonj@ceu.hu

Research Associate
Cotsen Institute of Archaeology
University of California
Los Angeles, U.S.A.

Eszter Spät, PhD
Medieval Studies Department
Central European University
Nádor u. 9.
H-1051 Budapest, Hungary
spateszter@yahoo.com

Paula Zsidi
Director
Aquincum Museum,
Záhony u. 4.
H-1031 Budapest, Hungary
zsidi.paula@aquincum.hu

www.ingramcontent.com/pod-product-compliance
Lightning Source LLC
Chambersburg PA
CBHW061001030426
42334CB00033B/3313